Educational

Architecture

in Ohio

Educational

From One-Room
Schools and Carnegie
Libraries to Community
Education Villages

Architecture in Ohio

Virginia E. McCormick

The Kent State

University Press

Kent, Ohio, & London

© 2001 by The Kent State
University Press, Kent, Ohio 44242
All rights reserved
Library of Congress Catalog Card
Number 00-036877
ISBN 0-87338-666-3
Manufactured in the United States
of America

07 06 05 04 03 02 01   5 4 3 2 1

Library of Congress Cataloging-in-Publication Data
McCormick, Virginia E.
(Virginia Evans), 1934–
Educational architecture in Ohio : from
one-room schools and Carnegie libraries
to community education villages /
Virginia Evans McCormick.
p.   cm.
Includes bibliographical references and index.
ISBN 0-87338-666-3 (cloth : alk. paper) ∞
1. School buildings—Ohio—History.
2. Public buildings—Ohio—History. I. Title.
LB3218.03 M33 2000
727'.09771—dc21   00-036877

British Library Cataloging-in-Publication
data are available.

For Robert,

perceptive critic

&

best friend

Contents

Acknowledgments

This book evolved from an Ohio Historic Preservation Office project that attempted to provide educational context for individuals and groups interested in nominating an educational property for the National Register of Historic Places. This included the development of a timeline of educational highlights, an annotated list of educational sites on the National Register of Historic Places, and an annotated bibliography of educational resources. When it became evident that there was a wealth of material deserving of a wider audience and broader scope, no one could have been more supportive than Barbara Powers, head of the Division of Planning, Inventory, and Registration. She planted the seed and nurtured its growth in many ways, reviewing the entire manuscript and sharpening its focus significantly. Many members of the Ohio Historic Preservation Office staff have been supportive along the way, but I am particularly grateful to Stephen Gordon and Nathalie Wright for their encyclopedic memories regarding the numerous properties in the Ohio Historic Inventory and their abilities to call up the information I was seeking.

Several people offered encouragement regarding the desirability of examining educational history from an architectural perspective, but I admit that if I had realized the difficulties of this project from the beginning, I probably would not have attempted it. Life late in the twentieth century has become quite specialized. There is little common expertise between school superintendents and architects, public librarians and university professors, local historians and architectural historians, educational historians and historic preservationists. I found myself forced to rely upon historians, educators, architects, or librarians who could critique specific items or sections and hope that I was synthesizing these into an appropriate whole.

My second confession is that I owe an incredible debt to many people—beginning with the archives and library staff of the Ohio Historical Society, where I spent countless hours and found people such as Matthew Benz, John Hass, Tom House, Tom Rieder, Tom Starbuck, and Ann Thomas particularly knowledgeable and helpful.

Traveling throughout Ohio, I found librarians and archivists to be an invaluable resource. Sometimes they alerted me to information I would likely have missed, like Kay Schlicting of the Ohio Wesleyan University Archives who called my attention to the Hebrew inscriptions on the University Hall arch, or Jeffrey R. Herold, director of the Bucyrus Public Library, who knew a local resident who had a photo card of the original Bucyrus Library interior and arranged for me to borrow it. Sometimes they went well beyond the call of duty in searching materials, as did Sheila Darrow, the Central State University archivist who combed through years of Wilberforce University trustees minutes to find the name of the African American faculty member who was the Galloway Hall architect, or Marge Billman of the Huron Public Library who arranged for me to see a home video made during the construction of McCormick School. I will never forget the generosity and trust of people such as Bev Boroff of the Marsh Foundation and Linda Blicke, curator of the Bucyrus Historical Society, who loaned me irreplaceable early school yearbooks.

At the risk of omitting names, let me express my thanks to the many others who helped me acquire information and photographs or reviewed sections of the manuscript: Denise Monbarren, College of Wooster Archives; Rai Goerler, director, and Bertha Ihnat of the Ohio State University Archives; Lois Szudy, director, and Stephen Grinch, archivist, Otterbein College Library; Beth A. Weinhardt, Local History Department, Westerville Public Library; Sandy Warren, Springfield South High School; Jeffrey T. Darbee, historic preservation consultant, Columbus; James C. Marshall and Greg Miller, Local History Department, Lucas County Public Library, Toledo; Joyce Baer, Westwood Branch director, Sylvia Verdun Metzinger, Rare Books Division, and Mary Kay Levesay, Branch Library Services of the Public Library of Cincinnati and Hamilton County; Mary Windau, retired teacher, Huron School; Catherine Wilson, Local History Department, Greene County Public Library; Roland M. Baumann and Tammy Martin, Oberlin College Archives; Jami E. Peelle, special collections librarian, Kenyon College; Audrey Mackiewicz, Huron Historical Society; Lucy McCarren, Harveysburg Historical Society; Sybil Galer, director, and

Kelly Foust, Findlay–Hancock County Public Library; Frances A. Fleet, Tiffin University Library; Rosalie Adams, Seneca County Museum; Lea Bissell, secretary, Twinsburg Historical Society; Marjorie Brown, curator, Butler County Historical Society; Sharon Buxton, registrar, Johnson-Humerickhouse Museum; Joyce Alig, Mercer County Historical Society; Julie Klema, librarian, and Jack Alston, director of communications, Burgess and Niple, Limited; Susan N. Hill, director, Paulding County Carnegie Library; Ruth Krabach, librarian, Rick Aronholt, facilities coordinator, and Ralph Johnson, superintendent, New Albany–Plain Local Schools; Ruth A. Lesko, marketing director, Lesko Associates, Architects, and Planners; Rosa Stultz, vice president, Columbus Association for the Performing Arts; Virginia King, Granville; Robert A. Flischel, Robert Flischel Photography, Cincinnati; Mary Klei, curator, and Mary W. Payne, director, Warren County Historical Society Museum; Steve Middleton, architect, formerly with SEM Partners; John Butterfield, retired assistant superintendent, Worthington Schools; Pamela L. Pletcher, archivist, Mahoning Valley Historical Society; Sheperd Black, Ohio University Archives; Robert Richmond and Sally Richmond, Morgan County Historical Society; Nina Myatt, curator, Antiochana Collection, Antioch College; Pam Bessel, Ohio Wesleyan University Public Relations Office; Ron Sterling, executive director, Canton Preservation Society; Richard Fleischman, Richard Fleischman Architects; W. J. Weber, librarian, Stark County Historical Society; Diana Druback, librarian, Fine Arts Library, The Ohio State University; Michael Ruffing, archivist, M. Callaghan Zunt, director, Carnegie West Branch, and Amy Dawson, Photo Collections, Cleveland Public Library; Mary Ann James and Rebecca Hamilton, Stepping Stone House, Portsmouth; J. M. Newman, Visual Collection, Columbus Metropolitan Library; James E. Price, executive secretary-treasurer, Marsh Foundation; Mary Bridget Reilly, Public Relations Office, University of Cincinnati; Eugenia G. Beecher, Lane Public Library, Hamilton; Linda Blicke, curator, Bucyrus Historical Society; Betty Jones, Poland Township Historical Society; H. Roger Grant, Department of History, Clemson University; Sam Ashworth, curator, Middletown Historical Society; Nancy Birk, special collections librarian, Kent State University; Dan Strain, principal, Edward Lee McClain High School, Greenfield; Mary Oliver, curator, Montgomery County Historical Society; John Sanford, Wright State University Library.

I appreciate the skill of Ken Snider of Photographic Techniques, Columbus, in producing useful illustrations from old reports and yearbooks. My special thanks go to John Hubbell, director of The Kent State University Press for seeing value in and supporting this project, and to managing editor Erin L. Holman for shepherding it through the editorial process, to copy editor Toni Mortimer for raising the questions that force clarity, and to Will Underwood for creating the visual interpretation. They are a pleasure to work with, and their capabilities have been invaluable, but I assume full responsibility for any errors that may remain.

As always, I benefited immeasurably from the support and advice of my husband, Bob, whose expertise as an educator was tapped at every stage along the way. Completion would have been impossible without his patience and understanding.

Introduction

Even for those whose only acquaintance with one-room schools is their restoration as a museum, these buildings hold a mystique—a sense of nostalgia for a simpler time and place that perhaps exists only in our imagination. Wayne E. Fuller, who has researched them as extensively as anyone, contends that the typical Midwestern one-room school was the most symbolic representation of community enterprise—its site, form, construction, and use determined by the people it served.[1] That past is gone, but the concept that an educated population is the essential ingredient for democratic government has never been stronger. Schools encompass the commonly shared childhood experiences that define our culture, and for architectural historians, educational historians, historic preservationists, and local historians this book seeks to describe educational progress as it is reflected in the architecture of its buildings.

For many persons across the landscape of rural and small-town America there are also fond memories of hours spent in their local library—in many communities across the country remembered among older citizens simply as "the Carnegie," for the philanthropist who so greatly influenced the American public library culture. Novelist Helen Hooven Santmyer found "all Carnegie libraries are so alike that one's memories hardly seem associated with an individual set of yellow-brick walls, white stone trim, and granite steps." Yet her inner child recalls "rough stone through a summer dress, the sun on one's back, the pull of skates on shoe soles, and accepts as identical one's own and all others' experiences."[2] For children of Santmyer's era, the library was a special place—an adult place where children experienced the privilege of reading and borrowing books—an emotional as well as physical place. Ohio ranked third in the Carnegie funds states received for libraries and fifth in the number of such buildings constructed; but during the phenomenal growth of public libraries in the early twentieth century even more Ohio libraries were built with funds from local taxes and local donors.[3] The first countywide library in the country reached outlying communities with book boxes in general stores. Urban libraries provided bookmobiles that were treasured by children and others without transportation. However, Carnegie libraries have, like one-room schools, become a symbol of shared educational experience.

Such experience is, of course, far more complex than the middle-class memories of local historians and best-selling novelists, but educators recognize that emotional attachments to the learning environment often have a significant impact.[4] Public schools and public libraries have been the most tangible providers of the knowledge that created the American melting pot which assimilated immigrants from diverse cultures. The design of buildings to transmit knowledge—private and public schools, colleges for the academic elite, public libraries for lifelong learning, nineteenth-century opera houses, and twentieth-century museums—provides physical evidence regarding a society's cultural values that is as fascinating as any archaeological excavation of an ancient habitation site.

The wonder of an archaeologist carefully brushing residue from a jeweled artifact is no greater than that of a knowledgeable observer discovering the symbolic treasures imbedded in educational architecture. Although designed by the same architects in similar Richardsonian Romanesque style and erected the same year, the Hebrew inscriptions from Solomon's Temple in the foundation arch of Ohio Wesleyan's University Hall proclaim its religious foundation as surely as the forty layers of Ohio bedrock stratified in Ohio State University's Orton Hall convey the scientific base of this new institution with a statewide land-grant mission.

Standing in the open end of the quadrangle formed by Kauke, Severance, and Scovel Halls, one can admire the collegiate Gothic unity of the College of Wooster campus and realize that the space between these buildings and their vitrified brick construction reflect the resolution of an institution which only a year before their construction lost everything—chapel, classrooms, library, literary society, and dormitory rooms—in a fire that destroyed Old Main. These buildings are a survival statement and a declaration that such tragedy must not be repeated.

Admiring a photograph of Galloway Hall—the Wilberforce University gem destroyed by a tornado in 1974—one is struck by its appearance, a massive tower entry with a tripartite facade to the left defined by window groupings, and a temple facade with a Greek Revival pediment to the right. For anyone who misses the symbolism, mottoes on the frieze refer to the mind, body, work, and spirit that defined the philosophy of educators at the turn of the twentieth century—concepts popularized by the Head, Heart, Hands, and Health of the 4-H Club movement that originated with a township school superintendent just a few miles north.

The impressive stone carvings of the Gothic-arched entry of the 1899 classroom building at the Ohio School for the Deaf include the stylized faces of deaf-mute children—as they were called at the time—topped by a motto, "Religion, morality, and knowledge being necessary to good government and the happiness of mankind, schools and the means of education shall forever be encouraged."[5] This quotation from the Northwest Ordinance of 1787 is evidence that more than a century later the state re-acknowledged its responsibility to provide educational opportunities, especially for physically disadvantaged children.

Ohio offers an excellent perspective for viewing and interpreting educational architecture across the span of the nineteenth and twentieth centuries. The heritage of its pioneer settlers included the original colonies from Virginia to New England, and the diversity of its immigrants from the nineteenth century to the present has significantly affected its educational institutions, both public and private. Its strategic geographic position created a funnel for westward migration from Missouri to Minnesota and made its educational history typical of much of America. With a few innovative exceptions that have attracted national attention, Ohio's educational architecture is representative of the Midwestern states and reflects mainstream American taste.

Professional educators have always maintained that school buildings and their equipment should be considered accessories to the educational process.[6] Subscribing to this belief that form is dictated by function, the present volume focuses on education and its changing goals, methodologies, and audiences and utilizes educational architecture as the perspective for viewing movement from subscription schools to public schools, from one-room schools to graded schools, from isolated district schools to larger and larger centralized schools, and from the philosophy of students as recipients to current emphasis on their active participation in the acquisition of knowledge. The architecture of higher education provides testimony regarding the philosophies of specific institutions and has tended in both the nineteenth and the twentieth centuries to reflect the highest artistic aspirations of the community. The evolution of public library buildings demonstrates striking philosophical change in concepts about lifelong learning and public access to information.

Such currents of educational change are illustrated within the perspective of dramatically shifting concepts of architectural fashion. Ohio's early common schools—both private and public—were vernacular structures of a generic form equally suitable for residential, commercial, religious, or educational use. The earliest academy and college buildings reflect the Federal style of the New Englanders who led early educational efforts in the state and viewed Yale University as their model. It is a continuing architectural influence in the state's two oldest institutions of higher education, Ohio University and Miami University.

A majority of the state's pre–Civil War academy and college buildings reflect the Greek Revival architecture that paid homage to democracy's dependence upon an educated citizenry and bestowed prestige on the elite students admitted to such temples of learning where classical studies thrived. Fine examples of this survive in Western Reserve Academy at Hudson, Norwalk Female Seminary (now converted for residential use), and Founders Hall at Heidelberg College. Although Gothic architecture was not widely used in Ohio's educational buildings, there were notable exceptions that reflected America's reliance on British fashion, such as Bexley Hall at Kenyon College and Hughes High School and Woodward High School at Cincinnati that became nationally admired examples—although neither survives today.

Sufficient one-room schools—most from the latter part of the nineteenth century—have survived as residences and museums to reveal the diversity of their vernacular architecture. Modest frame buildings like Ragersville School in Tuscarawas County typify an early vernacular period, while late-nineteenth-century buildings like the brick Washington Heights School in Hamilton County and the stone South Ridge School in Lorain County both display high-quality craftsmanship. Unique examples such as the octagon-shaped school at Florence Corners reflect individual craftsmen applying creativity to standard plan books. There is ample evidence that nineteenth-century carpenters and masons, even in rural areas, were acquainted with architectural fashions through commercial plan books and incorporated elements of Greek Revival style, such as pediments and pilasters, or Italianate elements, such as bracketed cornices or window hood-molds, into their school buildings.

The preferred architectural style in the construction boom that followed the Civil War was Italianate, and variations appeared in elementary school, high school, and college buildings. It was a style well suited to an era of rising educational professionalism when large classrooms placed neat rows of students before an authoritarian teacher. Surviving buildings, such as Cummins School at Cincinnati and Sycamore School at Sandusky, show the diversity of construction materials and quality of craftsmanship associated with this style, even though they have been converted for contemporary use as offices or residential apartments. Few Victorian Gothic buildings survive, but superb examples—such as Oberlin School at Oberlin, Miami Street School at Tiffin, and Campbell Street School at Sandusky—have all entered their second century of service with solid craftsmanship that neither the twentieth nor this century can afford to replicate.

By the latter part of the nineteenth century, fashion swung to the robust style of Richardsonian Romanesque architecture for public schools, college buildings, and public libraries—the last a new concept on the educational landscape. Notable surviving examples range from Emerson School at Westerville to Orton Hall at Ohio State University, Warder Public Library at Springfield, and Sorg's Opera House at Middletown. Architecture had recently become a recognized profession, with practitioners of this period greatly influenced by John Ruskin's passionate plea for artistic effort, not just mechanical solutions.[7]

This led to a neoclassical revival that prevailed in educational architecture through the early decades of the twentieth century, with Georgian Revival and Second-Renaissance styles dominating. Leading architects began to look to various classical sources for different styles of buildings— a concept well illustrated in Cass Gilbert's design for Allen Memorial Art Museum at Oberlin College and Edward B. Green's Italian Renaissance inspiration for Dayton Art Institute.[8] With premier architects training in Europe, beaux-arts classicism became increasingly popular, particularly for public buildings such as libraries. Springfield High School and the Cleveland Public Library are illustrative, with the latter specifically related to the city beautiful movement that developed following the Columbian Exposition of 1893.

Such influences in design coincided with progressive educational reforms emphasizing democratic rather than authoritarian educational philosophies. John Dewey's writings reflecting work at the University of Chicago laboratory school synthesized Platonic philosophy with Jean Jacques Rousseau's Enlightenment, creating a new educational psychology that balanced the intellectual and practical phases of experience.[9] Vocational education experiences required the inclusion of rooms equipped for specific purposes such as domestic science, mechanical arts, and business education. And increasing concerns for fire safety quickly replaced the monumental three-story, nineteenth-century structures with horizontal buildings providing multiple exits.

Few educational buildings employed the art deco or art moderne styles that were more commonly associated with commercial construction, although there are interesting exceptions such as Toledo Public Library and McCormick School at Huron, the latter reflecting wartime steel shortages in its poured concrete construction. Post–World War II construction, to accommodate the baby boom, focused on utilitarian materials and speedy methods—with some critics contending architects were creating classrooms, hallways, and cafeterias with so little individuality they might as well have used cookie cutters.[10] Such "factories for the mass production of learning" are now perceived as a major reason that students, parents, and teachers feel little pride in such community buildings and place little value on the learning experiences that occur within them.[11]

Recent collaborations between educators and architects are producing modern and postmodern buildings that respond to society's need for flexible space, communications technology, and resource centers open to the entire community—and occasionally creating buildings that evoke emotional excitement among teachers, librarians, and students of all ages.[12] The modular flexibility of Mariemont High School and the campus complex of the Perry Community Education Village have received national attention. Innovative designs—such as the deconstructionist style of the Wexner Center for the Visual Arts at Ohio State University and the Aronoff Center for Design and Art at the University of Cincinnati, or the cubist style of the Center for the Visual Arts at the University of Toledo—have received far more attention in the architectural community than among educational professionals. It is perhaps too soon to rate their lasting impact, but they have focused national and international attention on three of the state's public universities.

It is fair to question how specific buildings were selected for discussion in this book. Inclusion should not be perceived as an endorsement of quality, although some buildings typify a significant development in educational practice and some reflect an architectural ideal that was cited as a model for professional educators and architects. A few represent both. The purpose of this work is to provide an educational and historical context for educators, architectural historians, and community leaders involved in decisions regarding the preservation and utilization of historic educational structures and to raise thought-provoking questions among educators, architects, and decision-making trustees and board members about the functional and aesthetic significance of educational architecture and the cultural values it displays.

Where possible, surviving buildings have been chosen—particularly those listed on the National Register of Historic Places. But some razed structures are included, simply because they reflect a significant educational concept or architectural interpretation. A conscious effort has been made to portray the state's geographical diversity, urban and rural environments, and the chronological span from statehood in 1803 to the present. Considering the thousands of educational structures that serve or have served the state, the selection process was admittedly arbitrary but hopefully rational.

As local builders gave way to professional architects during the last decades of the nineteenth century, the tendency was to use respected local talent even for major educational projects—architects such as Samuel Hannaford and Frederick W. Garber of Cincinnati, George F. Hammond, Frank R. Walker, and Harry E. Weeks of Cleveland, Guy Tilden of Canton, Joseph W. Yost and Frank L. Packard of Columbus, Alfred Hahn of Toledo, and Albert Pretzinger of Dayton. Many public schools and libraries felt and continue to feel obligated to employ local architects for publicly funded projects and sometimes find it economically beneficial to retain an individual architect or firm over a period of years—like Frank S. Barnum in Cleveland, Edwin M. Gee in Toledo, or Howard Dwight Smith in Columbus. For projects seeking to make an architectural statement, nationally recognized architects have been employed—such as William Tinsley of Indianapolis, William B. Ittner of Saint Louis, George F. Shepley of Boston, Cass Gilbert and Peter Eisenman of New York, Minoru Yamasaki of Detroit, and Frank O. Gehry of Santa Monica, California. Recently, as educational buildings have become a recognized specialization within architecture, Ohio firms such as Lesko Associates of Cleveland and Burgess and Niple of Columbus have acquired a wide reputation, as have out-of-state firms, such as Perkins and Will of Chicago, who often work in partnership with a local firm.

When one reviews the state's educational architecture across a period of time, it is impossible to ignore the significant role local benefactors have played in creating innovative architectural treasures. This is evident from the Hughes and Woodward bequests that made it possible for Cincinnati to build in the 1850s two of the most admired high schools in the country to the Brumback gift that in 1901 created at Van Wert the first countywide library system in the United States; the 1915 McClain donation that provided Greenfield with an elementary school, high school, and vocational complex that was admired by much larger cities and copied across the nation; the 1928 Carnell gift that gave Dayton an art institute unequaled by any city of its size in the country; and the 1988 Wexner gift that inspired Ohio State University to erect one of the most praised and controversial art complexes in the country. For better or worse—and there are many who would argue that public buildings should not reflect the desires of a single wealthy individual—there appears to be a freedom of creative expression associated with private funding that may be more difficult to achieve when architects work with committees representing a variety of constituencies.

The ancient proverb that maintains one picture is worth a thousand words holds much validity for educational architecture and Ohio offers an excellent perspective for its study.

One | Academies, Seminaries, & Institutes

The Northwest Ordinance of 1787 was neither the first nor the last time that politicians committed themselves to educational goals but failed to provide the necessary funds. When the Continental Congress established a territorial government northwest of the Ohio River, the legislators proclaimed, "Religion, morality, and knowledge being necessary to good government and the happiness of mankind, schools and the means of education shall be forever encouraged."[1]

As the federal government began surveying land for sale in the 1790s, section sixteen—1/36th of each township—was set aside for the support of public schools within the township. The framers of the Ohio Constitution reaffirmed this dictum in 1802, and they added that no law should prevent the poor from equal participation in such schools endowed by the government. But in spite of these sentiments, rental income from 640 acres of land—in most cases virgin forest—was far too little to support public schools for all the children in frontier communities. Parents who wanted their children to be able to read the Bible, write a letter, or compute the value of farm produce being offered for sale were forced to enroll them in a subscription school and pay for each scholar who attended.[2]

These were the first schools, described in glowing terms when county histories were written several decades later. In 1789 Rev. Daniel Story was engaged to teach at Marietta and Bathsheba Rouse, daughter of an Ohio Company settler, at Belpre—making them the first teachers among the pioneer settlers in the new territory.[3] Such subscription schools were usually conducted for eight- to twelve-week terms in winter or summer between

spring planting and autumn harvest. The log buildings that accommodated them were crude structures that no longer exist.

A rare log survivor, although it is larger and more carefully constructed
than early common schools, is Reverend Thomas's Select School, a steeple-
notched log building at Shandon in Butler County. This 30 x 22–foot structure was the two-story home and school of Rev. Thomas Thomas, pastor
of Whitewater Congregational Church in this Welsh settlement. Ministers
were often the most educated persons in pioneer communities, and it was
not unusual for one to teach a subscription school in his home as a source
of income. In the 1820s this congregation had two ministers who conducted dual Sunday school and church services in Welsh and English. In
the subscription school, Reverend Thomas taught advanced grammar,
geography, and mathematics—including algebra and geometry, while his
wife taught the girls plain and ornamental sewing.[4]

Although church-sponsored academies soon became common, it was
rare for one privately run by an individual minister to survive for any length
of time. A notable exception was Twinsburg Institute, founded in 1828 by
Rev. Samuel Bissell, a Yale graduate and Congregational Church minister.
Although it was never chartered by the state and received no public funds,
by midcentury it occupied four buildings, employed seven teachers, and
had enrolled approximately three hundred students—including Seneca,
Ottawa, and Patawatomie youths.[5] Financial difficulties during the Civil
War, when qualified teachers and students were scarce, required the sale
of the buildings. Yet after the war, at the age of seventy, Bissell started
over, constructing a new stone building—doing most of the manual labor
himself. Its simple vernacular construction attests to the proprietor's unique
goal of providing classical instruction for modest tuition, allowing Native
American students not only to enroll but to work around the premises
for their board. Its seven-bay, two-story size, however, defined the expec-
tations of an old-fashioned teacher who continued to teach a number of
years longer.

In 1808 the Ohio legislature officially chartered (a legal requirement for
joint ownership of property) the first academies: Dayton, Chillicothe, and
Worthington Academies.[6] These communities aspired to furnish a classical
education beyond the three Rs, and each soon constructed an appropriate
building—with local residents subscribing materials such as bricks, boards,
and shingles, or labor such as carpentry or chopping wood for the brick
kilns.[7] Daniel Bishop was contracted on September 29, 1808, to erect Worthington Academy, agreeing to complete the brick walls and chimneys of
this 53 x 27–foot, two-story Federal style building by December first. He

REVEREND THOMAS'S SELECT SCHOOL
c. 1819
Steeple-notched log
Builder: Unknown
Shandon (Butler Co.)
Photo by Virginia E. McCormick

TWINSBURG INSTITUTE
1867
Vernacular
Builder: Samuel Bissell
Twinsburg (Summit Co.)
Courtesy of Twinsburg Historical Society

was to receive $3.00 for each thousand bricks laid, $1.50 for each brick arch over windows and doors, and $20.00 for "painting and penciling said walls." Local residents agreed to build the scaffolding and deliver bricks, lime, and sand "within a convenient distance" as needed.[8]

This was one of the first brick buildings for education in the state and undoubtedly reflects the common process used in constructing many of the early-nineteenth-century academies, seminaries, and colleges. These were community enterprises and subscriptions from local residents were often made in terms of materials and labor rather than cash, since the latter was extremely scarce on the frontier. Only skilled labor such as masonry or finish carpentry was contracted and paid for in cash or goods. Such vernacular buildings constructed by local builder-carpenters were usually generic, Federal I-shaped structures, a single room deep—equally suitable for residential, commercial, or educational use.[9] Whether brick or frame, they were typically two stories high with a three- or five-bay facade—a rectangle with gable ends that any skilled carpenter had learned as an apprentice to design to the desired dimensions. Within a decade the Worthington community had nearly identical buildings serving as a residence/tavern, a commercial building with separate entries for three businesses, and a Masonic lodge. School buildings were not yet designed for their specific function.

By 1811 Worthington Academy had hired John Kilbourn, who had received his "A.B. degree from Vermont University."[10] The local newspaper advertised four academy terms annually at $1.50 per term for small children "who do not write"; $2.00 for a basic grammar curriculum of spelling, reading, writing, and common arithmetic; $3.00 for a course of study including geography, history, English grammar and composition, surveying, and navigation; and $4.00 for an advanced curriculum of higher mathematics, Latin, Greek, rhetoric, logic, natural and moral philosophy, and astronomy.[11] Such diversity was representative of early academies that could not survive on their advanced classical studies alone.

However, the Lancaster Seminary, chartered by a group of Cincinnati business leaders in 1815, reflected that city's educational leadership in creating a coeducational school that would incorporate the Lancasterian philosophy of employing master teachers for great numbers of students and utilizing older students as monitors for the younger ones.[12] The concept appealed to early-nineteenth-century business leaders, who found attractive the economy this method offered for teaching basic employment skills in reading, writing, and arithmetic. An appropriately grand building was erected in Cincinnati with a colonnaded central portico and separate wings for boys and girls—a building with a capacity of eleven hundred students.[13]

GRANVILLE ACADEMY
1833
Federal
Builder: ? Gerard Bancroft
Granville (Licking Co.)
Drawing by Horace King, courtesy of
Virginia King

After 1863 remodeling into single story for
Welsh Congregational Church
Photo by Virginia E. McCormick
[from slide]

CHESTER ACADEMY
1822–34
Federal
Builder: Unknown
Chester (Meigs Co.)
Photo by Virginia E. McCormick

Most early academies, however, were not designed by architects but by local builders with access to plan books. Various communities did strive for an element that would distinguish their school. When in 1834 the Education Society of Painesville contracted with Jonathan Goldsmith to build a 44 x 36–foot, two-story brick academy for one thousand dollars, they committed an extra ten dollars for tinning the cupola. Few of these early-nineteenth-century brick and frame academies have survived, but Granville Academy, a frame building that originally had four rooms on two floors and an impressive gable-end entry with fanlight, was remodeled in 1863 for use as a Welsh church and the windows elongated for a single-story sanctuary. This academy was a girls' school sponsored by the Congregational Church; catalogs show 65 students in 1835 and 175 by 1837, a sign of its excellent reputation and the lack of public secondary schools.[14]

Chester Academy in Meigs County was unusual in being chartered as Stephen Strong's Manual Labor Seminary to provide instruction "in the

WESTERN RESERVE COLLEGE/
ACADEMY CHAPEL
1835–36
Greek Revival
Architect/Builder: Simeon Porter
Hudson (Summit Co.)
Photo from National Register file,
courtesy of Ohio Historic Preservation
Office

various branches of useful knowledge," but it did not have a sectarian religious affiliation.[15] Strong's father had been involved in the salt industry that drew the first settlers north from the Ohio River, and Stephen was one of several brothers who served in county leadership roles—traveling to Columbus to campaign for the creation of Meigs County in 1819 and serving in the Ohio House of Representatives in 1826–27. Ironically, Stephen Strong died the year the academy legislation passed, but a brick building was erected on public land next to the county courthouse, which was then at Chester. The building hugs the hillside with three stories in front, two in the rear. When the county seat moved to Pomeroy in 1841, Chester's prosperity declined. However, this building served for a number of years as Meigs County High School and Teacher's Institute, preparing teachers for local one-room schools—fourteen in Chester Township alone.[16]

Federal style architecture continued to be popular in Ohio, but by the 1830s academies that aspired to provide a classical education were beginning to erect buildings in the Greek Revival style brought west by New Englanders. Such buildings reinforced the concept that these institutions offered a classical curriculum and embraced the ideals of Athenian democracy—such as purity, wisdom, and independence.[17] An outstanding surviving example of such Greek Revival style is Western Reserve College/Academy Chapel at Hudson.[18] Master builder Simeon Porter conceived a Greek Revival row of buildings for Western Reserve College/Academy, with particular attention on the chapel, which was dedicated at the August 1836 commencement. For architectural inspiration, trustees of the college looked toward Yale, the alma mater of their new president, Rev. George E. Pierce. Yale had instituted the concept of a campus where building fronts faced outward toward the street, presenting the community with an impressive academic row quite different from the closed quadrangles common to elite English universities.[19]

At Western Reserve, instead of a free-standing portico, engaged Doric pilasters define the facade of the chapel and are repeated on the side walls as piers with Georgian elliptical arches. The original three-stage tower—probably from a Asher Benjamin pattern book—has now been reduced and reinforced but retains the simplicity of design associated with New England Congregational churches.[20] Advertisements of the period refer to the male department of Hudson Academy and the Seminary for Young Ladies—parallel departments each offering a twelve-week term for $3.00 to $5.00, depending upon the curriculum.[21] During 1837–38, North College Hall—a dormitory for theological students—and the first astronomical observatory west of the Alleghenies were completed. Western Reserve was

LEBANON ACADEMY
1844
Greek Revival
Builder: Unknown
Lebanon (Warren Co.)
Photo by Virginia E. McCormick

Building in use as National Normal
University, with original windows and cupola
Courtesy of Warren County Historical Society

purposely establishing itself as a contender for the title of "Yale of the West" with its row of buildings aligned as they had been at their president's alma mater.[22]

Lebanon Academy, built a few years later, is a more modest interpretation of Greek Revival style executed by local builders. The simplicity of its unadorned pediment and the pilasters that define its facade remain, but the removal of its belfry and the remodeled windows destroy much of the style's integrity. Unlike the early Granville Academy and Hudson Academy, Lebanon Academy was coeducational, with early catalogs showing nearly equal numbers of male and female students—mostly from the local area.[23] Many of them became teachers, and within a decade this building became the first home of National Normal University—one of the largest and most highly regarded teacher training institutions as education moved toward professional status.[24]

It is noteworthy that in this era dominated by subscription schools there were some efforts by religious groups to provide education for African American youth. The only surviving structure representing such early endeavors is a vernacular, single-story brick building at Harveysburg— funded in part by the Grove Quaker Meeting —in which Elizabeth Harvey began teaching a school for "free Negroes" during the 1830s.[25] Most such ventures were short lived, but this community established by North Carolina Quakers fleeing the institution of slavery welcomed black residents, and fifty years after the school's erection there were fifty-four black or mulatto students recorded as attending school in the community.[26]

But perhaps the largest and best-known school for African Americans in Ohio in the early nineteenth century was Emlen Institute at Carthagena.[27] This school was established by Augustus Wattles, who migrated from Connecticut to Cincinnati and was disturbed by the number of former slaves and their children streaming north across the Ohio River to freedom without any opportunity to secure an education to support themselves. In Mercer County, Wattles and some associates began buying land for resale to persons of color so they might become farmers—an aspiration that may seem limited today, but it was a progressive opportunity for land ownership in the nineteenth century. In 1836 he established a manual labor school with an initial enrollment of seven boys. By 1840 this school had grown to more than fifty students, and Wattles made connection with the executors of the estate of Samuel Emlen, a New Jersey businessman whose will left twenty thousand dollars to educate black and Native American youth in mechanical arts, agriculture, and Christian religion. In 1843 the Emlen trustees erected at Carthagena a five-bay brick school building with stepped

HARVEY'S FREE NEGRO SCHOOL
1831
Vernacular
Builder: Unknown
Harveysburg (Warren Co.)
Photo by Virginia E. McCormick

EMLEN INSTITUTE
c. 1843
Federal
Architect/Builder: Unknown
Carthagena (Mercer Co.)
Drawing by Henry Howe, *Historical Collections of Ohio*

gables on either end, probably utilizing as masons and carpenters some of the former slaves who lived in the community. Although the school initially prospered, its setting was too remote to attract qualified staff, and in 1857 the trustees removed it to Philadelphia.

In this time period, educational opportunities beyond the common school were usually segregated by sex, but boarding facilities for female students also typically employed classical architecture. One example was Putnam Classical Institute at Zanesville, launched by Sarah Sturges Buckingham with a ten-thousand-dollar bequest from her mother's will.[28] This was a unique institution in an era when the trustees responsible for administering educational institutions were universally male. Beginning in 1835 with fifteen students, Putnam Classical Institute was incorporated by the Ohio legislature the following year, and in the autumn of 1838 moved into a three-story, 110 x 45–foot building with double parlors, an office, dining room, kitchen, school hall, library, and recitation and music rooms. It was expected that the young ladies attending would be taught the social graces and skills such as drawing, painting, and playing the piano. Putnam Classical Institute supported this cultural image with an imposing Greek Revival building with a projecting central bay, engaged Doric pilasters, and a classical frieze and pediment. Inside it employed the latest in technology, with wood- or coal-burning grates for heat and gas for illumination in all rooms.

Although seminaries for young ladies existed in a number of Ohio cities before 1850, most were administered by male trustees and were frequently affiliated with a religious denomination. One of the largest and best known was Steubenville Female Seminary, which occupied an imposing building overlooking the Ohio River and during seven decades of operation produced more than five thousand graduates, including a significant number of Presbyterian missionaries.[29]

A smaller but elegant surviving building is Norwalk Female Seminary, a Greek Revival masterpiece with two fluted Ionic columns in antis flanked by square pilasters at the corners.[30] With Presbyterian minister Joseph Hayes as superintendent, Mrs. Hayes as a teacher of drawing—an acceptable role for a married lady in the mid-nineteenth century—and two assistants, it operated for less than a decade before falling to the competition of a public high school.[31]

Portsmouth Young Ladies Seminary reflects a slightly later time period with an architectural transition from Greek Revival to the Italianate elements introduced in the years immediately preceding the Civil War. Although the entry retains Greek Revival influence with a Corinthian-

PUTNAM CLASSICAL INSTITUTE
1837–38
Greek Revival
Architect/Builder: Unknown
Zanesville (Muskingum Co.)
Drawing by Henry Howe, *Historical Collections of Ohio*

NORWALK FEMALE SEMINARY
1847–48
Greek Revival
Builder: George Manahan
Norwalk (Huron Co.)
Photo by Virginia E. McCormick

columned portico, the height and asymmetrical mass of the building, slender rectangular windows, low-pitched hip roof, and three-part mullion attic windows defined by a belt course typify the growing popularity of Italianate style. From the exterior, the seminary appears to be an impressive private residence—which it later became for many years—but from the end of the Civil War until the 1890s it served as a female seminary. Like the female seminary at Norwalk, Portsmouth displays the concept of a nineteenth-century finishing school for young ladies with an appropriately domestic style of architecture. At its zenith, six instructors taught music, history, English literature, and modern languages to the daughters of Portsmouth families who had prospered from the coal and iron ore industries.[32]

By the mid-nineteenth century, Ohio produced sufficient wealth for benevolent philanthropists to establish schools to their personal specifications. One of the earliest and most interesting was "Little Antioch" School at Yellow Springs. It was built at the same time as Antioch College to serve as a private school for young children—particularly the daughters of Judge William Mills, who platted the village and developed a resort around the sulphur springs purported to have healthful powers. Mills was among those who were instrumental in attracting Horace Mann—at the time the nation's leading educator—as president of the college.[33] The resort village had aspirations for educational excellence and cultural elegance that were abundantly reflected in this extraordinary Gothic Revival building, which is undoubtedly the most elaborate one-room school ever constructed in Ohio. Hiram Brown, a master carpenter who had helped build the Greene County courthouse and the Mills home in Yellow Springs, was reportedly given carte blanche for the school; and he created a miniature medieval castle with pinnacles at each corner and an octagonal bell tower complete with crenelations—all in a 26 x 30–foot school building.[34] "Little Antioch" incorporated the turrets of New York City's Free Academy and the tower of Cincinnati's Hughes High School—both featured as models by Henry Barnard, the mid-nineteenth century's leading authority on school architecture.[35] Mills and Brown were certainly flaunting Yellow Springs's cultural awareness.

In Youngstown only a year later, the will of Judge William Rayen left funds to construct an academy that was to be free to students regardless of their race or religious belief. Unlike most academies and colleges of the period, Rayen's will prohibited the teaching of "the peculiar religious tenets or doctrines of any denomination or sect whatever," but at the same time it specified that "no others be employed as teachers than those of

1850 advertisement from *Norwalk Reflector*

PORTSMOUTH YOUNG LADIES SEMINARY
1858
Transitional Greek Revival/Italianate
Architect/Builder: Unknown
Portsmouth (Scioto Co.)
Photo by Virginia E. McCormick

"LITTLE ANTIOCH" SCHOOL
1853
Gothic Revival
Builder: Hiram Brown
Yellow Springs (Greene Co.)
Photo from Antiochana Collection,
Antioch College, courtesy of *Timeline*

RAYEN SCHOOL
1866
Classical Revival
Architect: Simeon Porter
Youngstown (Mahoning Co.)
Courtesy of Mahoning Valley Historical
Society

good moral character and habits." Yet it required a special act of the Ohio legislature to allow such a privately endowed academy to be publicly owned and operated. By the time trustees were appointed and a building constructed, free secondary education was theoretically available to local children of any creed or color, so Rayen School opened in 1866 as a public high school. It is an elegant Greek Revival structure—one of the few in Ohio with a central Roman dome-shaped cupola complete with lantern—designed by Simeon Porter, the preeminent early-nineteenth-century architect of the Western Reserve. The brick pilasters are the work of Ross Berry, a free African American mason who was born in Pennsylvania, and the fluted Ionic columns of its portico are by master carpenter Daniel V. Tilden.[36] Whether it was the private endowment or its classical elegance, it is one of the few schools of its age to survive in a major urban center.

One of the largest and best known of Ohio's privately endowed elementary/secondary educational institutions is Marsh Foundation School at Van Wert, opened in 1925 as a boarding facility for orphaned and abandoned youth from northwestern Ohio. George H. Marsh began his career with the Eagle Stave Factory and reportedly increased his assets as a riverboat gambler on sales trips to New Orleans before he progressed to extensive investments in banks, real estate, and railroads. Typical of the early-twentieth-century benevolent philanthropists, Marsh's bequest of four million dollars and a fourteen-hundred-acre farm provided agricultural land and mechanical shops for learning vocational skills. Six Jacobethan style buildings clustered in a campus like setting were designed for the site by Toledo architects Langdon, Hohly, and Gram, establishing a prestigious environment that was intended to inspire the boarding students aged five to sixteen who had experienced little luxury or beauty in their lives. It is typical of the beaux-arts progressivism of the early twentieth century, which believed that individuals could be shaped by their environment.

Marsh Foundation School's first yearbook in 1927 reveals the school's progressive philosophy by picturing elementary students working at movable desks that could be arranged for interactive group work—more than two decades after Dewey described the difficulty of finding desks for "work" rather than for "listening" but when nearly all public schools still had rows of desks bolted to the floor. A dramatic example of Dewey's philosophy was the auto mechanics class given to both boys and girls in the fifth through the eighth grades—expecting that they would learn how an automobile worked by dismantling and reassembling one.[37] Another

MARSH FOUNDATION SCHOOL
1925
Jacobethan
Architects: Langdon, Hohly and Gram
Van Wert (Van Wert Co.)
Photos by Virginia E. McCormick

Dormitory under construction, with manual
training class assisting the builders
Photo from 1927 report, courtesy of the
Marsh Foundation

project—still standing as significant testimony to the success of this philosophy—was Marsh Hall, a two-story brick dormitory for high school boys that the older boys assisted in constructing as part of a class project.[38]

Although private academies continue to operate throughout the state, the rise of public high schools caused the demise of many early ones and the evolution of others into colleges and universities.

Elementary classroom with movable
desks/chairs, 1920s
Photo from 1927 report, courtesy of
the Marsh Foundation

Auto mechanics class for fifth to eighth grade
boys and girls
Photo from 1927 report, courtesy of the
Marsh Foundation

Two | One-Room Schools

The pioneer schools that were glowingly described in county histories are long gone—crude log structures that were never intended to be anything but a temporary accommodation on the frontier. Descriptions of a neighborhood school built in 1814 at Venice in Butler County and one built in 1835 in Adams Township in Washington County suggest, however, a remarkably similar design prevailed in various geographic regions of the state for much of the early nineteenth century.[1] These early log schools were rectangular buildings about 16 or 18 x 20 feet. The crudest had a dirt floor but most boasted a puncheon floor of split logs, a door hung on wooden hinges, and at the end opposite the entry a large fieldstone fireplace that was inefficient in producing heat. The chimney and the cracks between the logs that formed the walls were chinked with mud that required frequent renewal. On each side were two or three small windows, covered in the most rustic buildings with greased paper, but more commonly covered with four "lights"—glass panes about 8 x 10 inches in size. Beneath the windows a writing desk was formed by a board about eighteen or twenty inches wide and ten or twelve feet long that was supported by wooden pegs stuck at a slant into the log wall. The seats for scholars were split-log benches without backs that were made by attaching legs to slabs like those that composed the puncheon floor.

Public education in Ohio did not begin until legislation in 1825 established a property tax to support public schools and required townships to form school districts with directors elected by local voters.[2] But these funds were insufficient in most cases to construct buildings and pay teachers and

RAGERSVILLE SCHOOL
1830
Vernacular/Greek Revival elements
Builder: Michael Swagler
Ragersville (Tuscarawas Co.)
Photo by J. D. Brown, National Register
file, courtesy of Ohio Historic Preservation
Office

Interior with central stove and double-student desks
Photo by J. D. Brown, National Register
file, courtesy of Ohio Historic
Preservation Office

most schools continued to be erected by community labor, gradually pro-ducing a network of one-room schools within a two-mile walking distance of every student. On the eve of World War I, half of the school children throughout the United States were enrolled in the country's 212,000 one-room school buildings—nearly ten thousand of them in Ohio.[3]

The rapidly diminishing examples of these one-room schools that sur-vive across Ohio are not the first but usually the second or third building constructed—schools remembered with nostalgia by old-timers who at-tended them in the late nineteenth and early twentieth centuries. Some fondly recalled, "the hilarity of playtime antics, the embarrassment of class-room error, the tenseness of intrigue, the intimacy, and the awakening of youthful romance!"[4] Others saw the disparity between the educational of-ferings of the rural one-room schools of this period and the larger, graded urban schools with a diverse course of study and lamented their isolated one-room school as "a barren temple of arts."[5] Both viewpoints were valid.

Ragersville School in Tuscarawas County is one of the earliest and best-preserved Ohio examples of the basic one-room schools that became the basis for organizing and developing communities throughout the Midwest. It was built at a propitious location "in the forks of the roads, one leading to New Philadelphia and the other to Coshocton," that was conveyed to the local school directors for $1.00 by Michael Swagler and Mary Swagler on September 18, 1830—two weeks after their brother-in-law Conrad Rager filed a plat for an adjacent town containing twenty-two one-acre lots.[6] School building and town building typically proceeded hand in hand. Michael Swagler was one of the township trustees who divided the town-ship into four school districts the previous December and it is likely that he and Rager, with other neighbors such as school directors Peter Kern and Eli Walker, were responsible for this building's construction. As was common at the time, the land and building were a gift "to be used for school pur-poses so long as the inhabitants of said district wish to occupy the same for school purposes." If the school was later closed or moved, the deed speci-fied that the land would revert to Swagler or his heirs. This particular deed contained a more unusual provision for the school building "to be free for all gospel preachers to preach in at anytime when it . . . [does] not interfere with the teacher or his scholars' privileges."[7] The aspiring com-munity as yet had no regular minister or a religious congregation to support a building.

Local carpenters were capable of constructing vernacular frame schools like Ragersville from their own simple sketches. Within a few years there

OURANT'S SCHOOL
1871
Vernacular
Builder: Unknown
Cadiz (Harrison Co.)
Photo by J. D. Brown, National Register file,
courtesy of Ohio Historic Preservation Office

Interior with central stove and double-student
desks
Photo by J. D. Brown, National Register file,
courtesy of Ohio Historic Preservation Office

Double-student desks recommended
by the Commissioner of Common
Schools in 1868
Drawing from Ohio School Report, 1868–69

were at least eight nearly identical buildings in this township, some slightly larger and having four windows per side. Like the log buildings that preceded them, this generic rectangular form served for either church or school, and by eliminating the central side windows and adding partitions—and perhaps steps to a sleeping loft—such a building could serve as a residence. Ragersville School's classic simplicity consists of a four-panel door with a four-light transom above, a gable facade accented by plain frieze returns, a trio of nine-over-six double-hung windows on either side with wood slip sills and simple surrounds—all reflecting an 1830s awareness of Greek Revival design interpreted by local carpenters. The building remained in use for forty years, with the belfry and interior appointments such as the beaded ceiling and horizontal wainscoting reflecting later additions.

Henry Barnard, the Connecticut superintendent who became the first U.S. Commissioner of Education, favored the Greek Revival architecture of his New England Congregational heritage. He believed that every schoolhouse should be a temple consecrated to the physical, intellectual, and moral culture of every child in the community.[8]

Such frame schoolhouses continued to be built and used throughout Ohio for much of the nineteenth century—although the siding of the early ones was not necessarily painted but often left to weather to a natural gray. Built the year that Ragersville was closed, Ourant's School in nearby Harrison County exhibits unadorned shiplap siding but reflects advancing technology with its standing-seam metal roof and egg and dart ornamentation on its pressed metal ceiling. This building continued in use until 1941, complete with double desks for two children, separate outdoor privies for boys and girls, coal shed, and Boomer #4 stove from the Massillon Stove Company.[9]

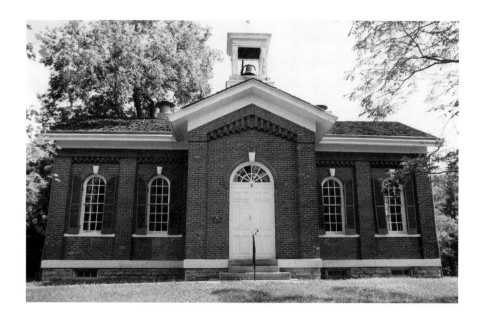

WASHINGTON HEIGHTS SCHOOL
1873
Neoclassical/Italianate
Architect/Builder: Unknown
Indian Hills (Hamilton Co.)
Photos by Virginia E. McCormick

The contrast between Ourant's School and the elegant brick craftsmanship of Washington Heights School, completed two years later at Indian Hills in suburban Cincinnati, reveals the evolving disparity between rural and urban education in Ohio, even for one-room schools. Washington Heights's 53 x 26–foot classroom opened with an enrollment of fifty-two students—noticeably larger than the common 32 or 36 x 24–foot building designed to accommodate about forty students, who would be within range of the teacher's voice.[10] Its projecting vestibule with double-door entry and a circular fanlight is echoed in the round-arched windows accented by a double row of headers and a center keystone. Alternate rows of bricks set at different depths give the gables a trim resembling Romanesque billeting. The building's interior is typical of the 1870s, with painted tongue-and-groove wainscoting to a height of three feet and above this five feet of plasterboard coated with lampblack to form a writing surface.[11] Its belfry with a two-hundred-pound bell cast by the Buckeye Bell Foundry in Cincinnati was added in 1879, about the time large schoolhouse bells were becoming a status symbol for many Midwestern communities.[12]

Brick schoolhouses were constructed in some Ohio communities from an early date—depending upon the availability of a skilled mason—but their number increased dramatically after the passage of extensive school legislation in 1853 following revision of Ohio's constitution. The position of state commissioner of common schools was created and a state tax was approved to establish a school trust fund. Responsibility for local school funds and ownership of school properties was assigned to newly created township school boards composed of one representative from each subdistrict.[13] This authority to own land and school buildings offered far more stability than previous leases or gifts from benevolent farmers anxious to have a school convenient to their children.

The state commissioner placed great emphasis on buildings, reporting "the ultimate success of our whole system of Common Schools depends as much on a thorough reform in the construction, furniture, and care of school houses, as upon any other single circumstance whatever." State Commissioner Barney urged school directors to remind local citizens that the expense of providing a suitable school building would not recur for a generation and commended half the districts in the state for providing "convenient, and in some cases, elegant, school houses."[14] From 1853 to 1858 the number of school buildings statewide more than doubled, from 5,984 to 12,602, with an average value of $340.[15]

This would have included Poland Center School in Mahoning County, a typical 22 x 32–foot building but with its basic Greek Revival form

POLAND CENTER SCHOOL
1858
Transitional Greek Revival/Italianate
Builder: Unknown
Poland (Mahoning Co.)
Photo by Virginia E. McCormick

SCIOTO TOWNSHIP DISTRICT #2 SCHOOL
1888
Vernacular
Builders: Ater and Kern
Orient (Pickaway Co.)
Photo by Virginia E. McCormick

distinguished by Tuscan pilasters with molded wooden capitals that reflect the rising popularity of the Italianate influence—even on the Western Reserve where Greek Revival residential architecture was prevalent. This building's soft red brick is laid in common bond with sandy mortar joints exposing bits of unmixed lime. Its most unique feature is a fluted cast-iron column in the center of the interior that supports the ridge and emulates the increasingly sophisticated technology railroads were making available even to small communities.[16]

Echoing the priority that communities placed on educating their children, many of the one-room schools built during the last quarter of the nineteenth century were brick—often with distinctive characteristics that local builders incorporated. Scioto Township District #2 School in Pickaway County is in many ways typical of schools in the state—yet identical to no other. At 28 x 40 feet with three windows on either side, it conformed to the standard rectangular mode, providing a separate cloakroom for boys and girls on either side of a recessed entry—as progressive educators recommended. But builders Ater and Kern distinguished their school with corbelling on the exterior walls and segmental-arched windows and an entry arch accented by two rows of brick headers. And they expressed a pride that was rare among one-room school builders by inscribing their names in stone on the completed structure.[17]

Parochial schools for the Catholic Church were for the most part similar to public schools, with brick buildings being particularly popular in the northwestern region of the state where there was a substantial population of German immigrants. The Cassella schools in Mercer County have arched windows that indicate the skilled workmanship of late-nineteenth-century masons and two distinct doorways on the gable facade, a feature some districts preferred so boys and girls could line up separately to enter the building. Several of the schools in this German Catholic community boasted a cross rather than a belfry on their gable facade. When one building became insufficient for the number of students, local citizens made the practical choice of erecting an identical building beside it to provide the convenience of primary and advanced grammar classes in separate one-room schools.[18]

Such buildings are remarkably comparable to a design in James Johonnot's popular manual on schoolhouse construction that featured alternative exterior treatments for a double-entry school that would accommodate sixty pupils at double-student desks.[19] This design included separate vestibules for boys' and girls' outer clothing, two stoves in opposite corners, and a small recitation room between the vestibules—a feature that seems

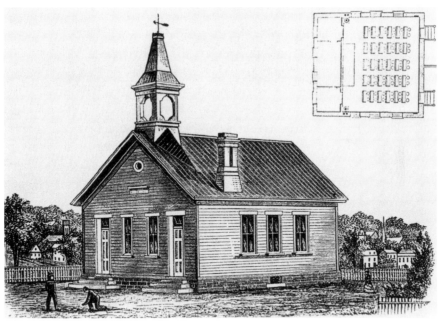

CASSELLA CATHOLIC CHURCH SCHOOL
1880 and 1893
Vernacular
Builders: Unknown
Cassella (Mercer Co.)
Photo by Virginia E. McCormick

Model one-room school from 1872 plan book
with cloakrooms, corner stoves, and double-
student desks for sixty students
Drawing from James Johonnot, *Schoolhouses*

incomprehensible to an experienced teacher well aware of the activities in which children might indulge if she were for any period of time to absent herself from a group of students in the classroom.

It was not uncommon for local builders and school directors to assert their cultural awareness in the style of a local school. An unparalleled example is Florence Corners School built in the 1850s in Erie County. Octagonal buildings are generally attributed to Orson S. Fowler, who in 1849 promoted the concept of octagon homes as a method for reducing building costs and increasing sunlight and ventilation.[20] Actually the form had been used much earlier, with as many as twenty such Dutch Reformed churches constructed in the Hudson River Valley before 1750.[21] Although it closely resembles an octagonal school built at Etna, New York, in 1825, Florence Corners School may owe its origin to a design by Town and Davis that appeared in Henry Barnard's widely distributed *School Architecture*.[22]

Erie County masons were skilled workmen of the sandstone common to that area and this building erected by the Collingwood brothers exhibits a high level of ashlar construction expertise.[23] Random cut stone eighteen inches thick forms walls twelve feet in length on each octagonal side. Florence Corners's symmetry is emphasized by a shingled roof that rises at a 30-degree pitch to a louvered cupola at the apex. One side contains a vestibule entry and the opposite side has a solid wall for the teacher's desk, while each of the remaining six sides has a central nine-over-nine double-hung window. Such schools normally had a stove in the center with two rows of desks circling the wall on either side of the teacher's desk—often with boys on the outer row and girls on the inner, and the smallest children near the stove. Abandoned as a school around the turn of the twentieth century, this unique building has continued to serve the community as a town hall.[24]

The geology a few miles south of Lake Erie left much of this region a legacy of sandstone formed by dunes overlying a shale base and being compressed over thousands of years. Sandstone seams one hundred or more feet deep offered a million cubic feet per acre of this prized building material. During the latter half of the nineteenth century, Lorain County quarried Amherst blue sandstone for the finest buildings on the continent—the courthouse in Cleveland, Astor family mansions in New York City, college buildings at Princeton University, and the parliament buildings in Ottawa, Canada, among others.[25]

The directors of South Ridge School near Amherst chose this variety of sandstone for their local school—a masterpiece of one-room school craftsmanship. This rock-faced ashlar building features unusually narrow

FLORENCE CORNERS SCHOOL
1850s
Octagonal
Builders: William Collingwood and Ransom Collingwood
Florence (Erie Co.)
Photo by Virginia E. McCormick

SOUTH RIDGE SCHOOL
1896
Vernacular
Architect/Builder: Unknown
Amherst Township (Lorain Co.)
Photo by Virginia E. McCormick

two-over-two double-hung windows paired beneath smooth stone pediments, a pattern repeated in the double-leaf entry. The imbricated slate roof was repeated on the pyramidal cupola.[26]

It was a building constructed to last for centuries, but when it was erected in 1896 progressive educators were already questioning the conceptual validity of the one-room school experience. Throughout the last half of the nineteenth century, various state commissioners of common schools devoted efforts to improving the design of school buildings, frequently including good examples in their annual reports. Unlike the vernacular buildings throughout the state, these were architectural renderings, and as late as the 1880s, plans for one-room schools were included along with the increasingly more prevalent graded schools. A building designed by Columbus architects Terrell and Morris for the Madison Township school directors in Franklin County was cited in 1884 as a fine example. It featured pressed brick arches and stone trim in the newly popular Richardsonian Romanesque style more common to much larger public buildings. Madison Township School was commended for its seating capacity of forty-eight to fifty pupils, slate roof and blackboards, and double flues for venting smoke from the stove and for providing fresh air. Such elegance cost $2,000, well above the state's average one-room building at the time.[27]

Far more representative was the October 15, 1885, contract between the Meigsville Township school directors in Morgan County and J. W. Allard for the construction of Oak Grove School. It was to be 28 x 30 feet in size and 12 feet high with a slate roof, white oak or pine floor, four windows—each with twelve lights of glass 10 x 16 inches in size—on each side, four-panel shutters for each window, a four-panel door with a three-light transom above, and the building was to be painted with three coats of "best white lead and linseed oil." Allard was to be paid $270 for materials including doors and windows, $80 for roofing, $65 for plastering, $35 for paint, $100 for labor, $45 for stonework including old stone (from the foundation of a previous school on the site). The total of $595 was to be paid by February 20, 1886, presumably when the building was expected to be completed.[28] In rural areas local school directors specified construction details decades after professional architects had assumed this responsibility for urban districts.

The Meigsville Township school was similar in size to Science Hill School at Alliance, which was built in 1870 and continued in use until 1956—the last one-room school in Stark County. This building was somewhat unusual in having seven large nine-over-one double-hung windows

MADISON TOWNSHIP SCHOOL
1884
Richardsonian Romanesque
Architects: Terrell and Morris
Grove City (Franklin Co.)
Lithograph from Ohio School Report, 1884

SCIENCE HILL SCHOOL
1870
Vernacular
Builder: Unknown
Alliance (Stark Co.)
Photo by J. D. Brown, National Register file,
courtesy of Ohio Historic Preservation Office

on the east side and no windows on the west side. Its belfry is accented by ornamental millwork and a turned finial. Now maintained as a museum it features typical late-nineteenth-century wainscoting and chalkboards, a teacher's desk and twenty-eight student desks, a potbellied stove, and a couple of bookcases.[29]

From the mid-nineteenth century on, state commissioners of common schools attempted to improve the physical characteristics of the one-room school—often with no more power at their disposal than the inspiration of the "bully pulpit" that was provided by their required annual report to the governor and state legislature. In 1861 Anson Smyth described the ideal classroom as having on its floor "Not an ink-drop, not one bit of paper, not one shaving of pen or pencil, can be seen . . . [teacher's] books and other articles are arranged with taste, and her example is imitated in every pupil's desk . . . window-blinds are so arranged as to admit the air and light . . . walls are hung with maps. . . . Upon portions of the blackboard, not needed for every-day use, there are seen drawings of animals, birds, trees, and flowers. . . . Large tumblers, and various other receptacles of flowers, are placed in the windows. . . . On the stove stands a pitcher, filled with wild flowers and rare grasses."[30]

One suspects few classrooms achieved this idyllic state even on the sunniest spring day, but as educational professionalism grew, more and more townships appointed superintendents to supervise and improve instruction. By the end of the century the one-room school was synonymous with "country school," and no one was more vocal about the disadvantaged status of rural schools than A. B. Graham, who in 1900 was appointed superintendent of the Springfield Township schools in Clark County. He immediately began improving their environments with painted or papered walls, persuaded the nearby Crowell Publishing Company to present each of the twelve schools with a set of six pictures to encourage art appreciation, took advantage of the boxes of books the state library circulated, and secured donations of trees and shrubs for landscaping the school grounds.[31]

Sometimes the one-room school of fond memory measured up to its image, and by the turn of the twentieth-century Ohio standards were above the national average. A 1914 survey by the U.S. Bureau of Education compiled 1,296 returns from two counties in each of eighteen states and found that 91 percent of the one-room schools were frame and 9 percent were brick or stone, with about half having slate blackboards and the other half painted wood for writing. The report recommended a 32 x 24–foot

Wallpapered interior, Sinking Creek School,
Springfield Township, Clark County
Photo by A. B. Graham from Springfield
Township Report, 1904

Book boxes rural schools could borrow from
the Ohio State University Traveling Library
Photo by A. B. Graham from Springfield
Township Report, 1904

Early-twentieth-century rural Van Wert
County school that boasted a bookcase
and organ
Photo from Saida Brumback Antrim and
Ernest Irving, *County Library.*

building to accommodate forty to forty-five pupils in five rows of desks, and provided plans for everything from sanitary privies to jacketed stoves.[32]

At the time, Ohio still had approximately nine thousand one-room schools, but consolidation was moving rapidly and the state no longer recommended designs for one-room schools, although a few isolated examples continued in operation until after World War II.[33] Some communities failed to survive after their one-room school closed. This was the price of progress, for many communities were defined by their school district boundaries.

Three | From Graded "Union Schools" to "Open-Space" Elementary Buildings

One of the most significant pieces of educational legislation in Ohio during the nineteenth century was the Akron Act of 1847. Akron was growing rapidly, and the previous year it enumerated within its boundaries 690 children between four and sixteen years of age, about half of whom attended public and private schools taught in a variety of rooms "temporarily hired and unsuited for the purpose in many respects." A committee organized by Reverend Jennings of the Congregational Church proposed a plan—which the Ohio legislature approved—to incorporate the town into a single school district with taxes to support free schools for all youth; elect a six-member board for their management; and make graded schools free to all, with qualifying examinations for those beyond the primary grades.[1] This became a model for graded schools throughout the state. Two years later the law was extended to any incorporated town or city if approved by a majority of its voters and in 1850 to all townships or special districts having at least five hundred inhabitants.

Although it was not immediately apparent, these laws began to illustrate the disparity between the educational opportunities in urban versus rural areas of the state, a disproportion that continues to the present day. In larger cities such as Cleveland, the swiftly changing standards for the construction of school buildings during the last half of the nineteenth century were dramatic. Cleveland rented space for public school classes until 1840, when two identical graded schools were built—one of them Prospect School, a forty-five-foot classical Georgian square with two entrances and two classrooms on each floor. It was equipped with wood-burning

stoves—until the 1850s when coal became standard—and pine benches which were replaced a few years later with double-student desks. This $3,500 building opened with 275 students divided into separate classes for boys and girls in both the primary and senior departments. A forty-four-week school year had five-and-a-half-day weeks of six hours per day. The male teacher for the senior boys was paid ten dollars per week and female teachers for the other three classes were each paid five dollars per week.[2]

In the 1850s, three-story buildings like Eagle Street, Mayflower Street, and Kentucky Street boasted a classical columned entry and pilasters culminating in elaborate pairs of brackets at the roofline. The design can probably be attributed to the architectural partnership of Charles W. Heard and Simeon Porter, the city's leading architects under contract to the Cleveland schools.[3] In Ohio's largest cities, public schools were achieving the status of temples of learning that had earlier been reserved only for private academies offering classical studies. These buildings with a capacity for 550 pupils had seven classrooms—three on each of the lower floors and a large room with smaller recitation rooms and a library on the third.[4]

During the 1860s and 1870s the Italianate style reigned supreme with the $45,000, eighteen-room Sterling Avenue building being acclaimed at its dedication in 1868 as the "finest school building in Ohio." With the school system growing by one thousand or more students annually, the design was replicated the next year in Rockwell, Saint Clair, and Orchard Schools—all

MAYFLOWER, EAGLE,
AND KENTUCKY STREET SCHOOLS
1854–55
Renaissance Revival
*Architects: Charles W. Heard
and Simeon Porter*
Cleveland (Cuyahoga Co.)
Lithograph from Cleveland School
Report, 1877

STERLING, ROCKWELL, ORCHARD,
AND SAINT CLAIR SCHOOLS
1868–70
Italianate
*Architects: Charles W. Heard
and Walter Blythe*
Cleveland (Cuyahoga Co.)
Lithograph from Cleveland School
Report, 1877

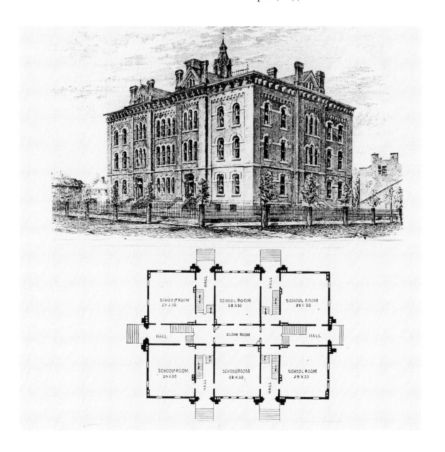

with six large classrooms on each of their three floors and six separate stairways surrounding a central cloakroom. These eighteen rooms seated over one thousand students in each school, with each 29 x 30–foot classroom accommodating up to fifty-six students. At Saint Clair School, one room held a German-speaking class and the remainder were divided from "A" grammar to "D" primary class levels.[5] These were elegant brick buildings with the pilasters of slightly projecting entry bays providing chimney flues. Rockwell's arched windows were accented by dripstones and keystones, and corbelled brick trim highlighted the bracketed cornice, while Sterling Avenue with the same interior plan boasted Gothic windows for a distinctive exterior. The superintendent displayed the cherry desks and the pictures and plants with which teachers and students adorned the walls and windows, asking "What child is there who is daily surrounded by such influences, who is not made the gentler and purer by them?"[6] It may sound like hyperbole, but he did report incidents of corporal punishment declined markedly.

Case School, completed 1875–76, employed a restrained Italianate design that suggested the coming transition to Second-Renaissance Revival architecture in its symmetry and the details of its horizontal planes. It was identical to Outhwaite School completed a year earlier, featuring the latest interior design that permitted each classroom its own cloakroom and provided light and ventilation from at least two sides.[7] Only the largest urban districts offered such extensive examples of progressive nineteenth-century school design, but on a smaller scale improvements were occurring statewide.

When a state commissioner of common schools was appointed in 1853 with the sweeping educational legislation that followed the state's second constitutional convention, one of his first recommendations was to make Henry Barnard's book on school architecture available to every school district so directors might have suitable plans for improving their school buildings.[8] "Union schools" consisted of two, three, four, or five graded classes—normally referred to as primary, secondary, intermediate, grammar, and high schools. Usually only the largest cities had a sufficient number of students within a convenient walking distance of the school building to enable them to offer all five classes—villages more commonly had only two or three departments.[9]

This is typified by the report from the New Philadelphia school district, which built a "commodious brick edifice" in 1849 at a cost of $4,085. The 75 x 40–foot building had two large rooms for primary and secondary classes on the first floor, and a grammar schoolroom and two smaller

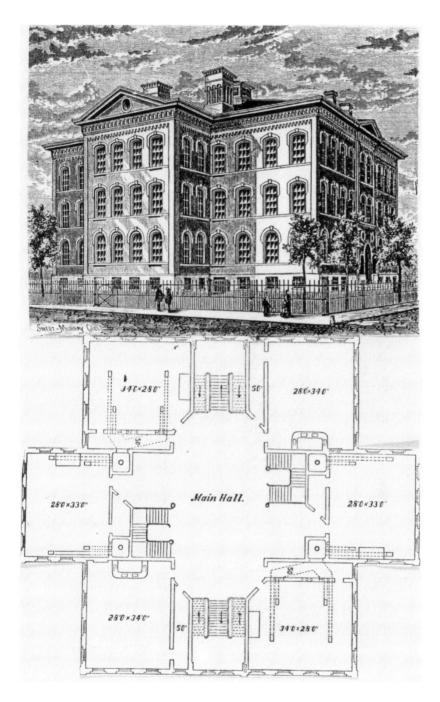

OUTHWAITE AND CASE
1874–76
Renaissance Revival
Architect: Unknown
Cleveland (Cuyahoga Co.)
Lithograph from Cleveland School Report, 1877

recitation rooms on the second floor. During three terms of thirteen weeks each, the average enrollment in these three classes was 384 students and the average daily attendance was 241, with one male teacher—probably in the more advanced grammar department—and two female teachers each term.[10] Graded classes were considered progressive even though each teacher was clearly instructing more than eighty students on a daily basis.

Two of these early union schools—one surviving and the other recently demolished—were 1855 and 1856 buildings in Coshocton and Worthington. The Coshocton building had a unique source of funding, originating with a petition from fifty-nine citizens to support a graded school by using all criminal fines imposed within the newly unified school district. A 30 x 80–foot building was completed by A. N. Milner for $4,500, although he reportedly lost money on the contract. It had an elegant nine-bay facade with Greek Revival elements such as brick pilasters dividing the window bays vertically. There were two rooms on each floor with a cloakroom between, served by an entry door with sidelights and trabeated transom. The belfry was completed a few years later—with funds derived from violations of the liquor law. Sycamore Street Union School served for seventy-five years before being converted to a museum and eventually razed.[11]

The Worthington building was smaller and reflected the changing fashion to Italianate architecture during the 1850s. It retains the form of earlier I-shaped structures with its single-room depth, but it features segmental-arched windows and doorways accented by a double row of headers. The roofline boasts a central gable and modest brackets at the eaves. The construction contract with Chambers and Smith was $1,955.82 for this two-story, four-room building.[12] The district was apparently planning for the future since there was an insufficient number of children to offer more than two grades—primary and intermediate classes in the first-floor classrooms; the upper story was leased to the Odd Fellows Lodge. With another $510 for landscaping and furnishings—such as constructing desks and privies, fencing the grounds, and graveling the walks—the total cost was more than five times the state average for a one-room school. However, Worthington residents probably avoided even higher costs by dealing with a local brickyard and carpenters. It is interesting to note that by contemporary standards it was evidently not considered a conflict of interest to pay local school directors William Bishop $6.50 for "procuring and sitting shade trees about the school house" and Homer Tuller $10.50 for supplying ten cords of wood for the two stoves. When more space was needed twenty years later, a new building was erected and this became the township hall.

SYCAMORE STREET UNION SCHOOL
1855
Vernacular/Greek Revival elements
Builder: A. N. Milner
Coshocton (Coshocton Co.)
Courtesy of the Johnson-Humrickhouse
Museum

UNION SCHOOL
1856
Italianate
Builders: Chambers and Smith
Worthington (Franklin Co.)
Photo by Virginia E. McCormick

In 1861 a building of similar size was completed for nonwhite students in Columbus at a cost of $3,000 including an adjacent playground.[13] To correct earlier inequities—with a move that today seems misguided and discriminatory—the revised educational code of the 1850s for the first time established a separate administrative and enrollment system in Ohio for nonwhite students. Tax funds were provided for the required "colored schools" where thirty or more such children were enumerated. In districts with fewer students, directors were given options to use such funds to provide "private instruction . . . an evening school . . . a vacation school" or to enroll nonwhite youth in the district common school "if no objections are raised against such an arrangement."[14]

Although cities such as Cincinnati developed an extensive network of "colored schools," by the end of the 1850s only 40 percent of African American youth statewide were enrolled and 21 percent regularly attended school compared to 72 percent and 40 percent for Caucasian youth between five and twenty-one years of age.[15] Many older youth of both races and sexes were in the labor force, but in the years prior to compulsory school attendance laws public schools routinely served only a minority of all eligible children.

The state commissioner described thirteen advantages and no disadvantages for graded schools—from cost efficiencies for buildings and teachers by hiring younger, less experienced teachers for the primary grades to better discipline and numerous curriculum benefits.[16] By 1857—only a decade after the Akron Act—eighty school districts in fifty of the state's counties reported the formation of union schools. School construction suffered during the Civil War, but during the final decades of the nineteenth century many districts erected school buildings that were the finest structures in the community—symbols of their cultural pride.

Nowhere was this more evident than in Bucyrus, a county seat town of approximately 4,500 persons with a substantial immigrant population from Bavaria, Württemberg, Saxony, Baden, Prussia, and Hesse-Darmstadt.[17] Until 1867 conservative citizens rejected tax levies for a union school, but when a $20,000 levy was finally approved, the school board selected Cleveland architect Alexander Koehler, a partner of Joseph M. Blackburn who designed the elegant Ohio School for the Deaf then under construction. Koehler designed the largest and finest union school in the state—a three-story, twenty-one room Italianate building with a nine–foot full basement, and an exhibition hall to seat five hundred persons. The massive 208 x 120–foot building crowned with a central dome was larger at the time than any collegiate building in the state.[18]

BUCYRUS SCHOOL
1868–69
Italianate
Architect: Alexander Koehler
Bucyrus (Crawford Co.)
Photo from the 1908 *Bucyrian,* courtesy of
the Bucyrus Historical Society

In their specifications the architects called for the highest quality materials—"All porches to outer doors to have cast iron fluted Corinthian columns, with molded base and enriched capitals" and all walls and ceilings "to be lathed and plastered with good three coat work," specifying that the mortar be made up eight days before it was applied to the walls and that it be made of "fresh burnt lime, clean screened sand, fresh slaughtered cow's hair," and "Eagle Vermont Purple Roofing Slate" in 16 x 22–inch sections.[19] The era of academies and one-room schools in which local school directors contracted for work in a "neat and workmanlike manner" had given way—in towns of any size—to the professional architect who designed the building and specified to builders exactly what materials and construction techniques were to be used. Bucyrus School had specifications for the excavation, stonework, brickwork, iron columns, plastering, carpenter and joiner work, stairs, painting, glass and glazing, and roofing.

But size and quality came at a price. Voters approved an additional $20,000 levy in November 1868—five months after the cornerstone was laid. Bucyrus Machine Works, the contractor, was eventually paid more than $50,000 and interior furnishings and landscaping the four-acre site added another $25,000. Voters felt betrayed that spending exceeded the tax levy and voted school board members out of office at the next election. The Ohio legislature passed legislation allowing the city council of any city under one hundred thousand people to borrow funds for school grounds and buildings and to levy a tax to repay the loan.[20] By the time the county history was published a decade later, however, it praised the gentlemen who, in "over-ruling the economical wishes of a wealthy community, succeeded in planning and furnishing for the public good, the largest and finest schoolhouse in Ohio."[21] But such bragging rights may have masked the building's utility, for it was demolished fifty years later—long before its elegant brick and stone construction would have failed—in favor of separate elementary and high school buildings.

Italianate architecture reigned as the most popular style for school buildings immediately following the Civil War. One of the most refined examples was Cummins School in Cincinnati, a district public school constructed in 1871 in the affluent Walnut Hills neighborhood, where William Howard Taft was then a teenager. Designed by Samuel Hannaford, Cincinnati's premier nineteenth-century architect, the vertical character of this three-and-a-half-story building is accented by slender rectangular windows and projecting bays that maximize natural light with a shallow double-E form. At a cost of $71,200 it reflected the highest quality construction of the

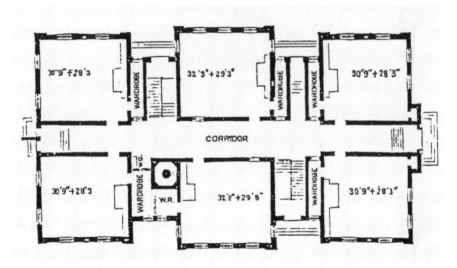

30'9" + 28'3		32'3" + 29'3"			30'9" + 28'3"
	WARDROBE		WARDROBE	WARDROBE	

CORRIDOR

30'9" + 28'3	WARDROBE WD.	W.R.	32'8" + 29'8"	WARDROBE	30'9" + 28'3"

CUMMINS SCHOOL
1871
Italianate
Architect: Samuel Hannaford
Cincinnati (Hamilton Co.)
Photo by Virginia E. McCormick

Innovative E-shaped design provided maximum light, ventilation, and wardrobes for each classroom.
Floor plan from National Register file, courtesy of Ohio Historic Preservation Office

day—iron for the elaborate window lintels and bracketed cornice, a slate roof, and brick privies in the rear. Eighteen classrooms—one offering instruction in German—provided 1,008 single seats, rather than the double-student desks commonly used at the time. There was also a principal's office, library, and apparatus room for scientific equipment for the intermediate classes. The fact that this building opened with stoves to heat each room but was designed so it could be converted to steam heat suggests that the architect and contractor were aware of new technology; perhaps the school directors were not yet convinced of its practicality. However, one of the building's technological innovations was the use of interior pivot blinds to control light.[22] Hannaford was critical of the graded district schools because he considered them "devoid of suggestions of art and beauty."[23] When offered the opportunity, he proved that good design and efficient function were compatible.

Sycamore School, built five years later at Sandusky, is similar in its Italianate details but achieves a distinctive appearance through the use of locally quarried blue stone crafted in "a simple solid wall with no extra furbelows and projections to catch dust and rain, is more beautiful than one redundant with flourishes."[24] The building's vertical mass is enhanced by a raised basement, elongated windows accented by keystone dripmolds, and a hipped roof culminating in ornately bracketed overhanging eaves. Sycamore was one of eight schools in the city at the time and stood impressively at the center of an entire city block. Its high-ceilinged classrooms featured pressed metal ceilings. In the 1890s it accommodated about 650 primary and grammar students in thirteen classrooms, and the durability of such stone structures is illustrated by its century of service as a school and its subsequent conversion into apartments in the 1980s.[25]

Oberlin School enumerated 1,052 school-age children when the cornerstone was laid in 1873 for an elegant Victorian Gothic union school to replace an 1851 building. Designed by Cleveland architect Walter Blythe, this structure of local Plum Creek brick is accented by Amherst blue sandstone with pointed-arched windows, buttressed corners, bracketed eaves, and a corbelled brick pediment. Its bell tower crowned by a forty-foot steeple was removed for safety reasons in 1940 but was recently restored when the building became a community arts center. On each of its three floors were four corner classrooms, each 27 x 34 feet in size and rising thirteen feet to pressed tin ceilings. Manufactured desks could be purchased at the time, rather than being individually crafted by local carpenters, and Oberlin School was furnished with typical oak desks mounted on black

SYCAMORE SCHOOL
1876
Italianate
Builder: H. E. Myer
Sandusky (Erie Co.)
Photo by Virginia E. McCormick

OBERLIN SCHOOL/ART CENTER
1873–74
Victorian Gothic
Architect: Walter Blythe
Oberlin (Lorain Co.)
Photo by Virginia E. McCormick

Manufactured desks of oak and iron were
typically bolted to the floor and had folding
seats for easy exit and entry.
Drawing from Ohio School Report, 1868–69

iron scrolled frames. It cost $40,500, including equipment and furnish-
ings, to provide this college town with a public school capable of offering a
curriculum from primary grades through high school. The first class grad-
uated in 1876.[26]

No state commissioner was more committed to improving school buildings than LeRoy Brown, who served during the 1880s. He was anxious to
assure that small towns, as well as large cities, could afford union schools
and included varied architectural plans in his annual reports. A $10,000
building designed by Elah Terrell and Company of Columbus was erected
in 1882 at Johnstown and the following year an identical building was constructed at Groveport. These two-story buildings were more modest
Gothic schools than the one at Oberlin, each with six classrooms designed
to seat forty students. All rooms were provided natural light both from
the rear and the left side, as recommended by progressive educators of the
day. Students entered through a corner bell tower crowned by a Gothic-
windowed spire that was the building's most artistic feature. The most
innovative was a folding partition between two second-floor classrooms
that could be opened to provide a large assembly or lecture area for advanced students.[27] One wonders if Terrell was influenced by the Akron
Plan churches that were becoming fashionable throughout Ohio, with
auditorium-style sanctuaries and folding doors that could partition the rear
into Sunday School classrooms.[28]

In Tiffin—a more populous community, and one with a college influence—Miami Street School was larger and its Gothic details more elaborate. Its three stories have projecting bays topped by gables with dormers, and intricate corbel trim on the recessed bays and central chimneys.
Mullion windows on the first and second floors are accented by radiating

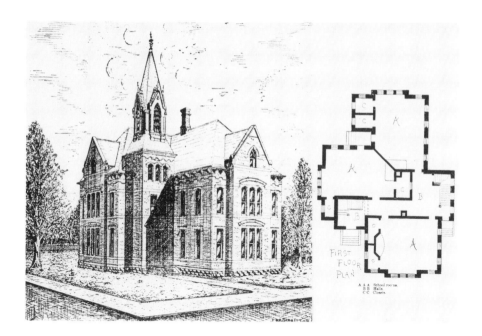

JOHNSTOWN AND GROVEPORT SCHOOLS
1882 and 1883
Victorian Gothic
Architect: Elah Terrell
Johnstown (Licking Co.), Groveport
(Franklin Co.)
Lithograph from Ohio School Report,
1885–86

MIAMI STREET SCHOOL
1884
Victorian Gothic
Builder: William H. Hollenberger
Tiffin (Seneca Co.)
Photo from Tiffin Superintendent's Report,
1873, courtesy of Seneca County Historical
Society

Columned arches crowned with spandrels
define stairways in the central hall.
Photo by Virginia E. McCormick

voussoirs, and an elliptical-arched entry is inscribed with its 1884 construction date.[29] The building served as a public school until 1956 when it was renovated to serve Tiffin University—an outgrowth of Heidelberg College's Department of Commerce.[30] It is a rare survivor from this period in which much of the interior woodwork has been maintained intact—including the unusual latticed arches leading to stairways and corridors from the octagonal center hall.

Exterior and interior similarities between Campbell Street School at Sandusky designed by J. C. Johnson of Fremont and Dunkirk School by J. C. Hopkins of Topeka, Kansas, suggest the universal characteristics that educational architecture had achieved by 1885. Both are square blocks with entrances on all four sides and four classrooms on each floor. Both were Victorian Gothic with emphasis on a clock tower of the type commonly found on county courthouses. The three-story Dunkirk building was one story higher and more intricately trimmed with details such as iron cresting along the roofline. But Campbell Street School—solidly constructed from the local sandstone—is the one still used for classes. Its clock tower is gone, but its exterior remains rich in Victorian details from the oculus windows

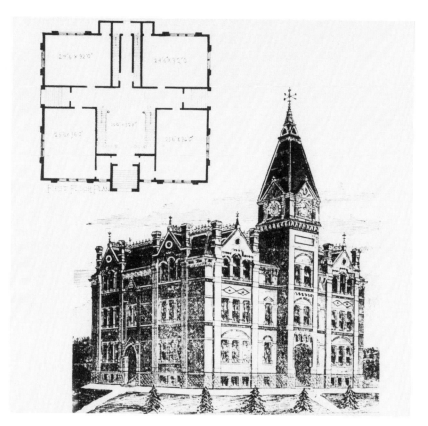

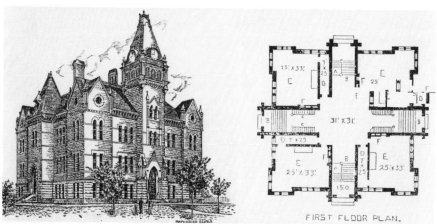

DUNKIRK SCHOOL
1884–85
Victorian Gothic
Architect: J. C. Hopkins
Dunkirk (Hardin Co.)
Lithograph from Ohio School Report,
1885–86

CAMPBELL STREET SCHOOL
1884–85
Victorian Gothic
Architect: J. C. Johnson
Sandusky (Erie Co.)
Lithograph from Ohio School Report,
1885–86

Current Campbell Street School minus clock
tower and chimneys
Photo by Virginia E. McCormick

of its corner gables to the elaborately carved Gothic entry. Technology was offering significant improvements by the 1880s. Campbell Street School boasted cloakrooms equipped with washstands and drinking fountains connected to the city waterworks. Both buildings had basements with coal-fired furnaces providing the latest in central heating—steam heat in each room of Campbell Street, hot-air flues and registers in Dunkirk.[31]

A decade later architectural fashion in educational buildings had begun to favor the Romanesque Revival style interpreted by Boston architect Henry Hobson Richardson.[32] These masonry buildings were usually rock-faced ashlar stone and featured segmental or semicircular arches, and Romanesque and Byzantine motifs such as foliate carving and open log-gia galleries. Richardson exploited the design elements of masonry—frequently employing a second color of stone to enhance doors and windows—but melded these elements in a unified style that subordinated materials and stylistic details to the monumental mass of the building.

Emerson School at Westerville is a fine example of the partnership be-tween noted Columbus architects Joseph W. Yost and Frank L. Packard,

Gothic entry with intricately carved stone details
Photo by Virginia E. McCormick

EMERSON SCHOOL
1896
Richardsonian Romanesque
Architects: Joseph W. Yost and
Frank L. Packard
Westerville (Franklin Co.)
Photo from National Register file, courtesy
of Ohio Historic Preservation Office

and it reflects the confidence of architects experienced enough to assimilate Richardsonian features into a design that was distinctly their own.[33] Constructed with Everal brick from the Westerville factory—which at the time employed twenty-three people and produced twenty-five thousand bricks a day—Emerson is trimmed with sandstone used for the high basement and the Richardsonian entry arch with basket handle trim. To emphasize the building's commitment to youth, the eternal faces of Emerson's children are sculpted in the stone of this arch—a boy on the left, a girl on the right. Turrets capped with metal spires flank an open-columned belfry. Triple flat-arched windows occupy each section of the first floor, while round-arched windows form an arcade on the second. Five-sided bays on either end of the building are accented by an oval window with decorative mullions on the top story. The theme of the dedication March 19, 1896, "I am Yesterday, Today, and Tomorrow," spoke not only to the thousands of children who would study within its walls but to the high quality of materials that would still be in use a century later. These include oak floors and wainscoting, brass hardware, slate blackboards, and wooden doors between two upper-floor classrooms that could be raised into the attic to open the space into an auditorium. Like in most villages and small towns, this was the only school and served the entire community from primary grades through high school—complete with its outdoor well and privies.[34]

Although it was built four years later, Willshire School designed by Kramer and Harpster for a smaller community reverts to an interesting interpretation of Richardsonian Romanesque features. The asymmetrical facade with bracketed eaves has a typical Richardsonian entry flanked by an octagonal tower on one side and a square bell tower on the other, with biforium ironwork decorating the belfry openings. Stone stringcourses and lintels combine with lower interior ceilings to give this two-story building a horizontal orientation in keeping with the flatness of its northwestern Ohio terrain.[35]

Walnut Street School in Wooster marks another architectural transition—toward Georgian and Second-Renaissance Revival style. Like many Ohio towns, Wooster conducted an extensive school rebuilding program in the last decade of the nineteenth and the first of the twentieth century. Some of the materials from an 1854 school on the same site were utilized in this eight-room 1902 building with full basement. Its distinguishing architectural feature is the Georgian-style Palladian window flanked by pilaster-framed rectangular windows and circular dating stones above the

Emerson School's Richardsonian arched
entry with twin towers and sculpted faces
of a young girl and boy on either side
Photos by Virginia E. McCormick

WILLSHIRE SCHOOL
1900
Romanesque Revival
Architects: Kramer and Harpster
Willshire (Van Wert Co.)
Photo by Virginia E. McCormick

balconied portico. This creates a dramatic focus for the landing on the interior staircase. Varied window treatments—rectangular on the first story and a round-arched arcade on the second—create a symmetrical facade emphasized by modillions at the cornice. The timeliness of such classical style is evident in Walnut Street School's reincarnation in the 1980s as Wayne County Center for the Arts.[36]

Similar trends in consolidation occurred in parochial schools. The transition from the Italianate style commonly associated with late-nineteenth-century Catholic school complexes to the Renaissance style can be seen in Saint Augustine School at Minster.[37] It has a typical raised basement and two stories with four rooms on each floor. The square four-stage tower boasts an entry flanked by fluted columns with Ionic capitals, and its roof is accented by dormers and a box cornice with paired brackets.[38] It was slightly more elaborate but similar to centralized Catholic schools nearby at

WALNUT STREET SCHOOL
1902
Second-Renaissance Revival
Architect: J. R. Webster
Wooster (Wayne Co.)
Photo by Virginia E. McCormick

Round-arched window and entry dramatize
this stairway.
Photo by Virginia E. McCormick

SAINT AUGUSTINE CATHOLIC SCHOOL/
MINSTER SCHOOL
1906
Renaissance Revival
Architect/Builder: Unknown
Minster (Auglaize Co.)
Photo by Virginia E. McCormick

Chickasaw and Saint Henry, suggesting that the diocese was utilizing the same designer.[39] Some have suggested that this may have been Andrew De-Curtins, who reportedly studied architecture in Milwaukee, or it may have been that local builders were adding decorative embellishments to a common interior plan.

These same decades were witnessing remarkable changes in country schools as well. A special act of the Ohio legislature in 1894 granted Kingsville in Ashtabula County the power to eliminate its subdistrict one-room schools and transport all children to a central township school.[40] It was an idea enthusiastically endorsed by educators but often resisted by local parents afraid of losing educational control and community identity. By 1898 township districts throughout the state were given legal authority to transport students and the tide toward consolidation had begun. No one pushed the concept more avidly than A. B. Graham, Ohio State University's first superintendent of agricultural extension. Graham surveyed the

HUNTINGTON TOWNSHIP SCHOOL
1911
Neoclassical
Builder: Unknown
Huntington Township (Lorain Co.)
Photo by Virginia E. McCormick

WATTERSON SCHOOL
1906–7
Second-Renaissance Revival
Architect: Frank S. Barnum
Cleveland (Cuyahoga Co.)
Photo by Steve McQuillan, National Register file, courtesy of Ohio Historic Preservation Office

state and published the results in a bulletin called "Centralized Schools in Ohio"—distributing over one hundred thousand copies to local school directors, teachers, and parents. He found that in 1905 thirty-two townships already had completely centralized their schools and another sixty subdistricts had started transporting their students to an adjoining district.[41]

In 1911 Huntington Township in Lorain County joined the trend. Its modest two-story neoclassical building on a high, raised basement had little architectural distinction beyond stone corner quoins and a projecting entry with its segmental arch surmounted by paired windows on the second floor.[42] But the building's important contribution was community identity. In the mid-nineteenth century, Huntington Township's crossroad commercial center was a thriving community of wagon makers and blacksmith shops, tinners, bootmakers, and shoemakers, and general stores and taverns serving some twelve hundred people. But it was bypassed by the Columbus, Cleveland, and Cincinnati Railroad in favor of nearby Wellington and Huntington Township's population was quickly cut in half. On August 10, 1915, the township held a homecoming celebration with approximately one thousand current and former residents congregating at Huntington Township School, the new central school building.[43] Centralized schools expanded opportunities for rural adults as well as youth and this building clearly expressed but was unsuccessful in achieving Huntington's hopes for a return to prosperity.

Even such locally applauded centralized schools reveal the dramatic disparity between rural and urban facilities. Frank S. Barnum, the architect who designed seventy-five schools for Cleveland between 1895 and 1917, demonstrated a rising architectural concern for fireproof structures in designing a Second-Renaissance Revival building to take advantage of a busy urban street corner.[44] Watterson School was an innovative L-shape with its main entrance on the inner angle to create a broad entry terrace and a park-like lawn with trees and shrubs. The building's dark brick is accented by terra cotta banding between floors and around the arched entry and the window arcade above. In a break with traditional nineteenth-century buildings featuring large lecture halls or auditoriums on the uppermost floor, Watterson's entry hall led directly to a two-story octagonal auditorium with a central skylight. Unique triangular staircases where the auditorium met the wings led to a second-floor hall curving from one end of the building to the other.[45]

Barnum was right to be concerned about safety. Ironically, it was at the nearby Lakeview School in suburban Collinwood on March 4, 1908,

Lakeview School at Collinwood, after the
March 4, 1908, fire, which killed 172 students
and two teachers
Photo card, courtesy of H. Roger Grant

LINCOLN ELEMENTARY SCHOOL
1915
Neoclassical
Architect: Edwin M. Gee
Toledo (Lucas Co.)
Photo from John J. Donovan, *School Architecture*

that a rapidly spreading fire caught panicked students "as if in a trap at the bottom of the rear stairway," killing 172 children and two teachers.[46] Lakeview was a typical three-story building with wood frame and brick face construction, containing thirty to forty pupils per classroom. Wooden floors, stairs, and banisters carried flames to all parts of the building, collapsing everything into the basement. It was a tragedy that brought immediate attention from educators and legislators throughout Ohio—and across the nation and the world, from Pittsburgh to Saint Louis, Paris to Berlin. Architects and school directors immediately began erecting fire escapes for large older buildings. They also started designing new structures to eliminate vast upper-floor lecture halls, wooden staircases, oiled hardwood floors, and open center halls from basements to third floors that served like chimneys in cases of fire. It was Barnum who designed the Collinwood Memorial School, a flat-roofed, two-story building with classroom windows only on one side—the recommended standard after electric lighting became available. Decorative brick was used to relieve the blankness of windowless exterior walls.[47]

During the early part of the twentieth century—with major cities employing professional architects and the United States Bureau of Education taking the lead on designs for school safety—such two-story brick neoclassical buildings became the fashionable architectural standard. Lincoln Elementary School, designed in 1915 by Edwin M. Gee, the Toledo city schools' architect, pays homage to Barnum's design for Watterson with its L-shape, but it has one wing shortened to accommodate the lot. Lincoln Elementary also places the auditorium directly in front of the main entry. Stone stringcourses provide a fire barrier while emphasizing the building's horizontal lines and enhancing its apparent size. From the exterior one can define the classroom spaces—even the firewalls backing the cloakrooms between classrooms. Both John J. Donovan and William C. Bruce selected it as an outstanding example of elementary school architecture.[48]

One of the innovative aspects of Lincoln Elementary School was the inclusion of a kindergarten room. Although early childhood education had been available in private schools for a half century, the first kindergarten in a public school opened in Cincinnati in 1905. Early-twentieth-century architects envisioned the ideal kindergarten room as an open space for singing, dancing, and games—twice the size of a typical classroom. Lincoln Elementary's was typical in having circles painted on the floor to guide students into correct position for activities, an artificial fireplace to provide a homelike atmosphere for story time, a piano for musical activities, and sand

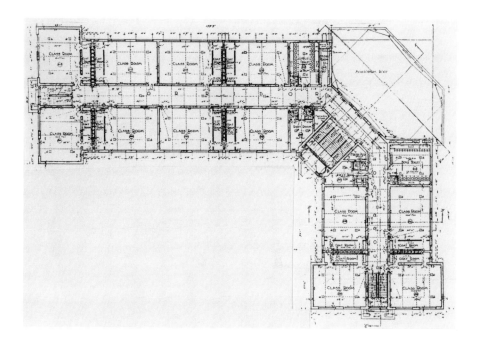

Lincoln Elementary School's L-shaped floor plan with firewalls between classrooms and a first-floor auditorium
Floor plan from John J. Donovan, *School Architecture*

Specially designed kindergarten room with circles and piano for musical games
Photo from John J. Donovan, *School Architecture*

tables for creative play. Particular attention was given to appropriately sized toilets, wardrobe hooks, and shelves for books and toys. Donovan urged architects to exercise their imagination "in making this room a little wonderland of childhood."[49]

Few new schools were erected during the Great Depression or during the material and labor shortages of World War II, so McCormick School at Huron is unusual in reflecting the art moderne style then popular in commercial structures such as hotels and factories but rarely used in public buildings such as schools. Similar to the art deco style in its geometric details, art moderne was more streamlined in form.[50] The curved corners and flat roof of the Huron school are typical, as is the use of the new glass block building material. Because of the wartime shortage of steel this building utilized concrete, which was mixed on site.[51]

The linear form of school construction continued through the building boom that followed World War II, but advancing technology and shifting educational concepts produced a dramatic change by the late 1960s and early 1970s. As buildings aged, the need for specialized facilities such as gymnasiums, music rooms, libraries, and those to encompass various types of vocational education that professional educators advocated during the early part of the twentieth century collided with the need for flexibility. Government standards increasingly recommended nonsupporting walls between classrooms to facilitate renovation.[52] Responding to a commitment from educators and school boards that education be dynamic, architects created open-space facilities designed to be shaped by the curriculum and teaching staff. They spoke confidently of flexibility for a building's fifty to one-hundred-year life span that seems naive only two or three decades later. Just as electricity had made it unnecessary to rely on natural light, air conditioning was now eliminating the need to rely on windows for ventilation, and technology was making it feasible to construct large open spaces uninterrupted by supporting walls or columns. Modules that could be defined with movable partitions became the recommended form for school buildings.[53]

Butternut Elementary School at North Olmsted is a compact, single-story K-6 elementary school designed for 660 students. It utilizes these principles with instructional modules—each with flanking classrooms, wardrobes, and small group work spaces—clustered around a large open study center adjacent to the entry courtyard. At the opposite end of the building are a multipurpose gymnasium/cafeteria, as well as art, music, and kindergarten rooms.[54] Such designs for team teaching became standard

MCCORMICK SCHOOL
1943
Art Moderne
Architects: Harold Parker and C. Edward Wolfe
Huron (Erie Co.)
Photo by Virginia E. McCormick

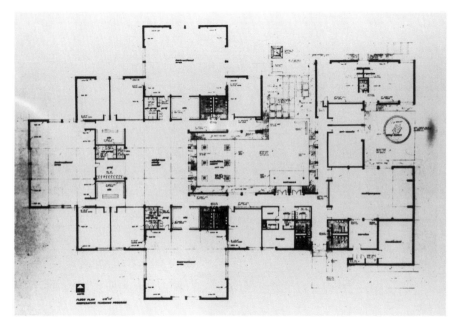

BUTTERNUT ELEMENTARY SCHOOL
1969
Open-Space Modern
Architects: Perkins and Will, and Lesko Associates, Architects and Planners
North Olmsted (Cuyahoga Co.)
Courtesy of Lesko Associates, Architects and Planners

Floor plan showing graded classroom clusters
Courtesy of Lesko Associates, Architects and Planners

WORTHINGTON PARK AND GRANBY
ELEMENTARY SCHOOLS
1988–89
Postmodern/Modular
Architects: SEM Partners
Worthington (Franklin Co.)
Photos by Virginia E. McCormick

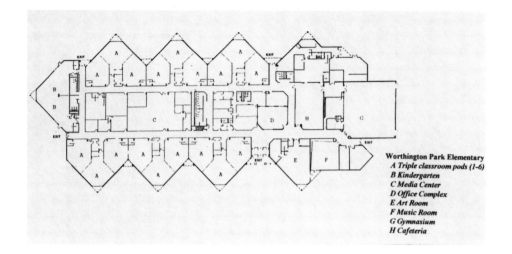

Worthington Park Elementary
A Triple classroom pods (1-6)
B Kindergarten
C Media Center
D Office Complex
E Art Room
F Music Room
G Gymnasium
H Cafeteria

Modular floor plan with triple classrooms for
six grades flanking a learning resources core and
art, music, and physical education facilities
at the end
Courtesy of Worthington Schools

during the last decades of the twentieth century, with a functional architectural style that shows little variation from one community to another.

Worthington Park School and Granby Elementary School at Worthington were cited by a panel of architects and school administrators as "stunning understated buildings with traditional overtones and a well-conceived compact plan."[55] Red brick and stylized Palladian windows echo the New England heritage of the community but are modernized with a bold limestone trim. Triangular modules cluster three classrooms for six grade levels in sets of team suites with retractable partitions permitting either separate class projects or team teaching.[56] Art and music rooms adjoin the gymnasium and cafeteria and can be joined or separated by a partition wall for maximum flexibility. A prototype of this design opened two years earlier and was replicated several times in this rapidly growing Columbus suburb because teachers and students liked the environment and it saved design costs for a district that opened seven new buildings within a decade.[57]

In a rapidly growing suburb near Cleveland, Solon Dual School is a unique design that unites Solon Middle School and Parkside Elementary School in related but independent buildings. Each has its own entrance and distinctive appearance—Solon has two stories and Parkside a single

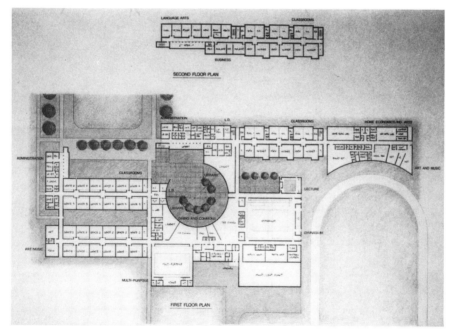

SOLON DUAL SCHOOL
1992
International Modern
Architects: Burgess and Niple
Solon (Cuyahoga Co.)
Photo by William Shenk, courtesy of Burgess
and Niple, Ltd.

Footprint with single-story elementary and
two-story middle school connected by dining
and library facilities
Architectural rendering, courtesy of Burgess
and Niple, Ltd.

floor—but for efficiency they share a mechanical plant, kitchen, and gymnasium. They also are unified by libraries and student and faculty dining rooms with views of a circular courtyard that creates a campus feeling. Bold combinations of brick and glass reflect international modern style in a flexible space that could be converted to serve a single student population from elementary to secondary levels should future needs demand it.[58]

Four | Secondary Schools

Although classical education flourished in some of Ohio's early academies and common schooling became a public responsibility with legislation in 1825, it was still rare in the mid-nineteenth century for a city to offer public education beyond the common schools. Cincinnati, Ohio's largest city, proclaiming itself the "Queen City of the West," was proud of its cultural awareness. It was the first in the state to offer musical education in the schools, the first to provide German students classes taught in their language, and the first to offer evening schools for working youth and young adults. It is not surprising that this city would establish a central high school in 1847, under the direction of Hiram H. Barney, who would in 1853 become the first state commissioner of common schools and lead a rapid movement for graded classes and improved school buildings.

In the 1820s—before public education—Thomas Hughes and William Woodward, two local farmers without heirs, made gifts of land to Cincinnati. Hughes specified that his property be used "for the education of the poor, destitute children whose parents or guardians are unable to pay for their schooling."[1] As tax funds became available for public schools, rents from the Hughes and Woodward properties were placed in a trust fund for secondary education. In 1852, with an annual income of $6,000 from this fund, Cincinnati made plans to construct two high schools in different sections of the city and name them for these benefactors. Each was a coeducational school with admission by open examinations.

Constructed at a cost of $20,000, Hughes High School was an elegant Tudor Gothic Revival building with a projecting gable entry flanked by

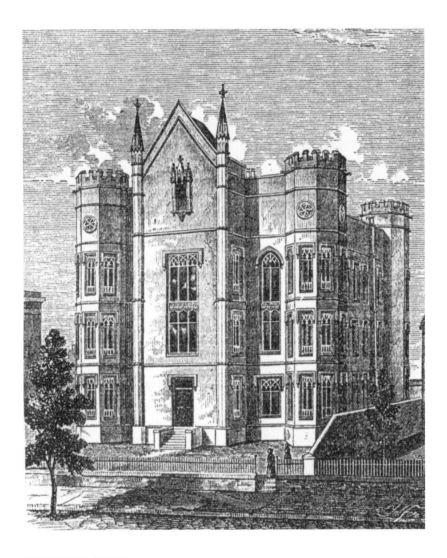

HUGHES HIGH SCHOOL
1852–53
Tudor Gothic
Architect: John B. Earnshaw
Cincinnati (Hamilton Co.)
Lithograph from Henry Barnard, *School Architecture*

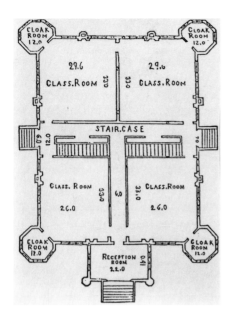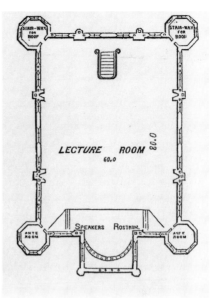

Floor plan with four classrooms per floor,
cloakrooms in the towers, and a lecture room
on the top floor
From Henry Barnard, *School Architecture*

slender turrets, inspired by the towers of Fotheringay Castle where Mary, Queen of the Scots spent the last years of her life. Crenellated octagonal towers in each corner presented the solid symmetry of a castle, but their interior provided practical amenities such as washrooms in the basement, cloakrooms for the lower-floor classrooms, and stairs to the roof from the third floor. A 60 x 80–foot lecture hall with a speaker's platform occupied the entire third floor and was open for community as well as school programs. It is ironic that one of the first Gothic educational buildings in Ohio to measure up to the "substantial and venerable" style that Paul Venable Turner described as resembling medieval cathedrals was designed not to serve a college but a public high school.[2] Hughes High School soon acquired a loyal core of alumni who were proud to have attended its hallowed halls and its status as a national model for educators was assured when Henry Barnard selected it for the frontispiece of his authoritative treatise on school architecture.[3]

When Woodward High School was completed two years later, the Gothic style was interpreted in terra cotta that architect John R. Hamilton had seen used in Italy—a poor decision because local manufacturers had not mastered its production and quality was poor. The number of classrooms was the same, although each was a little larger. The major design "improvement" was to move the stairways to the sides of the building for greater safety in case of fire and to have the corridors intersect on each floor in a central octagon.[4] During the 1850s each of these schools enrolled about two hundred students—almost equally divided between boys and girls. The principal of Hughes High School addressed the innovative practice of "mingling the sexes in the recitation" and spoke highly of its advantages, finding no evidence of "improper connections" being formed. At the time, Hughes High was serving primarily as an institution for teacher training, graduating about ten students per year and having sixty or more withdraw before receiving a degree—many to teach in local one-room district schools that annually employed more than two hundred teachers, the majority of them female.[5]

Cleveland also built two high schools during the 1850s—Central High School and West High School—both reflecting the rising influence of Romanesque architecture popularized by the Smithsonian building in Washington, D.C., as an economical but beautiful style appropriate for public buildings in a democratic society. Designed by Charles W. Heard and Simeon Porter with corner towers and Romanesque battlements of the style popularized by King's College in Cambridge, England, these Cleveland buildings were among the earliest to use cast-iron structural columns.[6]

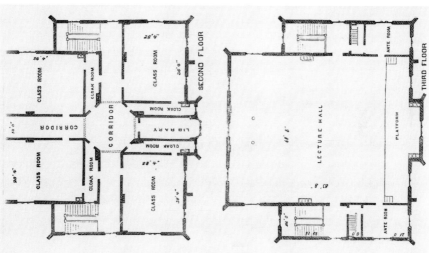

The first two floors had four classrooms around a central corridor, and there was a lecture hall on the third floor.
Floor plan from Cincinnati School Report, 1856

In the middle of the nineteenth century, few towns had either philanthropists or a local tax base to fund the construction of public high school buildings. Like many small villages, Yellow Springs was part of the Miami Township school district until 1858, when local citizens voted to establish a separate village district and made the economically prudent decision to offer primary, intermediate, and high school studies in three former one-room schools. A two-year-old one-room school on the south side of the village became Yellow Spring's first high school. Its vernacular interpretation of Greek Revival style with a gable roof accented by cornice returns, corbelled pilasters, and nine courses of corbelling at the entablature reflects quality one-room school craftsmanship. But this one room public school contrasted sharply with the lavish Gothic architecture of the nearby "Little Antioch" School—the subscription school Judge William Mills financed at approximately the same time. When Yellow Springs built a union school in 1873 to include primary through high school classes, the one-room building was abandoned as a high school and became the "colored school." With construction of a second room to create an L-shaped building, it served about sixty non white students per year until 1887 when legislation was enacted to racially integrate all Ohio public schools.[7]

Legislation requiring school attendance increased school enrollments dramatically and created needs for more and larger buildings. In 1877 the state legislature made twelve weeks of school attendance compulsory for all youth from eight to fourteen years of age, but there were exceptions for mentally deficient children, those needed in the labor force, or children residing more than two miles from a public school. In 1889 required attendance was increased to twenty weeks per year and fourteen-year-olds leaving school had to prove their ability to read and write.[8]

It was not unusual during this time for village union schools that offered high school–level courses to enroll qualified students from nearby township districts if they paid tuition. But Burton High School, constructed in 1884, exemplifies another trend. Through a special act of the legislature to create a township tax district, this $13,000 Victorian Gothic building offered instruction "free to all" qualified youth throughout the surrounding township. However, some students who enrolled lived beyond walking distance, and horse-drawn "kid-hacks" were employed to transport them.[9] A new era in consolidation and transportation had begun.

By the 1880s public high schools were common in Ohio's urban areas, and cities vied to have the latest technology and an architecturally designed building that reflected local civic pride. This coincided with rising professionalism among educators and a proliferation of teacher institutes and

YELLOW SPRINGS HIGH SCHOOL/SOUTH
"COLORED" SCHOOL
1856
Greek Revival
Builder: Unknown
Yellow Springs (Greene Co.)
Photo by Virginia E. McCormick

normal schools to improve teacher qualifications. Progressive districts now had superintendents to provide administrative leadership. Nowhere was this role more aptly illustrated architecturally than in the 1882 Elyria High School where the superintendent's office was "so located that by the use of pneumatic tubes, he has command of the entire building."[10]

State commissioner LeRoy Brown devoted much of his 1885 and 1886 reports to examples of school buildings that he considered worthy models. Three-story brick buildings with a raised stone foundation providing a lighted basement and classrooms on the upper floors were now the standard. Newark High School was one of the smaller ones—a cube 98 x 104 feet and 106 feet to the summit of its tower—but it was heated by steam, lighted by gas, and had water connections in every room. It still featured four classrooms per floor, but in the basement, in addition to the boiler room, were "two large gymnasiums, to be used in very cold or wet weather."[11] Physical exercise had become a health issue.

Akron High School was more elaborate—introducing the coming transition to Richardsonian Romanesque architecture with sandstone and terra cotta trim accenting window and entry arches. Its dominating feature was a 160-foot entry tower containing a 2,000-pound bell and a Seth Thomas clock with illuminated dials, a dramatic example of conspicuous display rather than educational function. The building provided eight classrooms on the main floor but on the second an assembly hall contained "six hundred and fifty opera chairs" and a large stage. Fire safety was a concern addressed by "a niche on each floor [that] contains one hundred feet of hose, with nozzle, connected with a stand-pipe extending to the roof." Both this building and a similar one in Canton by the same architects featured oak woodwork with bronze hardware, floors of hard maple, electric "call bells," and a Ruttan-Smead system of heating and ventilation with "dry closets"—an innovation in sanitary waste disposal that its makers claimed "solved the problem of what to do with sewage," particularly in cities or villages without a community-wide sewerage system.[12]

An even more elaborate High Victorian Gothic structure in Cleveland reveals the urgent need for areas with large Catholic populations to provide advanced education to prepare priests. Brother S. J. Wipfer was dispatched from Europe specifically to create plans for the building that became Saint Ignatius High School—later evolving into John Carroll University. Its asymmetrical appearance reflects a plan that was never completed, which would have made the tower a central entry flanked by another wing to the right.[13]

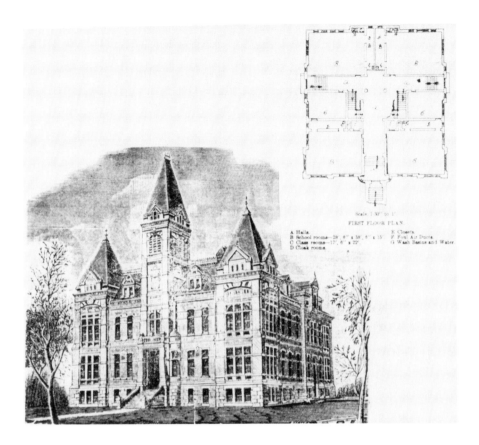

Scale, 1-32" to 1'
FIRST FLOOR PLAN.

A Halls.   E Closets.
B School rooms—28', 6" x 38', 6" x 15'.   F Foul Air Ducts.
C Class rooms—17', 6" x 22'.   G Wash Basins and Water.
D Cloak rooms.

NEWARK HIGH SCHOOL
1884–85
Victorian Gothic
Architect: Joseph W. Yost
Newark (Licking Co.)
Lithograph from Ohio School Report,
1885–86

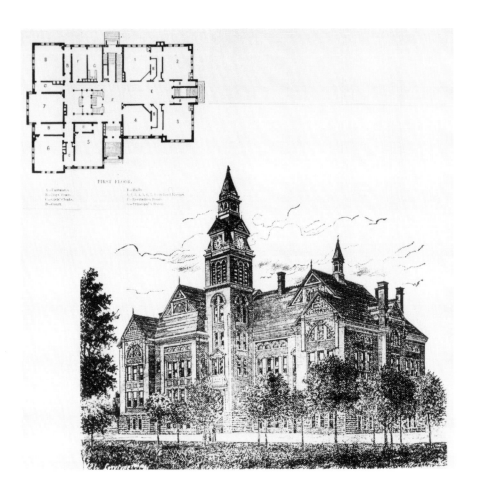

AKRON HIGH SCHOOL
1884–85
Victorian Gothic
Architects: Weary and Kramer
Akron (Summit Co.)
Lithograph from Ohio School Report,
1885–86

From 1889 to 1894 the Ohio legislature passed several laws that allowed local boards of education to open or rent school buildings for literary entertainments, school exhibitions, singing schools, or religious exercises.[14] As auditoriums became standard in urban high schools, they served not only assemblies of the student body for lectures, concerts, or dramatic productions but became increasingly important in smaller towns as cultural

SAINT IGNATIUS HIGH SCHOOL
1888–91
High Victorian Gothic
Architect: Brother S. J. Wipfer
Cleveland (Cuyahoga Co.)
Photo from National Register file, courtesy of
Ohio Historic Preservation Office

centers for the entire community—both for student productions and traveling performances. The beaux-arts design motifs of Piqua High School's auditorium emulate a nineteenth-century opera house. The serpentine form of the balcony with a paneled front leads to a deeply coffered ceiling. Paired pilasters and arcaded panels on the side walls contain silhouettes of historical figures in circular bas-relief garlands.[15] Such architectural features in public high schools made a clear statement that culture now belonged to the masses not just the elite.

By the turn of the century, the most progressive secondary schools interpreted their educational mission to include knowledge of literary, musical, and artistic masterpieces. Again, Cincinnati led the way with an organization to raise funds to beautify old Hughes High School. In 1903 the high school's art teacher, Miss Brite, proposed the formation of the Art League to "develop a love for the beautiful in environment," and with the help of alumni and friends—and contributions of five cents a month from many student members—the Art League began to acquire a rich collection of paintings, sculptures, murals, and tiled drinking fountains from the local Rookwood Pottery. When a new, larger Hughes High School building was dedicated in 1910, the president of the alumni association declared, "Our greatest pride is the public schools—our greatest boast that we are their products."[16] Public high schools were succeeding in creating the educated citizenry required for democratic government.

Nowhere was a community's pride in a new high school building more evident than in Springfield—Ohio's eighth largest city at the turn of the century—as the community basked in the honor of its native son Governor Asa Bushnell and a diversified commercial-industrial base that ranged from the Crowell Publishing Company to agricultural equipment manufacturer International Harvester.[17] In a competition that included architects from Cincinnati to Cleveland, Pittsburgh, and Chicago, Albert Pretzinger of Dayton won the contract with a beaux-arts/Georgian Revival design. His classical facade was suggestive of the Library of Congress and nicely complemented the adjacent elegant homes on Limestone Street and Fountain Street. Students of American neoclassicism will note a remarkable resemblance to Charles Bulfinch's design for the Massachusetts State House, which had in turn been influenced by London's Somerset House.[18] A projecting central block provided entry through a columned arcade on a raised terrace. Paired columns, quoins, and an accentuated cornice are typical of the beaux-arts style, but the building's dominant feature is a central dome defined by decorative metal ribs, illuminating an inner stained glass dome

Rookwood Pottery Fountain, Roselawn
Condon Elementary School, Cincinnati
Courtesy of Robert A. Flischel, © 1999,
Robert Flischel Photography

Rookwood Pottery Fountain designed by
C. Barnhorn, Hughes High School, Cincinnati
Courtesy of Robert A. Flischel, © 1999,
Robert Flischel Photography

that highlights what was originally a museum but is now the school library. When Springfield High School opened in 1911 with more than nine hundred students, it boasted an auditorium capable of seating twelve hundred persons and technological conveniences such as a large gymnasium that could be divided into separate facilities for boys and girls by a rolling partition, radiant steam heat, electric lighting, a vacuum cleaning system, a house telephone for each teacher, and "a clock in every room agreeing with the master clock in the principal's office."[19]

Ironically, one of the most progressive high school buildings of the early twentieth century was built in the small town of Greenfield—a legacy from local entrepreneur Edward Lee McClain, who began working in his father's harness shop at the age of thirteen, invented a superior horse-collar pad, and founded a manufacturing company with an international market that became the community's major employer. McClain's retirement goal was to provide his community with a state-of-the-art high school. When Greenfield citizens voted funding for a new elementary school as well, McClain made an additional donation for a vocational building, natatorium, and athletic field—completing a unique educational complex that made this town of six thousand persons a nationally recognized educational model.[20]

The men who made the dream a reality were Superintendent F. R. Harris, a native son who studied education at Harvard and returned home to implement his theories, and William B. Ittner, an architect for the Saint Louis city schools who was establishing a national reputation.[21] Buildings were razed to ready three city blocks conveniently near the center of town and a Georgian Revival style was chosen, which the architect believed provided "dignity, nobility and restraint." The two-story high school building with raised basement has auditorium and gymnasium wings to the rear that form a center courtyard, and separate entries to these facilities afford community access for evening or weekend events. Red brick is accented by Bedford sandstone keystones on the upper-story windows and the balustrade above, and the classical main entrance is flanked by pilasters with Ionic capitals and a decorative cartouche above a tripartite multipane window. The building's treasures are revealed in intricate details—Moravian tile panels with Latin inscriptions on each exterior corner, marble stairs in the main entry corridor which displays choice pieces from the building's art collection of 165 paintings, sculptures, and murals—three of the last painted specifically for this building by Boston artist Vesper Lincoln George.[22]

The vocational building provided rooms equipped to offer instruction in industrial arts, agriculture, domestic science, and commercial studies that

SPRINGFIELD HIGH SCHOOL
1909–11
Beaux-Arts
Architect: Albert Pretzinger
Springfield (Clark Co.)
Lithograph from 1980 rededication program,
courtesy of Springfield South High School

The colonnaded entry and dome intentionally
reflected the Library of Congress in
Washington, D.C.
Photo by Virginia E. McCormick

were financially supported by the Smith-Hughes Act enacted by Congress in 1917. An adjacent natatorium featured what was at the time the largest school swimming pool in the country, along with space for eight hundred spectators. A cafeteria seated two hundred and fifty students at one time—an innovative but necessary facility when students were being bused from outlying areas. The elementary building had a clinic equipped to offer physical examinations as well as to teach health and hygiene. The high school auditorium seated one thousand persons and was outfitted with a pipe organ in addition to radio and visual education apparatus.

When all three buildings were completed in 1923, wooden pergolas supported by Doric columns linked them, providing shelter for students walking from building to building or to the bus stop at the street. A statuary fountain in the courtyard created a soothing island of beauty. Ittner had created a landscaped educational campus that was applauded by the United States Bureau of Education and featured extensively in contemporary books on educational architecture.[23] A campus complex had been introduced for public schools that resembled the privileged retreats previously seen in America only for elite colleges modeled on the British examples of Oxford and Cambridge. Greenfield was cited as a model for centralized education with its cost of $950,000 for the three buildings—not including land and interior furnishings—or $432 per student at its capacity of 2,200. The district had acquired more for its money than some schools across the country paying more than twice as much per pupil, and it was attracting tuition-paying students from a hundred-square-mile area around the town.[24] Ohio's Patterson Law of 1902 had made it compulsory for school districts that had no high school to pay tuition for qualified students to attend another district—and facilities like Greenfield's were a major attraction.[25]

The neoclassical style was also chosen by the architectural firm of Garber and Woodward in 1919 for the Withrow High School complex in the Hyde Park area of Cincinnati.[26] The thirty-eight-acre site presented the challenge of rolling terrain bounded by two major thoroughfares as well as a diversified student population from "one of our best residential districts" to "children from a factory colony."[27] The site precluded a single building for all needs, but the architects responded creatively by designing multiple structures for the triangular site in classroom units for thirty pupils. Two or three units were combined to obtain gymnasiums for sixty to ninety students; and five or six units were joined to create small auditoriums that would seat 150 for music instruction or lantern lectures.

MCCLAIN HIGH SCHOOL
1915
Georgian Revival
Architect: William B. Ittner
Greenfield (Highland Co.)
Photo by Virginia E. McCormick

Entry is framed by pilasters and a semicircular
pediment displaying a cartouche.
Photo by Virginia E. McCormick

Main entry sculpture gallery
Photo from John J. Donovan, *School Architecture*

Library with mural by Vesper Lincoln George and lined with busts of authors
Photo by Stephen D. Iseman, from Edward Lee McClain High School Art Catalog, 1918

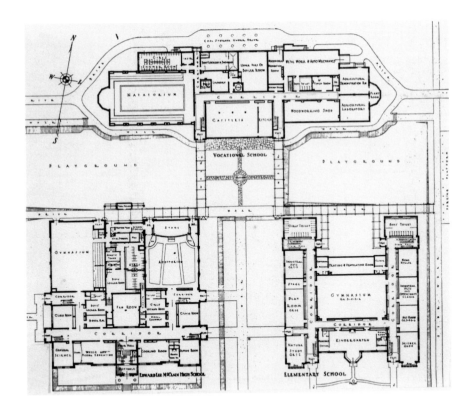

Greenfield Educational Complex—
elementary, high, and vocational schools
Architectural rendering from F. R. Harris
and William B. Ittner, *The Complete School at
Greenfield, Ohio*

WITHROW HIGH SCHOOL
1919
Neoclassical
Architects: Garber and Woodward
Cincinnati (Hamilton Co.)
Photo from *The American Architect–*
The Architectural Review, 1922

The three-story academic buildings, with the central entry from a portico supported by fluted columns, form a semicircular courtyard accented by a 114-foot clock tower with balustrades, corner urns, and a colonnaded cupola. The collegiate image of this complex reflects the beaux-arts emphasis on total environment, which is enhanced at this site by the approach across a Georgian style footbridge that spans a shallow ravine separating the site from the highway. Rising focus on physical education and facilities for competitive sports are noted in the impressive stadium and gymnasiums— the latter a building with round-arched windows accented by keystones, and a recessed porch in antis surmounted by a balustrade, dormers, and a lighted cupola. It was undoubtedly the most elegant school Cincinnati constructed during the building boom between World War I and the Great Depression. The auditorium, designed to seat the entire student body of eighteen hundred students, featured a classical frieze and a ceiling trimmed with moldings and medallions. Vocational training rooms boasted the latest technology, including gas stoves and porcelain sinks in the domestic science room.[28]

In an era of rapid consolidation, big was often equated with better, and the maximum was perhaps reached with McKinley High School at Canton—named to honor both the president and his sister, Anna, who taught for thirty years in the Canton schools. This 150-room building to serve four thousand students was the ultimate plan of George Francis Hammond, an MIT graduate and Cleveland architect who designed a number of

Entry bridge and clock tower
Photo by Virginia E. McCormick

Site plan from *The American Architect–
The Architectural Review,* 1922

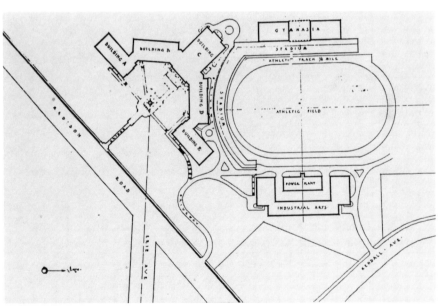

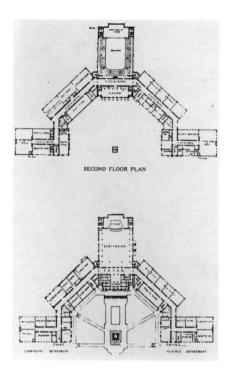

SECOND FLOOR PLAN

Withrow High School floor plans from
The American Architect—The Architectural Review,
1922

schools in the World War I era. The neoclassical revival building is of buff
brick accented by a stone entablature with modillions, and a single-story
portico with its pediment supported by Doric columns. Three structural
bays form an interior courtyard and side entries are from an arched arcade.
McKinley High School, too, contained an auditorium, cafeteria, two gymnasiums, and a swimming pool. This rapidly growing industrial city attracted a variety of eastern European immigrants, and, instead of smaller
schools in various parts of the city, this single massive high school building
was designed to provide the melting-pot culture that had become the
American ideal. McKinley High School proudly claimed the distinction of
being the largest high school in the United States.[29]

Beginning with the Columbian Exposition in Chicago in 1893, a number
of advocates of urban planning created what became known as the city
beautiful movement. It might, however, have been a disparaging remark
about the Columbus landscape that Alice Roosevelt Longworth made
while she was dedicating the McKinley statue on the west side of capitol
square in 1906 which motivated the capitol city to develop an urban plan
that included parkland and a civic center along the Scioto River front.[30]
Efforts were intensified by the extensive damage of the 1913 flood and the
first building erected in this area was Columbus Central High School in

MCKINLEY HIGH SCHOOL
1921
Neoclassical Revival
Architect: George F. Hammond
Canton (Stark Co.)
Courtesy of Stark County Historical Society

1923–24. The architect was again William B. Ittner, now resigned from the Saint Louis school system and working as a private consultant and considered by many "the most influential man in school architecture in the United States." During his career he designed approximately 430 schools in twenty-eight states.[31]

Central High School was an excellent example of the E-shaped school that became Ittner's trademark. The key elements were classrooms on only one side of interior corridors, and central auditoriums and gymnasiums flanked by courtyards for light. It was a flexible plan in which the lengths of all legs of the E could be adjusted to the site and the preferences of the client. An imposing eighteen-acre site on the riverfront was the perfect setting for this neoclassical revival building that took its inspiration from the public buildings of Athens and Rome. It set the pattern for subsequent civic center buildings, from Columbus City Hall to the Ohio State Departments Building.[32]

A classical entry supported by fluted Ionic columns was dramatized by an approach flanked by sunken courtyards with fountains on either side. Some of the building's unique features included a segmental-arched ceiling with skylights in the third-floor corridor that was designed to serve as an art gallery, drinking fountains with tile surrounds depicting historical and travel scenes, and a famous Emerson Burkhart mural entitled *Music* above the proscenium arch in the auditorium. This was painted a decade after the building's completion as part of the Public Works of Art Project during the Great Depression. Burkhart was paid $3,000 for painting this 13 x 70–foot mural that some teachers and parents found controversial because of the scantily clothed dancing nymphs.[33]

The postwar era also saw a building boom and centralization among parochial high schools. Hamilton Catholic High School was designed by Frederick G. Mueller, a local architect who became best known for the art deco municipal building he designed for Hamilton in the 1930s. This Catholic high school incorporated unusual Spanish colonial features intended to reflect the early Franciscan mission churches of the American Southwest in its variegated tiled roof, central octagonal tower, and an arched loggia emulating the style of Franciscan monasteries. A low hipped roof and wide overhanging eaves supported by slender horizontal brackets reinforce this image. A cartouche accents the central entry and projecting pavilions on either end are trimmed with cement quoins.[34]

Just a few years earlier, with the establishment in 1907 of a college of education at Ohio State University, Columbus, was on the leading edge of educational innovation. One of the major issues the National Education

CENTRAL HIGH SCHOOL
1924
Neoclassical Revival
Architect: William B. Ittner
Columbus (Franklin Co.)
Photo by Ross Hunt, National Register file,
courtesy of Ohio Historic Preservation Office

Courtyard entry with bridge and sunken
fountains
Photo by Ross Hunt, National Register file,
courtesy of Ohio Historic Preservation Office

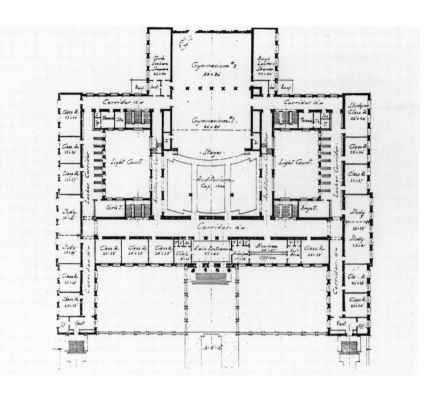

The E-shaped floor plan was an Ittner
trademark.
National Register file, courtesy of Ohio
Historic Preservation Office

Association (NEA) was discussing was a change from the prevailing eight-
four curriculum division of public schools to a six-three-three structure
that would better reflect the growing sophistication of students in the seventh and eighth grades as well as furnish a better transition to secondary
education. A. B. Graham, Ohio State's superintendent of extension, was
one of a five-member committee that in 1907 outlined the concept of a
junior high school and recommended that the NEA endorse it.[35]

In 1908–9, with university president William Oxley Thompson serving as a key member of the planning committee, Indianola Junior High
School—the first in the nation—was erected a block from the Ohio State
University Campus. It was a typical neoclassical building of the period with
a Palladian window above the entrance and an ornate metal cornice with
dentils and egg and dart motif.[36] In 1929 it was replaced by a modernistic,
three-story brick building a few blocks away designed by architect Howard Dwight Smith specifically for junior high students.[37] It has a pier and

HAMILTON CATHOLIC HIGH SCHOOL
1923
Spanish Mission Revival
Architect: Frederick G. Mueller
Hamilton (Butler Co.)
Photo by Bob McCracken, National Register
file, courtesy of Ohio Historic Preservation
Office

Colonnade entry gallery
Photo by Virginia E. McCormick

INDIANOLA JUNIOR HIGH SCHOOL
1908
Neoclassical
Architects: David Reibel and Sons
Columbus (Franklin Co.)
Photo by Virginia E. McCormick

INDIANOLA JUNIOR HIGH SCHOOL
1929
Modernistic
Architect: Howard Dwight Smith
Columbus (Franklin Co.)
Photo by Virginia E. McCormick

Entry arch and buffalo-head swag and animal
and bird sculptures by Erwin Frey
Photo by Virginia E. McCormick

Indian Chief Tahgahiute, sculptural motif
by Erwin Frey
Photo by Virginia E. McCormick

spandrel design with recessed segmental- and flat-arched windows and unusual decorative features such as balconies and terra cotta ornamentation. Visual keys to its mission are the sculptures by Ohio State professor Erwin Frey—best known for the statue of President Thompson in front of the Ohio State University Library. Indianola's adornments include a buffalo-head entry swag, a bas-relief sculpture of an Indian chief over the third story, and stone tiles carved with stylistic animal figures.[38] The interior was adorned with oak woodwork and wainscoting, ornamental plaster, a wood-burning fireplace, and leaded glass doors and bookcases. It is quality only a private school with a bountiful endowment could consider today, but the building is an interesting reflection of the university's commitment to the concept of a built environment that would inspire students during their transition from elementary to secondary studies.

The Immaculate Conception High School building completed at Celina in 1933 has a similar style, with a perpendicular effect created by stone columns of varied heights that dramatize the entry with its cross-tipped gable. It displays the tendency of conservative modernists to utilize a stripped-down, streamlined interpretation of historic styles. Diaper work of dark brick crosses beneath the windows accents each floor, and stone-tipped piers between them create the illusion of a well-wrapped box tied with ribbons.[39] Frederick DeCurtins, the architect of the building, was the grandson of Swiss immigrant Anton DeCurtins, the master carpenter who with his sons built and decorated numerous churches whose cross-tipped steeples still shine across the surrounding flatness of the northwestern Ohio landscape.[40]

After legislation in 1959 made it possible to form vocational education districts that cross local school district and/or county lines, the Penta County Joint Vocational District across five counties and seventeen school districts near Toledo became an early model for a joint vocational school. The federal government's declaration in 1962 of the Rossford Arms Depot as a surplus site provided the impetus to make the concept a reality. This fifty-five-acre property contained several small structures and a three-story building suitable for conversion to a classroom facility for approximately one thousand juniors and seniors who had completed basic requirements in their own school districts. The state board of education approved the facility in 1964 and the first students arrived in September 1965 to learn vocational skills developed in close cooperation with local industries, who often provided equipment, instructors, and job placement for graduates. Although it was 1976 before bids were taken for an educational resource

IMMACULATE CONCEPTION HIGH SCHOOL
1933
Modernistic
Architect: Frederick DeCurtins
Celina (Mercer Co.)
Photo by Virginia E. McCormick

Stylistic stone and brick piers with a simple
cross adorn the entry
Photo by Virginia E. McCormick

center, administrative offices, and additional classrooms, this facility as a model for vocational education had already hosted visits from legislators and school officials from around the country. As business and industry continually demanded more skilled workers, Owen Technical College was added next door—offering opportunity for vocational high school graduates to receive advanced technical training or for adult workers to upgrade their skills or retrain for new jobs.[41]

By the 1960s and 1970s open-space schools that offered a great deal of flexibility for team teaching or small group work were the latest manifestation of educational philosophy. Cincinnati architect Jack E. Hodell worked with faculty, parents, and students to produce a building that took unique advantage of a thirty-eight-acre rolling wooded site in suburban Mariemont, with entry across a bridge that preserved natural vegetation. This artfully designed building for eight hundred students in grades 9–12 is a cluster of hexagonal pods that could easily be expanded since common areas such as the gymnasium, auditorium, and cafeteria were designed for 1,200. The rolling terrain permitted construction of a two-story building with exterior access on both levels. Hexagonal units form open-space learning centers for related subjects such as English, social studies, or mathematics, while an administrative/guidance unit is adjacent and visible to a flexible student gathering space with lockers. Instrumental and vocal music rooms are part of the auditorium cluster for performance convenience, and the cafeteria/commons connects to the gymnasium for the accommodation of spectators during sporting events. A two-story library hexagon contains appropriate subject matter materials for the classrooms on each level—dramatically emphasizing the architect's commitment that the building's form should be dictated by its function and provide an atmosphere for teachers and students to share responsibility for the learning experience.[42]

School officials demonstrated that this 111,000-square-foot facility saved costs because it eliminated the corridors that comprise 20–25 percent of conventional school buildings. Administrators and teachers expressed pleasure that this structure enhanced team teaching. Architects addressed potential noise levels with acoustical tile ceilings and carpeted floors—causing one visiting reporter to note "education seems part of everyday carpeted America"—and students raised in the radio and television age found the activity and noise level acceptable.[43] The building was a model of community, educational, and architectural cooperation to insure that the building served their constituencies while maintaining a sensitive response to the surrounding natural environment.

PENTA COUNTY JOINT VOCATIONAL SCHOOL
1965–77
Modernistic
Architects: Richards, Bauer and Moorehead
Rossford (Wood Co.)
Photo by Virginia E. McCormick

Penta County Joint Vocational School reflects
its origins as a U.S. government depot.
Photo by Virginia E. McCormick

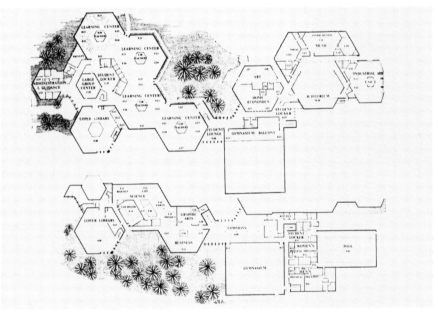

MARIEMONT HIGH SCHOOL
1969
Modular
Architects: Baxter, Hodell, Donnelly and Preston
Mariemont (Hamilton Co.)
Photo by Virginia E. McCormick

Plan shows open-space learning cores and environmental adaptation to the wooded hillside site.
Site floor plan from *Open-Space Schools*

WAPAKONETA HIGH SCHOOL
1989
Modern Rectilinear
*Architects: Lesko Associates, Architects
and Planners*
Wapakoneta (Auglaize Co.)
Courtesy of Lesko Associates, Architects and
Planners

Brick Indian-head mosaic by Cincinnati artist
John Nartker in entrance lobby
Photo by Virginia E. McCormick

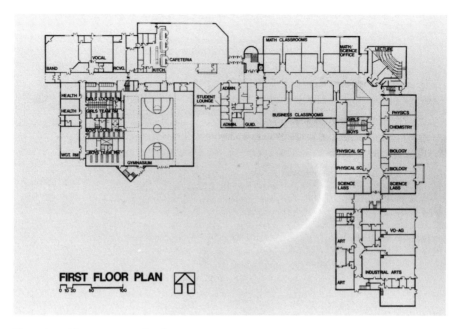

FIRST FLOOR PLAN

Floor plan with two-story academic core on
the right and cafeteria, music rooms, and
gymnasium to the left
Courtesy of Lesko Associates, Architects and
Planners

At Wapakoneta, a more traditional modernistic high school was designed by Lesko Associates; its horizontal lines of brick and glass echo the
spacious flatness of the northwestern Ohio landscape. A circular stair
tower—not unlike the silos that dot the surrounding countryside—defines
the main entrance where a glass-walled atrium separates the two floors of
classrooms and the media center from the cafeteria, gymnasium, and choir
and band rooms. The focal point of the lobby is a brick mosaic Indian head
that makes it clear this is the home of the Wapakoneta Redskins—an ironic
commemoration of the fact that this region is just north of the land the
Treaty of Greenville reserved for Native Americans in 1795.[44] But it is
a symbol of the importance competitive athletics play in modern school
building design, with a gymnasium seating 2,945 persons and serving multiple functions.[45]

For the industrial city of Massillon, the same architects designed Washington High School in an international modern style that breaks the masonry walls with bold horizontal bands of glass and aluminum that reflect
the region's industrial technology. The main entry is from a large paved and

MASSILLON WASHINGTON HIGH SCHOOL
1991
International Modern
*Architects: Lesko Associates,
Architects and Planners*
Massillon (Stark Co.)
Courtesy of Lesko Associates,
Architects and Planners

Amphitheater-style auditorium
Courtesy of Lesko Associates, Architects and
Planners

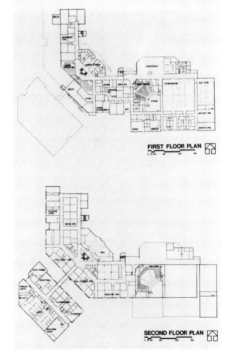

L-shaped floor plans showing classroom
and activity wings
Courtesy of Lesko Associates, Architects
and Planners

PERRY COMMUNITY EDUCATION VILLAGE
1993
Modernistic
Architects: Perkins and Will / Burgess and Niple
Perry (Lake Co.)
Courtesy of Burgess and Niple, Ltd.

landscaped plaza that serves as a hub directing traffic to specific areas such as classrooms, the cafeteria/commons, auditorium, or gymnasiums—the latter being easily separated from academic areas for community use after school hours.[46]

But a project that educators and architects nationwide consider extraordinary is Perry Community Education Village. It is an eighty-acre complex that began with a new high school but was designed from the beginning to include elementary and middle schools, a community fitness center, and an environmental education area with hiking trails—a dream made financially feasible by the construction of a nuclear power plant and the taxes it generated for the school district. Chicagoan Laurence Bradford Perkins established a reputation in educational architecture in 1940 with an innovative design for Crow Island School at Winnetka, Illinois, that utilized wings to define age groups and educational activities through design. This led to commissions around the country and recognition as a late-twentieth-century expert on educational architecture.[47] The Perry school complex is a collaborative architectural effort between Chicago-based Perkins and Will and Columbus-based Burgess and Niple that features a bold geometric interplay of vertical clock towers, a massive gymnasium cube, fan-shaped

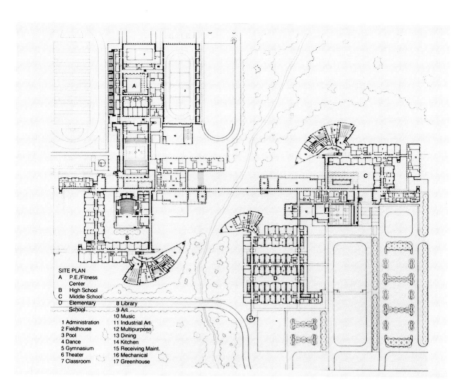

SITE PLAN
A   P.E./Fitness
    Center
B   High School
C   Middle School
D   Elementary
    School

1 Administration
2 Fieldhouse
3 Pool
4 Dance
5 Gymnasium
6 Theater
7 Classroom

8 Library
9 Art
10 Music
11 Industrial Art
12 Multipurpose
13 Dining
14 Kitchen
15 Receiving Maint.
16 Mechanical
17 Greenhouse

Site plan shows separate elementary, middle, and high school buildings and community fitness center linked by unique corner fans. Courtesy of Burgess and Niple, Ltd.

Structural steel combines with brick to create a sensation of movement in the crescent-shaped rooms.
Courtesy of Burgess and Niple, Ltd.

NEW ALBANY LEARNING COMMUNITY
1996
Neoclassical/Georgian Revival
Architects: Perkins and Will
New Albany (Franklin Co.)
Photo by Virginia E. McCormick

corner extensions with interlocking rooflines, and linear glass facades. Principle architect Ralph Johnson was elaborating on the school as village theme that Perkins and Will recently created for Troy, Michigan. It is a functional design for the twenty-first century, with an integrated information system using fiber optic cable to link all rooms with telephones, computers, and television monitors.[48] The education village offers an interesting modern comparison with the learning campuses of Greenfield's Edward Lee McClain High School and Cincinnati's Withrow High School approximately seven decades earlier, and it dramatically affirms public education's claim to a campus community for all citizens—a concept which until the twentieth century was reserved for the collegiate elite.

New Albany intentionally copied Thomas Jefferson's concept of an academic village in 1996 when it dedicated a high school, middle school, and library that were the first structures of the eighty-acre learning community campus. This resulted from a unique financial arrangement that forced developers to contribute to an incorporated entity so that existing farm and village property owners would not be unfairly taxed for facilities needed

Architecturally emulating the University of Virginia campus, the domed central library/information center serves students during the school day and adults in the evening.
Photo by Virginia E. McCormick

An aerial view shows the high school academic campus on the lower right, the athletic complex in the center left, and the elementary complex under construction near the top.
Courtesy of New Albany–Plain Local Schools

in response to rapid residential growth. Unlike Perry, this community selected classical architecture and unabashedly advertised, "If it feels familiar to you, its [sic] no accident. It bears more than a passing resemblance to Thomas Jefferson's own historic campus for the University of Virginia."[49] It is interesting that this revival of the University of Virginia rectangle—a longitudinal axis with a dominant focal point structure at one end and subsidiary buildings along the sides—should now be utilized in a community educational center as a status symbol.[50] The central library/information center serves students during the day and adults in the evenings and weekends. It features classical Doric columns supporting a central entry pediment, and a domed rotunda provides circular interior space surrounded by two-story book stacks—reminiscent of a Palladian villa. A key component of this campus is a state-of-the-art fiber optic computer network to all buildings, a video system to deliver multimedia formats to all classrooms, and a digital media laboratory to incorporate digital, graphic, video, or musical data for modeling or animation. Educational facility specialists Gary T. Moore and Jeffery A. Lackney call such spaces portfolio process studios, for preparing and exhibiting the individual or group projects that result when students are involved in determining how their learning will be evaluated.[51] The New Albany facility is a dramatic example of a rural village school district that had never enrolled a thousand students in its K–12 program until it was transformed in less than five years to a suburban school district with a campus bragging of its technological innovations, superior athletic complex, fifty-acre nature preserve for environmental studies, and its resemblance to Thomas Jefferson's neoclassical design for the grounds of the University of Virginia.

Whether the architectural interpretation emphasizes modernity or classicism, public education is opening the twentieth century with a striking commitment to serve the entire community.

Five | Colleges *&* Universities

The oldest college building in Ohio reflects a commitment to higher education even older than the state itself. In 1787 the United States Congress granted land for a university in the Northwest Territory, but it was 1804 before the new state of Ohio granted a charter to create Ohio University, and the summer of 1816 before the cornerstone was laid for the brick building now known as Cutler Hall—honoring Manessah Cutler, the Yale graduate and Marietta resident who was so influential in founding this university.[1] This Federal style building was designed and its construction supervised by Benjamin Corp, an Englishman who immigrated to Boston where he worked as a house joiner and carpenter before moving to Marietta in 1806. It is an elegant structure which Eric Johannesen believes was influenced by the Derby mansion in Salem, Massachusetts, with its fanlight entry surmounted by a Palladian window.[2] Cutler Hall also reflects civic architecture from Williamsburg to Philadelphia to Boston, with an elaborate cupola which Professor Frank J. Roos suggests was probably taken from Asher Benjamin's then recently published *American Builder's Companion*.[3] William Dean was awarded a contract for 37,000 bricks at $4.50 per thousand, and Christopher Herrolds and Daniel Herrolds for 27,964 feet of lumber at $1.12 per hundred. Completed in September 1818 at a cost of $18,800, it was a modest building compared to the academic village Thomas Jefferson was creating in the same period for the University of Virginia, but it defined a standard of classical simplicity for the first university on the Ohio frontier.[4] As enrollment prospered it was flanked in the 1830s by two complementary brick buildings with stepped gable ends, now known as Wilson Hall and McGuffey Hall. Together they form a college green that emulates the tripartite design of the eighteenth-century campus of The College of William and Mary, which in turn echoes the tradition of British country houses with flanking outbuildings that derived from Palladio's sixteenth-century Italian villas.[5] Ohio University thus copied the American colonial tradition of designing institutions of higher education on the medieval British model of learning communities where teachers and students lived and studied together. Such institutions not only required classrooms but dormitories, dining halls, and recreation facilities as well.

Federal architecture was also a source of inspiration to the founders of Miami University—chartered in 1809 to provide comparable opportunities in the western part of the state. The oldest surviving buildings on the campus are Elliott Hall and Stoddard Hall, brick dormitories completed in 1829 and 1835, respectively. They are classic examples of the American interpretation of refined elegance that the Adam brothers had made so fashionable in Great Britain. Identical in size—100 x 40 feet and three stories high—to the 1750 Connecticut Hall built at Yale University, the structures suggest a relationship by one or more of the trustees who were anxious to establish Miami as the "Yale of the West."[6] These simple Federal buildings, like those at Ohio University, originally flanked a more elaborate main building that no longer survives. One marvels at the current pristine appearance of these dormitories in which early student rooms ten feet wide were individually heated with a stove "fed with wood from the nearby forest."[7] They have certainly lived up to the trustees' request for buildings "which shall unite Cheapness of Construction with durability and Convenience."[8]

Both these state institutions looked to New England for architectural inspiration and local builders for its execution. Most institutions of higher education in Ohio throughout the nineteenth century, however, were established through private sponsorship—principally by religious denominations seeking to provide a source of educated clergy. The oldest of these is Kenyon College, established with funds solicited in England by Bishop Philander Chase of the Episcopal Church.[9] These gifts enabled Chase to purchase eight thousand acres of land in Knox County and move the school he had begun in 1824 at his home near Worthington—seeking space for contemplation in an idealized rural environment safely distant from urban temptations.[10] The Gothic Revival architecture he chose for Kenyon Hall, the main building which was erected between 1828 and 1836, emphasized the college's connection to the Church of England, whose architectural and liturgical heritage embraced this style.[11]

CUTLER HALL
1816–18
Federal
Architect: Benjamin Corp
Ohio University, Athens (Athens Co.)
Courtesy of the Ohio University Archives

The building anchors the college green today
as it has for nearly two centuries.
Courtesy of the Ohio University Archives

STODDARD HALL
1835
Federal
Builders: David Ritchey, William P. Vanhook,
and James T. Slack
Miami University, Oxford (Butler Co.)
Photo by Virginia E. McCormick

British Gothic architecture was beginning to influence American churches, but Kenyon Hall was the first Gothic collegiate building in America. It is a typical product of the early-nineteenth-century gentleman architect, designed by Rev. Norman Nash, an Episcopal minister responsible for several churches in eastern Pennsylvania, in collaboration with Bishop Chase who supervised its construction. The present building is a faithful reconstruction after a fire in 1949, and it remains an impressive native sandstone edifice with shallow arcades topped by pointed-arched windows, crenelations, and pinnacles. The building's crowning feature is a central 110-foot spire, created from a sketch reportedly provided to Chase by Charles Bulfinch when they met at a Washington social occasion while Bulfinch was working on the United States Capitol building.[12]

Chase left Kenyon before the building's end wings were completed, but Gothic architecture was firmly imprinted on the college. Bexley Hall, a building to house its theological seminary, was designed by Henry Roberts, a London architect who created a classical building with symmetrical

Photo from National Register file, courtesy of Ohio Historic Preservation Office

Nineteenth-century lithograph of Miami University shows Elliott Hall and Stoddard Hall to the left.
Photo from National Register file, courtesy of Ohio Historic Preservation Office

KENYON HALL
1828–36
Gothic Revival
Architects: Rev. Norman Nash and Rev. Philander Chase
Spire: Charles Bulfinch
Kenyon College, Gambier (Knox Co.)
Courtesy of the Ohio Historical Society

details such as paired round-arched windows. There is a distinctly Tudor Gothic quality in details such as the crenelated roof and a pointed-arched entry surmounted by a bow window flanked by projecting turrets. This building has been variously compared to Saint John's College at Cambridge, Hampton Court Palace, and the Houses of Parliament, but no one denies the sophistication of its design compared to the gentleman architects' execution of Kenyon Hall. The British influence on Kenyon College established what one college historian described condescendingly as "an architectural oasis" in the Midwest.[13]

The richness of Kenyon's Gothic design is symbolized in the Philomathean and Nu Pi Kappa Literary Society rooms in Ascension Hall. This building was designed in 1857 by William Tinsley, an Irish architect who immigrated to Cincinnati and quickly established himself as the Midwest's leading Victorian architect.[14] Its square tower entry flanked by gabled wings is a modest precursor to the Ohio School for the Deaf that he completed a decade later, but it clearly reflects the Tinsley trademark of a

BEXLEY HALL

1839–43

Tudor Gothic Revival

Architect: Henry Roberts

Kenyon College, Gambier (Knox Co.)

Courtesy of the Ohio Historical Society

ASCENSION HALL

1859–62

Gothic Revival

Architect: William Tinsley

Kenyon College, Gambier (Knox Co.)

Courtesy of the Ohio Historical Society

central block flanked by dependent wings. Literary society rooms echo one of the most significant aspects of the nineteenth-century collegiate experience—an emphasis on discussing and debating literary masterpieces and philosophical questions. Richly carved woodwork includes bracketed beams and ornamental screens with round- or pointed-arched arcades— the entirety indicating the elite atmosphere expected for young gentlemen who possessed the economic and intellectual resources to study and debate philosophical issues.

It is ironic that the oldest collegiate Greek Revival building in the state today, now known as Elliott Hall at Ohio Wesleyan University, was built as a luxury hotel rather than an educational facility. Yet this architectural style came to characterize education in the mid-nineteenth century. Sited adjacent to Delaware's sulphur spring, Mansion House was built in 1833 with dreams of becoming a fashionable health spa—the "Saratoga of the West." When this venture failed, Delaware Methodists successfully raised $10,000 to purchase this small, 52 x 62–foot luxury hotel and present it in 1842 to the Methodist Church to establish a college. It was a bargain price for an architectural gem that had cost $25,000 to construct only nine years earlier—with Frederick C. Welch, the principal carpenter-joiner, receiving $1,200 and 645 acres of land along the Scioto River. For a denomination whose origins in camp meetings preceded the formation of congregations, a resort becoming a religious college has a certain symbolism.[15]

Three-story Elliott Hall is a sophisticated classical design with a central arched entry flanked by two pairs of blind arches, surmounted on the upper floors by Doric columns supporting a recessed porch. It is capped by a Doric frieze and a hipped roof with a low square cupola accented by elliptical windows. The craftsmanship of both exterior and interior wood carving is unusually sophisticated for Ohio in 1833 and the origin of its design remains a mystery. But when the college received a gift in the 1850s to erect a new building with a library room, architect Morris Cadwallader paid Elliott Hall the supreme compliment of replicating it exactly in brick. In Sturges Hall the Doric columns are wooden, but the arched entry is stone.[16] Its completion in 1856 provided a symmetrical Doric front for the campus, with Elliott and Sturges Halls flanking a central chapel built four years earlier. The concept of a monumental front row dominated by a central chapel is commonly traced to John Trumbull's innovative plan for Yale University that was widely copied by eastern colleges such as Dartmouth, Brown, and Amherst.[17]

Ohio Wesleyan was not the only college in Ohio to adopt it. At Hudson, Western Reserve College was developing a monumental row centered on

ELLIOTT HALL
1833
Greek Revival
Builder: Frederick C. Welch
Ohio Wesleyan University, Delaware
(Delaware Co.)
Lithograph from Ohio Wesleyan Catalog, 1852

Photograph showing the building painted to
emphasize pilasters and frieze, 1908
Courtesy of the Ohio Historical Society

the Greek Revival chapel designed by Simeon Porter for the earlier academy.[18] Evolving to full collegiate status with Congregational Church support, the chapel—flanked by dormitories such as the 1837 North College Hall—reflects the central role of the church in such educational institutions. The simple Greek Revival style of four-story North College Hall provided for theological students four double residential suites per floor. Its exterior simplicity, distinguished only by stone piers and a carved lintel at the entry, contrasts with the Gothic elegance of its contemporary at Kenyon College and reflects an architectural distinction common among the churches of the Congregational and Episcopal denominations.[19]

Two of the purest Greek Revival collegiate buildings in the state reflect the geographic and religious diversity of Marietta College and Heidelberg College, and both play homage to Western Reserve College. Erwin Hall at Marietta was built a decade after Porter's chapel at Western Reserve, but it is a near replica—an example of architectural influence migrating within the state rather than from the New England origins of the Marietta pioneers. Reportedly designed by Rufus E. Harte, a local man who had attended Western Reserve Academy and Yale University, Erwin Hall was originally a multipurpose building containing chapel, lecture and recitation rooms, and literary society halls. It is distinguished by brick pilasters and a frieze that continues around the sides of the building, and it has a two-stage tower.[20] Although Marietta College evolved from Marietta Collegiate Institute and Western Teacher's Seminary, designed primarily to prepare teachers for common schools, it is interesting that its first building attempted to re-create the classical monumental row of Western Reserve College, which emphasized a classical and theological education.

Heidelberg College, founded in 1850 by the Evangelical and Reformed Church, reflects its German heritage in its name, but Founders Hall remains one of the most impressive Greek Revival buildings erected in the state—with a notable resemblance to North College Hall at Western Reserve but with refinements such as the projecting center facade crowned by a pediment with a fanlight window. Designed by a committee chaired by mathematics professor Jeremiah H. Good—a creative thinker whose 1852 home across the street was an octagon—this large three-story building with a half attic and basement conveyed a sense of delicacy in its details. It is a 104 x 47–foot rectangular brick structure distinguished by a projecting central section accented by monumental doorways in a series of three balconies. Horizontal attic windows in the frieze beneath the cornice are far more typical of domestic Greek Revival architecture but entirely appropriate for a multipurpose educational building originally containing thirty

"Classical row" composed of Elliott, Thompson, and Sturges Halls
STURGES HALL
1856
Greek Revival
Architect: Morris Cadwallader
Ohio Wesleyan University, Delaware (Delaware Co.)
Lithograph from Ohio Wesleyan Catalog, 1856

NORTH COLLEGE HALL
1837–38
Greek Revival
Architect: Simeon Porter
Western Reserve College/Academy, Hudson (Summit Co.)
Photo from National Register file, courtesy of Ohio Historic Preservation Office

ERWIN HALL
1845–50
Greek Revival
Architect/Builder: Rufus E. Harte
Marietta College, Marietta (Washington
Co.)
Lithograph from National Register file,
courtesy of Ohio Historic Preservation
Office

Gothic interior of Psi Gamma Literary
Society room at Marietta College is typical of
such nineteenth-century rooms.

FOUNDERS HALL
1852–58
Greek Revival
Architect: Jeremiah H. Good
Heidelberg College, Tiffin (Seneca Co.)
Photo by Virginia E. McCormick

residential, four lecture, six recitation, and two literary society rooms as well as chapel and library. The significance of this school's religious foundation was emphasized with a Bible and a copy of the Heidelberg catechism among the items placed in the cornerstone in 1852, but it was also oriented to the state and nation, with copies of the Ohio Constitution, 1850 census, and a set of U.S. coins.[21]

Such multipurpose Old Mains were typical of Ohio colleges in the era immediately preceding and following the Civil War, but their architecture presents a variety of styles. When Antioch Hall was built in 1852 it was a dramatic building making a statement about the concept and goals of this new coeducational college at Yellow Springs. Founded by a branch of Unitarians as a liberal nonsectarian Christian college, the school drew instant national recognition by attracting noted educator Horace Mann as its first president. A. M. Merrifield, a master builder from Worcester, Massachusetts, was a member of the planning committee, and even before a site was selected the plans for a main building with flanking dormitories for men and women illustrated the institution's aspirations for innovation.[22]

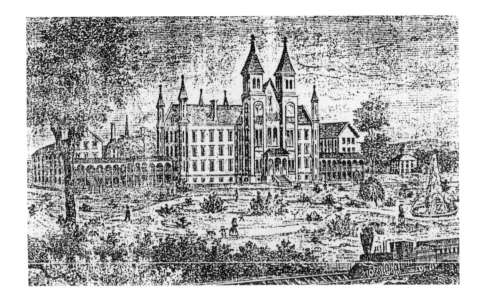

Antioch Hall was designed with peristyles to flanking dormitory wings.
Lithograph from Greene County map, 1855

Hall was actually built with freestanding dormitories on either side.
Lithograph from Greene County atlas, 1874

Although the Romanesque Revival style of Antioch Hall was new to Ohio, it has been persuasively demonstrated that it was derived from the plan for Davis Hall at Worcester Academy—a building erected by Merrifield's father or brother—which was modeled on the Smithsonian Institution building constructed at Washington, D.C., in 1846.[23] The four-story, 180-foot Antioch Hall—the same length as the White House—is a powerful Romanesque Revival interpretation that suggests the venerability of an old and honored institution. It exhibits the characteristic pairs of round-arched windows and rose windows, arched corbelling, an arched entry flanked by massive square towers with concave spires, and octagonal corner towers with concave spires. The symmetrical design was enhanced in the original plan that provided arched arcades—which were never built—connecting the main building to perpendicular dormitories on either side.[24] It was a design that clearly reflected its Italian influence, but without the arcades the flanking dormitories have no architectural distinction beyond the Palladian windows in their gable ends that had originally been intended to be viewed above the arched arcade.

COLLEGE HALL
1859
Italian Renaissance
Architect: Charles W. Heard
Lake Erie College, Painesville (Lake Co.)
Lithograph from National Register file,
courtesy of Ohio Historic Preservation Office

Photo card from National Register file,
courtesy of Ohio Historic Preservation Office

College Hall, designed a few years later by Cleveland architect Charles W. Heard for the Lake Erie College for Women, is the same size as Antioch Hall and bears some similarity in style, but its architectural details reflect the Italian Renaissance. A high basement gives this imposing structure a five-story facade dominated by a square entry tower. Both the building and tower feature typical Romanesque round-arched windows—singly, in pairs, or triples. The eaves of both the building and tower are bracketed in the newly fashionable Italianate style, and a portico is formed by wooden arcades with balustrades that connect the central tower to the end wings.[25] Johannesen has described the overall effect of this building as gracious and hospitable—suitable both for its use as a women's college and the resort atmosphere of the surrounding lakeside area east of Cleveland.[26] It provided living rooms, classrooms, library, dining hall, and social hall for 150 students and reportedly was influenced by the Mount Holyoke College campus that many of the Lake Erie staff had attended and aspired to emulate. Although fireplaces originally heated the rooms, by 1880 a furnace supplied steam heat and gas lights illuminated halls and public rooms.

College Hall—now known as Chapman Hall—at Mount Union College is an eclectic adaptation of Romanesque architecture that is interesting for several reasons. It is the only surviving Ohio collegiate building constructed during the Civil War, and it reflects how changing architectural fashions had influenced the mature work of Simeon Porter, by then a practicing architect in Cleveland but still recognized for his work twenty years earlier as a master builder of Greek Revival structures at Hudson. Mount Union College was chartered with the intent that scientific studies would parallel and be equal to the humanities and that enrollment would be open to students of either sex regardless of their race or color.[27]

It would appear that Porter was attempting to incorporate all these aspirations as well as his lifetime of construction experience into this single college building. It was technologically innovative in using cast-iron supporting columns within a Romanesque brick shell, with characteristic round-arched windows in pairs and triples and two oculi windows on either side. Entry is made through a gabled projection flanked by a pair of Gothic turrets; the eaves are decorated with an eclectic combination of corbelling on the sides and bracketing on the ends; and towers with battlements anchor the corners in a manner nearly identical to Porter's design for West High School in Cleveland.[28] An enlarged Greek Revival octagonal cupola is crowned by a dome that originally served as an astronomical observatory.[29] It was an extravagant building, successfully designed and built to attract the support of the Methodist Church.

CHAPMAN HALL
1862–64
Victorian/Romanesque Revival
Architect: Simeon Porter
Mount Union College, Alliance (Stark Co.)
Photo from National Register file, courtesy of
Ohio Historic Preservation Office

Another Methodist venture was the establishment of Wilberforce University—named in honor of the famed British abolitionist—to provide education for African American students. As they had done in establishing Ohio Wesleyan a decade earlier, the Cincinnati conference of the Methodist Episcopal Church paid $13,500 for Xenia Springs—a retreat for "taking the waters" that included a 54-acre timbered site with five mineral springs and $40,000 worth of buildings a few miles northeast of Xenia. The main structure—Tawana House—had a three-story central block with a cupola, a two-story gallery porch, and wings on either side that created the overall effect of a wedding cake. It faced a central green surrounded by cottages clustered around the focal fountain generated from one of the natural springs.[30] Four of the original twenty-four trustees were ministers of the African Methodist Episcopal (A.M.E.) Church and the institution quickly prospered. By 1859–60, the catalog showed 207 students at this site, but declining enrollments during the Civil War left the Methodists with considerable debt. In 1863 they sold the property to the A.M.E. Church, who rechartered the college under an African American administration.[31]

Two years later the main building was destroyed by a fire that originated with arsonists determined to drive the African American institution from the area. The community knew that most of the teachers and students were in town celebrating the fall of Richmond, but it was a coincidence that the same night President Abraham Lincoln would be assassinated. A.M.E. church members and supporters as diverse as the U.S. Freedmen's Bureau, The American Unitarian Association, and the estate of Supreme Court Justice Salmon P. Chase helped Wilberforce rebuild. What became known as Shorter Hall was a three-story brick building with eight recitation rooms, one lecture room, library, museum, dormitories for eighty students, basement kitchen, dining room, and laundry and staff rooms. Opened in June 1867—although it was yet unplastered and unpainted—its segmental-arched hoodmolds and ninety-two-foot central cupola show the popular Italianate style of the period, but pediment dormers flanked by chimneys and round-arched dormers reflect a unique vernacular blending of Greek Revival with Italianate elements.[32] It was a building that boldly stated Wilberforce was here to stay.

The institution prospered, and in 1905–6 Galloway Hall, a more elaborate Italian Renaissance administrative building, was completed—with an asymmetrical clock and bell tower, corner quoins, and a hipped roof with a modillion cornice. This was the design of Professor Lowell W. Baker,

Tawana House at Xenia Springs was a retreat flanked by cottages when the Methodists purchased it in 1856 for Wilberforce University.
Courtesy of the Ohio Historical Society

SHORTER HALL
1866–67
Victorian
Achitect: Unknown
Wilberforce University, Wilberforce (Greene Co.)
Drawing by Henry Howe, *Historical Collections of Ohio*

director of the college's department of building trades, which included a three-year carpentry program that taught design drafting as well as construction skills.[33] Flat-arched windows on the first floor and round-arched on the second are grouped in trios on one side, while on the other side floor-length round-headed windows beneath a classical pediment create a temple-like facade. The design was clearly intended to reflect the importance that turn-of-the-century educators placed on total training of mind and body. On the frieze of the tripartite facade, where one would expect classical decoration, are the mottoes, "A sound body, a trained hand, a trained mind," and on the temple side, "A true spirit." These are the concepts made famous by the "Head, Heart, Hands, and Health" of the 4-H Club movement that had recently originated a few miles to the north.[34] Galloway Hall was primarily a modern trades building lighted by electricity and heated by steam, but its 1,200-seat auditorium contained a proscenium arch and a fine pipe organ.[35] The Ohio legislature had granted Wilberforce funding for a normal school to train African American teachers and an industrial department with facilities to teach carpentry and building trades to young men and sewing and domestic skills to young women—a policy that was deemed benevolent in the 1880s but appears racist and sexist today. The only enduring portion of this elegant building is the upper tower— which survived the April 1974 tornado that devastated the Wilberforce campus and is now incorporated in a modern alumni center at Central State University. It is a small reminder of a building whose architecture, more than any other in Ohio, displayed educators' commitments to training mind, body, and spirit.

Towers Hall, erected at Otterbein College from 1870 to 1872, exemplifies High Victorian Gothic architecture in a collegiate setting, but it reflects the end of an era of massive main buildings. Professional architects were now universally employed to design major educational buildings and one imagines Robert T. Brookes—although little is known of his career in Cleveland and Columbus—as a confident man, aggressively composing an asymmetrical building dominated by three distinctively different towers. Pointed windows and doorways combine with corner buttresses to emphasize its Gothic character, but in a far more massive and vertical manner than the early Gothic Revival buildings of Kenyon College. Johannesen notes the sculptural quality of Towers Hall—cubes, octagons, and pyramids all cast in dramatic juxtaposition to each other.[36] Although this 170 x 107–foot building basically conforms to the Tinsley plan with a large central block and dependent wings,[37] it was still a multipurpose Old Main, replacing a

GALLOWAY HALL
1905–6
Italian Renaissance
Architect: Prof. Lowell W. Baker
Wilberforce University, Wilberforce
(Greene Co.)
Photo card, courtesy of the Ohio Historical
Society

Tower salvaged from the tornado that
destroyed Galloway Hall, now part of the
alumni center at Central State University
Photo by Virginia E. McCormick

TOWERS HALL
1872
High Victorian Gothic
Architect: Robert T. Brookes
Otterbein College, Westerville (Franklin Co.)
Courtesy of Otterbein College Archives

smaller, earlier building that had burned. Towers Hall contained the traditional mix of lecture and recitation rooms—each heated by its own coal
stove—and a chapel for eight hundred persons.

The four literary society rooms on Towers's upper floor had carved
woodwork that echoed the High Victorian Gothic elegance of the building's pointed-arched windows.[38] Entry to the Philomathean room was
through massive birch doors embedded with multiple colors of leaded glass.
It was furnished in 1891 with the advice of Columbus architect Frank L.
Packard in regard to stained glass windows, woodwork, frescoes, and carpet.
Contemporary photos show a room adorned with blue and gold Brussels
carpet, a life-size oil portrait of William Shakespeare, and a painted dado
and frieze with a Latin motto that translates, "To inquire is our zeal."[39] The
literary societies that preceded modern social fraternities and sororities intentionally cultivated an elite mystique, but the building reflects a postwar
industrial era when the nation—including higher education—was poised
on the brink of exuberant expansion.

The Philomathean Literary Society room as it
appeared from 1891 to 1905, with interior
designed by Frank L. Packard
Courtesy of Otterbein College Archives

Stained glass doors to Philomathean Literary
Society room
Photo by Virginia E. McCormick

This would soon be reflected in the robust elements of the Richardson-ian Romanesque architecture that became immensely popular for public buildings. An interesting adaptation of this style to higher education can be seen in Orton Hall at Ohio State University and University Hall at Ohio Wesleyan University—both completed in 1893 and both designed by the Columbus architectural firm of Joseph W. Yost and Frank L. Packard.[40]

The new land-grant university campus at Columbus was developing in a form new to Ohio but consistent with the "free, liberal, picturesque" plan Frederick Law Olmsted recommended for Cornell University, to follow the terrain rather than rigid lines. He had a remarkable influence on land-grant college planning in the 1860s and 1870s, and Ohio State University's Oval is a park-like setting similar to Olmsted's designs for Kansas State, Michigan State, and Iowa State Universities.[41]

Orton Hall—named for Ohio State's first president and Ohio's first state geologist—dramatically symbolized the scientific role in the state's new land-grant university. Forty types of Ohio stone, arranged in strati-graphic order with the oldest limestones in the lower part of the building and the younger sandstones above, provide a geologic record of the state. The building's massive round-arched entry is balanced by a round conical-roofed tower on one side and projecting gable on the other. Lime-stone steps quarried from nearby Marble Cliff reveal an assortment of fossils of vanished marine life. Twenty-five gargoyles circling the top of the tower are intricately crafted to represent the heads of extinct animals of this region—ichthyosaurs, dinosaurs, pterosaurs, titanotheres—keeping a whimsical eye on campus activities across the Oval. Window styles range from the pointed-arched to trabeated, their variety contributing to the overall unity of this asymmetrical design.[42] The geological elements appro-priately define the unique mission of the state's only land-grant university to disseminate scientific research to people throughout the state.[43]

The typical Richardsonian entry arch of Ohio Wesleyan's University Hall is similar to Orton Hall's, but foundation stones on either side are inscribed in Hebrew—"Boaz," he comes in power, and "Jachin," he establishes—in accordance with King Solomon's temple.[44] From a cornerstone in-scribed "Christ the Chief Cornerstone," to a cross and Bible carved in the stone entry, no one could miss the symbolism of this university's sponsor-ship by the Methodist Church. The building's main feature was Gray Chapel, with two thousand opera-style seats to accommodate the entire student body for required daily chapel services. Its highlights were a dome 126 feet in circumference fitted with Venetian glass frescoes painted by

ORTON HALL
1893
Richardsonian Romanesque
Architects: Joseph W. Yost and Frank L. Packard
Ohio State University, Columbus
(Franklin Co.)
Courtesy of the Ohio State University
Archives

Tower with gargoyles representing extinct
animals of the region
Photo by Virginia E. McCormick

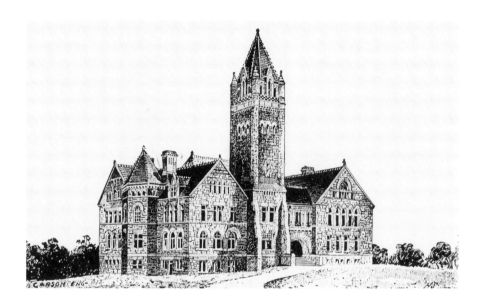

UNIVERSITY HALL
1893
Richardsonian Romanesque
Architects: Joseph W. Yost and Frank L. Packard
Ohio Wesleyan University, Delaware
(Delaware Co.)
Lithograph from Ohio Wesleyan Catalog,
1892–93

Christian Jensen, a Columbus immigrant from Munich who was experienced in painting Bavarian theaters, and a $13,000 pipe organ specifically designed for the chapel by the Roosevelt Organ Works of New York City.[45]

As the nineteenth century came to a close, so did the era of the collegiate Old Main that could encompass all academic and administrative needs of the faculty and students. Both the number and size of Ohio's institutions of higher education were thriving. The need for a new age is dramatically symbolized by the College of Wooster where a devastating fire December 11, 1901, destroyed the main college building, and led to an immediate decision by trustees and alumni to rebuild separate administrative and academic buildings in fireproof vitrified brick so that such a monumental loss could never be repeated.

Kauke, Severance, and Scovel Halls were dedicated on the first anniversary of the catastrophic fire—designed by Lansing C. Holden in the picturesque Tudor Gothic style that became a unifying architectural theme for all subsequent construction on this campus, from dormitories to chapel

Hebrew inscriptions on University Hall
entry arch
Photos by Virginia E. McCormick

Domed interior of Gray Chapel at the
beginning of the twentieth century
Courtesy of Ohio Wesleyan University
Archives

KAUKE HALL
1902
Tudor Gothic/Collegiate Gothic
*Architects: Lansing C. Holden and
George C. Nimmons*
College of Wooster, Wooster
(Wayne Co.)
Lithograph from College of Wooster Catalog,
1907–8

Tower entry of Kauke Hall
Photo by Virginia E. McCormick

to gymnasium.[46] Holden was certainly acquainted with Cope and Stewardson's recent designs for Princeton University, and by replicating this architectural style perhaps he sought to acquire the scholarly introspection and
clubby elitism Professor Woodrow Wilson was creating there.[47] Kauke Hall
forms a half quadrangle whose projecting wings define the central campus
green, which leads directly to Severance and Scovel Halls. A projecting
entry block with octagonal crenelated towers features a pointed-arched
stone entry with terra cotta trim. Typical Gothic features include the stone
doorway and window dripstones, a copper domed cupola, recessed wooden

Reconstructed campus, with college green
extending from U-shaped Kauke, Scovel,
and Severance Halls in the foreground
Lithograph from College of Wooster Catalog,
1907–8

Scovel Hall entry detail
Photo by Virginia E. McCormick

doors with carved panels and decorative hinges, sculptured botanical motifs, and roofs defined by step gables or crenelations. In emulating its more prestigious sister institution at Princeton, this Presbyterian college established in Ohio a style that has often been copied as Collegiate Gothic. The College of Wooster's Tudor Gothic gate towers create a symbolic and psychological boundary between the college and the world outside that bears some resemblance to the unified architectural quadrangles of the British universities at Oxford and Cambridge, as Wooster's catalog proudly proclaimed. Although the architecture reflected tradition, Severance and Scovel were designed to serve progressive scientific departments—chemistry and physics, biology and geology—with lecture rooms including "automatic devices for darkening and all modern conveniences for lecture illustrations."[48]

Professionalism among teachers had been growing throughout the last half of the nineteenth century and several private normal schools had arisen for the purpose of training teachers, but it was an act by the Ohio legislature in 1910 that created the first two state normal colleges in northern Ohio and provided $150,000 for buildings. Competition was keen for a site in northeastern Ohio—which had no state-supported schools like Ohio University and Miami University—and the gift of a fifty-three-acre farm from William Stewart Kent secured the location.[49] George Francis Hammond, an architect who had studied at MIT and worked in Boston before moving to Cleveland, created a master plan.[50] He conceived a crescent of neoclassical revival buildings following the crest of a wooded ridge that was the central topographic feature of the Kent farm site—conforming to a typical beaux-arts plan that evolved in the wake of the Columbian Exposition.[51] The administration building—which received the addition of a Greek temple facade of eight pilasters, an entablature, and pediment in 1929 when the normal school became Kent State College—is flanked by Kent Hall, with an entry of fluted Ionic columns, and Merrill Hall, which adjusts to the slope with a podium of wide steps. Together with Lowry and Moulton Halls, all completed before 1915, the classic simplicity of this crescent of five buildings established a restrained but dignified standard for teacher education.[52]

It was far more challenging to change an existing campus with varied buildings to a beaux-arts form that employed symmetry, focal points, and geometric clarity, but that is what Oberlin College attempted, in consultation with the Olmsted brothers, sons of famed landscape architect Frederick Law Olmsted.[53] They conceived a master plan for the Oberlin campus around a typical New England village green—creating what one college

LOWRY, MERRILL, ADMINISTRATION,
AND KENT HALLS
1911–14
Neoclassical Revival
Architect: George Francis Hammond
Kent State University, Kent (Portage Co.)
Courtesy of Kent State University Archives

Moulton Hall typifies the neoclassical revival
style of the Kent State crescent.
Photo from National Register file, courtesy of
Ohio Historic Preservation Office

historian has described as "a largely twentieth century college campus surrounded by a nineteenth century Ohio village."[54] A key to the implementation of this plan was the retention of nationally recognized architect Cass Gilbert as college architect.[55] Although the plan was doomed by compromises that prevented the demolition of buildings, Gilbert's distinctive imprint can be seen in several campus buildings, particularly the northern Italian Renaissance classicism of Allen Memorial Art Museum. Buff sandstone is accented by red sandstone trim and the arched loggia and red tiled roof complete the Mediterranean style.[56] World War I was making Gilbert an intense nationalist and Geoffrey Blodgett points out that Gilbert's architectural range narrowed as he attempted to impose his interpretation of appropriate classical design for public buildings.[57] Allen Memorial Art Museum is the purest example of Gilbert's concept for the campus, and its location and style illustrates his desire to bridge the boundary between campus and community. It is interesting to note the striking similarities between this building and his design for the Detroit Public Library or the art institute Edward B. Green would design for Dayton a decade later.

It is appropriate that Pontifical College Josephinum—the only pontifical seminary in the world outside of Italy—should reflect High Romanesque Revival architecture. The imposing building north of Columbus is seven hundred feet in length and has a gabled center block defined by square towers topped by copper domes. But its most striking feature is a 180-foot tower with buttresses on the lower levels rising to turrets and a louvered belfry crowned with a copper dome featuring a cross at the pinnacle. Designed by the Saint Louis architectural firm of F. A. Ludwig, the carved wooden entry doors, sculpted stone masonry, and stained glass reveal the superb craftsmanship that $1,500,000 could purchase during the Great Depression. The Josephinum evolved from an orphanage founded by Father Joseph Jessing for German Catholic boys, hoping many would prepare for the priesthood. At its opening, this building of more than three hundred rooms provided living quarters, classrooms, chapel, library, and gymnasium for four hundred students from elementary to advanced levels—in contrast to the massive Old Main buildings being forsaken by most other colleges. Today the building is a durable and visible symbol of faith, serving as a Catholic liberal arts college and theological seminary. The inscription from Rom. 8:31 on Father Jessing's nearby statue inquires: "Si Deus Pro Nobis—Quis Contra Nos?" If God is for us, who can be against us?[58]

The enrollment surge in higher education following World War II resulted in massive construction programs at both private and public colleges and universities—often with utilitarian buildings exhibiting little sense of

ALLEN MEMORIAL ART MUSEUM
1917
Second-Renaissance Revival
Architect: Cass Gilbert
Oberlin College, Oberlin (Lorain Co.)
Photo by Virginia E. McCormick

PONTIFICAL COLLEGE JOSEPHINUM
1929–31
High Romanesque Revival
Architects: F. A. Ludwig and Co.
Pontifical College Josephinum, Columbus
(Franklin Co.)
Photo by Virginia E. McCormick

JEROME LIBRARY
1965–67
Modernistic
Architect: Carl E. Bentz
Bowling Green State University, Bowling
Green (Wood Co.)
Photos by Virginia E. McCormick

style. It is worth noting two buildings constructed at Bowling Green State University during the turbulent 1960s that attempted within a modest budget to speak artistically and functionally to student demands for a voice in the issues that affected them. The nine-story Jerome Library—named for the president who led the university through this chaotic period—was designed by state architect Carl E. Bentz, with functional open stacks and subject matter groupings to make it user friendly. What raises it from an utilitarian nonentity and creates the image of a tree of knowledge rising from the flat northwestern Ohio landscape are the curving entry terraces and the nonobjective murals designed for the east and west towers by

SADDLEMIRE STUDENT SERVICES BUILDING
1966–68
Miesian Circular
Architects: Sanborn, Steketee, Otis and Evans
Bowling Green State University, Bowling
Green (Wood Co.)
Photos by Virginia E. McCormick

The Don Drumm mural captures the peace
symbolism of the 1960s.
Photo by Virginia E. McCormick

Akron artist Don Drumm while he was serving the university as an artist-in-residence. Drumm outlined, and construction crews sandblasted into the precast concrete, the abstract figures that symbolize the size and variety of educational ideas.[59]

A few steps away, Saddlemire Student Services Building suggests the landing of a flying saucer—a popular obsession of the 1960s. This is the home of the student bookstore, the dean of students and related guidance and counseling functions, student publications, student government, a center for international students, and financial aid and placement services. Toledo architects from Sanborn, Steketee, Otis, and Evans worked closely with students on the design, selecting a Miesian circular form that would symbolize the centrality of individual students in the university environment. Movable partitions throughout the interior provide flexibility, and doors on the ground floor open to offer performance space facing a concrete amphitheater on one side—or shelter for lines waiting to enter the adjacent bookstore at the beginning of the term. A colorful Drumm mural circles the wall, with a crest in the center featuring half—the peaceful half—of the American eagle and a Latin motto giving tongue-in-cheek expression to the American values for "mother and apple pie."[60] It is a unique

SINCLAIR COMMUNITY COLLEGE
1969–75
Modernistic
Architects: Edward Durell Stone and Sullivan,
Leclider and Jay
Dayton (Montgomery Co.)
Photos by Virginia E. McCormick

example of a building for students designed with students. Such a building on a state university campus would have been unthinkable in the 1930s, when the international style of modern architecture was controversial. But in the post–World War II era, the Bauhaus concept of motion in architecture became appropriate for the dynamic and changing nature of college campuses embroiled in the controversial U.S. role in Southeast Asia.[61]

Another response to the baby boom generation was the rise of community colleges offering two-year associate degrees and career-oriented technical programs for commuting students. It was as distinctive a part of the American populist tradition as the land-grant colleges a century earlier, and it demanded new forms to accommodate nontraditional commuting students. Unlike the nineteenth-century residential colleges that sought isolation for scholarly contemplation, the community college depended upon becoming an integral, physical part of the daily life of its community.[62] One of the first was Sinclair Community College at Dayton, which traces its history to an evening school the Young Men's Christian Association (YMCA) originated in 1887. This had evolved into a junior college awarding associate degrees by the time the Montgomery County commissioners chartered a community college district that local voters and the Ohio Board of Regents approved in 1966. Dayton was in the midst of an urban renewal program and twenty acres were acquired for a downtown campus in a situation similar to the then recently completed Chicago Circle campus of the University of Illinois.[63] There the architect had conceived a microenvironment of diverse building heights and shapes linked by pedestrian corridors that influenced the modernistic Sinclair Community College master plan. Designed by New York architect Edward Durell Stone, the college was built as a variety of building cubes in harmony with the downtown Dayton skyline. From a 1966 core of little more than two thousand students using temporary facilities around the city—with local residents paying as little as ten dollars per semester-hour of credit—the college launched a $22 million building project with approximately half from the local tax levy and half from state and federal funds.[64]

In the same period of frenzied growth, Detroit architect Minoru Yamasaki designed the striking King Memorial Hall and Bibbons Conservatory of Music for Oberlin College in a unifying new formalist style. They are a dramatic architectural departure from other buildings on this campus, but they complement each other at one corner of the campus green and exploit the technological potential of steel-reinforced quartz-aggregate panels. With a contemporary hint of the pointed-Gothic arch, the unique window treatments—grillwork for King and "shutters" for Bibbons—

BIBBONS CONSERVATORY OF MUSIC
AND KING MEMORIAL HALL
1964
New Formalism
Architect: Minoru Yamasaki
Oberlin College, Oberlin (Lorain Co.)
Photos by Virginia E. McCormick

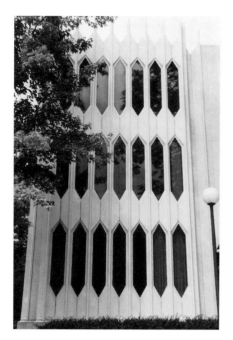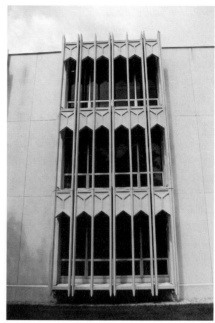

Window details
Photos by Virginia E. McCormick

were intended to be practical in controlling light and aesthetically pleasing in providing a delicacy that reduces the mass of these buildings. The conservatory complex includes a courtyard with a reflecting pool surrounded by a concert hall, studio theater, and nearly two hundred practice rooms.[65] They complete a picture of architectural diversity at Oberlin College that contrasts with a campus such as Miami University that is atypical in choosing to maintain architectural unity by demanding that new structures conform with its original Federal and Georgian Revival buildings.

Architects of modern college buildings are more commonly faced with the need to design a functional modern structure that will blend with the architectural styles of buildings from a variety of previous periods. Olin Library designed by Boston architects Paul Peng-Chen Sun and Geoffrey Freeman for Kenyon College is an excellent example of such a challenge.[66] Precast aggregate panels were utilized in a postmodern design reflective of the Gothic buildings around it, but its artistic answer to a difficult problem is a geometric glass atrium that unites Olin with Chalmers Library, a rectilinear building that one critic described as having "all the exterior charm of an industrial-strength, 1950s flat-roofed box."[67] The three-story atrium tower changes shape on each level, uniting the two buildings with a barrel

OLIN LIBRARY
1984–86
Postmodern
Architects: Paul Peng-Chen Sun and Geoffrey
Freeman of Sheply, Bulfinch, Richardson and Abbot
Kenyon College, Gambier (Knox Co.)
Photo by Virginia E. McCormick

Atrium tower
Photo by Virginia E. McCormick

OHIO AEROSPACE INSTITUTE
1992
Cubist
Architect: Richard Fleischman
Brook Park (Cuyahoga Co.)
Courtesy of Richard Fleischman Architects

stairway and effectively concealing the undistinguished Chalmers facade while utilizing its functional space with service areas and stacks.[68]

An innovative structure for a novel educational consortium is the Ohio Aerospace Institute, a unique education and research facility for graduate and continuing education in aerospace studies. It is affiliated with NASA Research Center, recently renamed for Ohio space pioneer John Glenn, and it includes an organizational structure staffed by faculty representing nine universities, together with government and private agencies. Richard Fleischman designed abstract glass-walled components to form a building that reflects the creative mission of the aerospace institute. Entry is through a three-story atrium that leads to a first-floor lecture room equipped with the latest communications technology. Classrooms and seminar rooms occupy the second floor and administrative staff offices the third—each offset to overlook the floor below. Structural metal grids contrast with curving glass walls in a manner that defies any occupant of this structure not to be technologically inventive. Advanced materials such as argon gas window coatings to increase thermal efficiency and reflective glass for office privacy

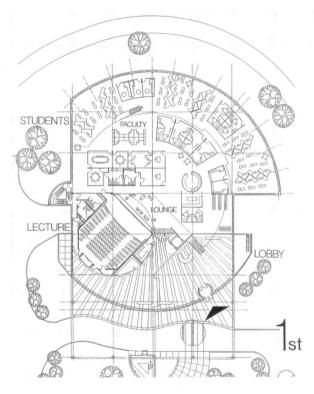

As shown in this view of the library, interior spaces flow visually between the floors. Photo courtesy of Richard Fleischman Architects

First-floor plan showing public and private divisions of space
Courtesy of Richard Fleischman Architects

were utilized to create functional interior spaces. As a sculpture on the landscape, this building displays the excitement of the aerospace enterprise.[69]

Few buildings symbolize the neomodernist movement more dramatically than the Wexner Center for the Visual Arts at Ohio State University. Funded primarily by a gift from retail clothing magnate Leslie H. Wexner, this deconstructionist building is a bold statement by internationally recognized architect, Peter Eisenman. It is a controversial design that focused on the intersecting grids of the city of Columbus and the campus—closing and occupying the site that had been the university's main entrance for more than a century. Dark brown and red brick is used to create towers evoking images of the former armory on this location that symbolized the land-grant university's role in military education. But the Wexner towers have been "split and peeled" to open them to new possibilities. Walkways under a canopy of white girders that suggest scaffolding allow one to walk through the building without entering, and the grids as reflected in a glass curtain wall convey a conceptually unfinished structure open to future prospect. One critic described the varied shapes of this building as giant chess pieces set against the surrounding environment—allowing adjacent buildings and spaces to echo and contrast. Even the symbolism of the surrounding landscape, from a grove of buckeye trees on one side to clumps of prairie grasses on another, was part of the design to blend existing and created environments with the intention that they will become blurred by time. Eisenman characterized it as a nonbuilding, an archaeological earthwork whose essential elements are scaffolding and landscaping.[70]

It is appropriate that a building for studies in the creative arts should be the venue for testing the limits of architectural innovation, but it has fittingly been the subject of serious research into questions regarding the degree to which signature architecture functions effectively for the intended users. Professor Jack L. Nasar of the university's Department of City and Regional Planning has pursued the question: what happens when the critics leave town?[71] He found that despite the compliments of many architects, users, and passersby, the Wexner Center has been an expensive building to construct and maintain. It is a design that attracts graffiti, provides gallery spaces that are frequently dysfunctional, and entrances which are so effectively concealed that both students and gallery visitors have been noted walking away in confusion.

A similar desire to encourage architectural innovation led to the commission for Frank O. Gehry's cubist design for the University of Toledo Center for the Visual Arts which is physically attached to the Toledo Museum

WEXNER CENTER FOR THE VISUAL ARTS
1988
Deconstructionist
Architects: Peter Eisenman / Richard Trott
Ohio State University, Columbus
(Franklin Co.)
Courtesy of the Ohio State University
Archives

An architectural rendering of the Wexner
Center in relation to Weigel Hall and Mershon
Auditorium shows how the deconstructionist
design reflects the original armory building on
this site.
Courtesy of the Ohio State University
Archives

of Art, where the college department originated in 1921. The building forms an integrated space for a reference library, studio work spaces, and exhibition galleries. Like most Gehry buildings—and bearing a resemblance to his Guggenheim Museum at Balboa, Spain—Toledo's Center for the Visual Arts is a collision of fragmented geometric forms always shifting from different perspectives, which one critic described as "powerful essays in primal geometric form."[72] The intent was for the building to be an individual entity rather than an addition to the impressive neoclassical museum it adjoins. Visually the building appears to be a massive sculpture of stacked boxes of varying sizes and shapes, all clad in lead-coated copper that in some lights resembles mottled stone from a nearby quarry. Entry to the buildings is made through a curtain wall of green tinted glass that reflects an expanse of lawn and pays tribute to Toledo's role in the glass industry. Although staff and students have expressed both positive and negative reactions regarding the functional quality of the space, the building has served as a catalyst for both the university and the city—exploring the boundaries between architecture and art and reinforcing the educational partnership between museum and university. It is a building that aspires to become art by allowing people who walk through or work in it to feel they are inside a giant sculpture—with glass screen walls making users an ever-changing part of the picture.[73]

A similar desire to serve as a catalyst for artistic creativity led the University of Cincinnati to select Peter Eisenman to design the Aronoff Center for Design and Art for the university's acclaimed College of Design, Architecture, Art and Planning. Its objective was to challenge and transform the way people are educated: to discourage the design of the superficial and the inconsequential.[74] The Aronoff Center bears some resemblance to Eisenman's Wexner Center, but this was the firm's first computer-generated project and it dramatically illustrates this technology's capacity for freeing an architect's creativity and mastering the problems of a difficult site. The Aronoff Center is a structure with no traditional facade. Instead it offers an undulating wave of colorful cubes containing studios, auditoriums, and offices that follow the contour of the hillside and curve around existing college buildings in a manner one critic described as "catching and containing them like a mitt."[75] It hugs its hilly setting, twisting and shifting attention inward on multiple levels, demonstrating Eisenman's philosophy that a building which houses an architecture school should explore and embody the discourse of the school itself, taking risks just as students are expected to take risks.[76]

CENTER FOR THE VISUAL ARTS
1993
Cubist
Architect: Frank O. Gehry and Associates
University of Toledo, Toledo (Lucas Co.)
Photo by Virginia E. McCormick

Glass curtain wall reflects the significance of
Toledo's glass industry.
Photo by Virginia E. McCormick

The building generates both praise and criticism for the iconoclastic architect once described as an "Elmer Gantry character" capable of persuading clients to invest in nothing more than but nothing less than form.[77] Nevertheless, the Aronoff Center is a keystone in the university's 1989 master plan to transform an urban campus into an integrated whole. President Steger was committed "to increase appreciation of our campus through signature buildings created by the best, brightest, and most accomplished architects working today." It brought the campus international recognition when the *New York Times* cited it as one of the outstanding buildings of the year when it opened in 1996 and labeled the University of Cincinnati "one of the most architecturally dynamic campuses in America today."[78] But it is the spatial experience of the interior—with bridges and galleries following the natural hillside from one functional level to another—that makes the Aronoff Center exceptional. Professor David Gosling has noted that the 400-level atrium is one of those rare architectural spaces that needs to be filled with people to appear at its best.[79]

Ohio's diverse collegiate landscape is rich with both nineteenth- and twentieth-century architectural symbolism. It seems appropriate that colleges and universities should be on the cutting edge of architectural innovation—particularly in their libraries, art and design, and architecture facilities. Bountiful aesthetic environments encourage students to respond creatively and physical structures powerfully reveal an institution's self-concept, but such buildings raise thought-provoking questions about the convergence of architectural aesthetics and public policy. What are the respective roles of architects, donors, or taxpayers, and faculty and students in the design of collegiate buildings?

ARONOFF CENTER FOR DESIGN AND ART
1993–96
Deconstructionist
Architect: Peter Eisenman
University of Cincinnati, Cincinnati
(Hamilton Co.)
Photo by Shannah Cahoe, courtesy of the
University of Cincinnati

The geometric qualities of the central lounge
are enhanced by the ever-changing presence
of students and faculty.
Photo by Dottie Stover, courtesy of the
University of Cincinnati

Six | Special Educational Institutions

A unique aspect of nineteenth-century educational practice was the attempt to provide appropriate facilities and learning experiences for youth with physical disabilities such as blindness or deafness. This was a benevolent position spearheaded by leading ministers and physicians who believed such youth deserved opportunities to render them productive citizens.

Rev. James Hoge, of the Columbus Presbyterian Church, is credited with encouraging the legislation that in 1827 created the Ohio Asylum for Educating the Deaf and Dumb—a name later changed to the Ohio School for the Deaf. This was the fifth such school in the country and classes were held in the church until a modest building was completed in 1834 and enlarged a decade later.[1] But it was woefully inadequate by 1864 when the legislature approved plans for a brick building "of plain and substantial construction" to accommodate 350 students plus staff. Architect Joseph M. Blackburn described the planned style as "Franco-Italian"—a symmetrical building with round-arched windows, a three-story veranda flanked by wings defined by square towers with corner quoins and bracketed eaves reflecting the Italian influence, and French-inspired mansard roofs accented by dormers.[2] Although ground was broken June 30, 1864, and it was anticipated that the new building would be ready for classes in September 1866, numerous construction obstacles and delays—and a typhoid epidemic at the institution in the spring of 1867, which some related to ventilation and sewer problems associated with the construction—led to Blackburn's dismissal shortly before the project was completed.[3] When the $650,000 building opened

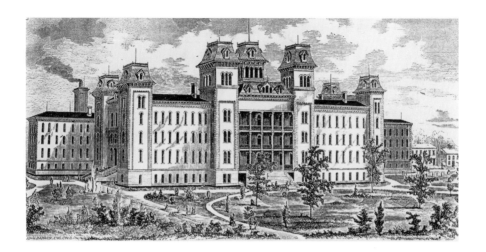

Ohio School for the Deaf lithograph by
John Barrick from Superintendent's Report,
1870

OHIO SCHOOL FOR THE DEAF
1864–69
French/Italian Renaissance Revival
Architect: Joseph M. Blackburn
Columbus (Franklin Co.)
Courtesy of the Columbus Public Library

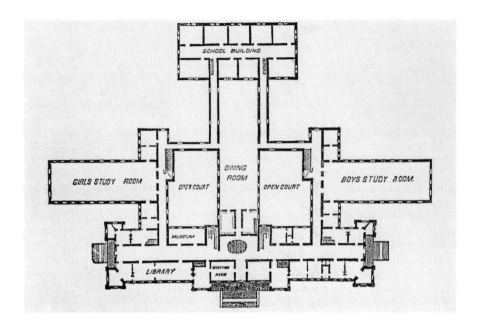

Floor plan shows separate dormitory wings
for boys and girls.
From Superintendent's Report, 1870

February 11, 1869, it served 235 students from across the state, but within a
year the number grew to 303 youth from ten to twenty years of age.

Ohio was proud of the school's appearance and the scope of the programs it offered. With a 270-foot facade, the building had seven mansard-
roofed towers, with a spiral staircase in the center one that presented
visitors a magnificent view of the city. In addition to the requisite school-
rooms, offices, and dormitories, the complex had a full kitchen and dining
room, as well as a library, chapel, hospital, and its own heating plant and
laundry.[4] Sewing, shoe making, and printing were among the skills taught,
and students published their own weekly journal, the "Mute's Chronicle."
Pictures of the dining room, main lounge, and one of the dormitories reflect a benevolent Victorian institution—where it was believed the state
could educate students with special needs better than their parents and local
schools.

Unfortunately this 1869 building was destroyed by fire, but a similar
Gothic masterpiece survives, one designed by Cincinnati and Indianapolis
architect William Tinsley for the Ohio School for the Blind. This institution was founded a decade later than the School for the Deaf, but it too was
outgrowing its facilities by the end of the Civil War. During this period of

Ohio School for the Deaf decorated for the
Northwest Centennial celebration
Courtesy of the Columbus Public Library

civic exuberance, Governor Rutherford B. Hayes's administration launched a variety of building projects, including the land-grant university campus. Although construction of the school for the blind began in the spring of 1870, it was not ready for occupation until four years later.[5] Described by the architect as "Old English, of the later period of Elizabeth," this building had curvilineal gables, pyramidal towers, paired windows, an arcaded piazza, stringcourses, and quoins—all surmounted by a belvedere accented by wrought iron cresting.[6]

Designed for 250 students and staff, the building provided individual student rooms—each with 750 cubic feet of space—as well as classrooms for a literary department that offered courses from basic reading, writing, and arithmetic to advanced geometry, Latin, philosophy, and rhetoric. The music department offered vocal instruction and instrumental studies in piano, organ, and violin. An industrial department taught broom making, cane seating, sewing, knitting, and crocheting, all toward the goal of outfitting students with skills that would allow them to earn an income.

The other nineteenth-century survivor of these state schools is an 1898–99 classroom building designed for the Ohio School for the Deaf by Columbus architects Richards, McCarty and Bulford.[7] The French influence upon its Gothic architecture is not typical for Ohio, but its lavishly decorated twin towers, Flemish gables, and massive entry with intricately carved stonework are unusually fine examples of late-nineteenth-century craftsmanship. A reporter at the 1899 dedication described this "architectural gem" as "the most ornate and elaborately appointed school of its kind . . . in the world."[8] Administrators and politicians made a conscious decision to build on an adjoining site to the 1869 building to allow students to be close to city activities and interact with the people around them rather than isolate the hearing impaired with a new school in a rural location.

One of the most striking features of this building is a gothic arched entry lined with faces of "deaf-mute" children—as they were then known—and crowned by the motto "Religion, morality, and knowledge being necessary to good government and the happiness of mankind, schools and the means of education shall forever be encouraged." This quotation from the Northwest Ordinance of 1787 is a powerful statement that with this building the state was recommitting itself to provide educational opportunities for all children, even those with physical disabilities. It was a progressive building for the time, with features for physical and vocational education that would not become common in most public schools for several decades. Among the thirty-six classrooms were facilities specifically equipped to train students to earn a living—a sewing department,

OHIO SCHOOL FOR THE BLIND
1869–74
Victorian Gothic/Second Empire
Architect: William Tinsley
Columbus (Franklin Co.)
Lithograph from Superintendent's Report,
1874

School as it currently appears, with towers
removed for safety reasons
Photo by Virginia E. McCormick

OHIO SCHOOL FOR THE DEAF
1899
Flemish Gothic/Chateauesque
Architects: Richards, McCarty and Bulford
Columbus (Franklin Co.)
Photo from National Register file, courtesy of
the Ohio Historic Preservation Office

Gable detail of side entry
Photo by Virginia E. McCormick

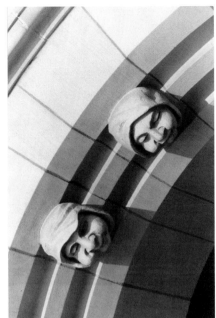

Entry, with quotation from the Northwest
Ordinance of 1787 and the faces of
"deaf-mute" children
Photos by Virginia E. McCormick

art room, carpenter shop, tailor shop, and book bindery. There was also a 47 x 50–foot gymnasium adjacent to a swimming pool and showers for both boys and girls.[9]

Such massive institutional structures seem an anachronism today—when students with physical disabilities are routinely mainstreamed into local public school classes or taught in workshops to read braille or communicate through sign language. But these buildings are testimony to an early public commitment to serve students with special needs.

Seven | Libraries

The first library in the Northwest Territory is generally attributed to Colonel Israel Putnam, who about 1795 moved his family to Belpre, a few miles from the Marietta settlement founded by his cousin Rufus Putnam. A $10 receipt from Jonathan Stone for a share in Putnam Family Library is an example—although more expensive than typical—of the frontier period when some early groups of settlers organized library associations and sold subscriptions for the privilege of borrowing books. Putnam's library eventually contained about eighty-five volumes and evolved into Belpre Farmers Library, a subscription library that lasted more than twenty years.[1] Numerous others followed across the state during the first part of the nineteenth century—including Cincinnati Library that sold $340 shares as early as 1802, and the famous Coonskin Library established at Amesville by pioneers who used proceeds from the sales of animal skins to buy books and pay their subscription fees.[2] Many of these early libraries operated from a settler's home, store, or tavern. The bylaws established in 1803 by subscribers of Worthington Library set quarterly meetings when books would be offered to the highest bidder, with each subscriber entitled "to draw two volumes whenever there are books enough."[3] Although many libraries were chartered by the Ohio legislature during the first half of the nineteenth century, all of these were subscription societies whose facilities never exceeded a few bookshelves or perhaps a reading room in a commercial establishment or academy. None were free to the general public or owned a building of their own.

Public support for libraries first appeared in conjunction with schools, when the Ohio legislature in 1846 authorized every school district the right to levy a tax not to exceed $30 annually for the support of a school library. Public libraries can trace their origin to legislation seven years later, requiring every school district to levy a ¹⁄₁₀th mill tax for the support of a school library and entitling each family in the district to use one volume at a time from the school library—although one assumes the selection of books was related to the educational curriculum for youth rather than general reading for adults.

By the mid-nineteenth century, Boston had established a public library to complement the public school system and allow anyone to "continue intellectual privileges throughout life."[4] Its concept of a combined reference and circulating library open to the public was controversial at the time, but it has now become the basis for public libraries throughout the country.

In 1866 Clark Lane, a wealthy manufacturer at Hamilton, Ohio, offered the city $10,000 to build a public library. But after failing to generate support he paid for a building to be erected, and he placed his niece in charge of its free reading room. This early philanthropic effort resulted in an architecturally unique octagonal building—a design Lane had utilized three years earlier in his home across the street. One of the benefits proponents of the octagonal design emphasized was an abundance of light from every direction, and this may well have influenced Lane's decision for the library. Although local sources credit Lane for the design, it is likely that he and the builder had access to plan books such as Orson S. Fowler's octagon residences or Henry Barnard's book published in Cincinnati which included plans for an octagonal school.[5] Lane Public Library is architecturally sophisticated for an Ohio county seat town in the 1860s, with the Romanesque effect of paired front windows arched with a round window at the apex. The central cupola boasts stained glass windows and a unique book and quill weathervane. When citizens voted in 1868 to accept responsibility for maintaining the library, Lane donated the building to the city, to serve first as a public reference library and since 1879 as a free circulating library, which through additions and renovations the city continues to maintain with pride.[6]

Cincinnati, Ohio's largest city, was the first Ohio community to erect a purpose-built public library. In 1870 the city unveiled an ornate reading hall with multiple book alcoves encircling a 105 x 75–foot reading room lighted by skylights fifty-five feet above.[7] The library's elegance resembled the Astor Library in New York City and reveals its origins in the libraries

LANE PUBLIC LIBRARY
1866
Romanesque Octagon
Designer: Clark Lane
Hamilton (Butler Co.)
Photo by Pat Brown Studios Photography,
courtesy of Lane Public Library

Paired arched windows crowned by a circle
on each face of the octagon and a repeat
of the octagon form in the cupola are the
building's distinguishing characteristics.
Photo by Virginia E. McCormick

maintained by medieval monasteries, but its librarian, William Frederick Poole, lamented the wasted space, the need for workers to climb ladders to retrieve books, and the heat damage to book bindings in the high galleries.

Although eleven Ohio cities developed free public libraries in the decade preceding the formation of the American Library Association (ALA) in 1876, Cincinnati was the only one to construct a building before librarians used their association's collective voice to contribute their opinions to the physical layout of libraries designed by architects.[8] The double-galleried book halls of scholarly societies derived from European universities, which had been influenced by medieval monasteries. Public librarians found them impossible to supervise from a single discharge desk and exhausting for clerks to retrieve books.[9] Justin Windsor, of the Boston library, bemoaned "architectural enormities" like the Cincinnati building, and he advised library boards to spend more money on the purchase of books and less on "architectural flutings and bas-reliefs for aesthetic effect."[10] Public librarians were proud guardians of their "great collections to which the multitudes have access."[11] But architects were also achieving professionalism in the last quarter of the century and arguments of aesthetics versus practical function sometimes generated mutual contempt. Poole, who moved from Cincinnati to Chicago and served as ALA president, advocated comfortably sized library rooms lighted by side windows, with 16-foot ceilings that allowed air circulation above freestanding bookshelves accessible to adults from the floor.[12]

Many Ohio county seat towns developed library associations that operated public reading rooms, typically staffed by volunteers from the leading women of the community, and sometimes with the space or funds for books contributed by leading businessmen. In 1875 only 10 percent of public libraries across the nation were housed in specially designed structures, but the profits that northern industrialists made during the Civil War unleashed a wave of philanthropy for library construction. By the turn of the century, hundreds of communities nationwide boasted library buildings, more than 80 percent of them endowed by philanthropists.[13]

Such was the case in Springfield, Ohio, where a library association was incorporated in 1872, with Benjamin Warder as one of the largest stockholders. After receiving a financial pledge from Warder to erect a building in memory of his parents and two decades of nurturing public support to maintain a library, the Boston architectural firm of Shepley, Rutan, and Coolidge was engaged to design a building in the fashionable Richardsonian Romanesque style. Although some Midwestern architects parodied

READING ROOM, CINCINNATI PUBLIC LIBRARY
1874
Gothic Revival
Architect: James W. McLaughlin
Cincinnati (Hamilton Co.)
Lithograph from *Public Libraries in the United
States of America*, 1876

WARDER PUBLIC LIBRARY
1890
Richardsonian Romanesque
Architects: Shepley, Rutan and Coolidge
Springfield (Clark Co.)
Photo by Virginia E. McCormick

Henry Hobson Richardson in the decade following his death, or created vernacular interpretations of his style, Warder Public Library is a faithful interpretation of Richardson's style by his son-in-law's firm.[14]

The L-shaped plan is executed in buff Amherst limestone with brown Worcester sandstone trim, an excellent example of the polychromatic style that John Ruskin advocated to create walls that reflect natural themes, such as the colorful veins of earth and stone revealed in mountainous regions.[15] The reentrant angle of the building with a turret to accommodate stairs and the triple-arched entry arcade accented by terra cotta medallions are reminiscent of Converse Memorial Building in Malden, Massachusetts—the last library Richardson designed.[16] The interior corner is dominated by a 71-foot tower, seventy-one feet in diameter, that culminates in a cone-shaped red tile roof with a terra cotta finial. Each gable wing is accented by a trio of arched windows, and the impressively paneled read-ing room featured a massive fireplace. When the $125,000 building

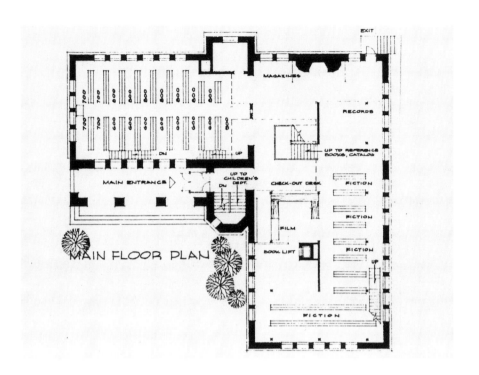

Floor plan of the building as it appeared
shortly before it was abandoned for library use
From National Register file, courtesy of Ohio
Historic Preservation Office

Arcade entry with typical Richardsonian
terra-cotta trim
Photo by Virginia E. McCormick

Entry column stone sculpture of child's face,
Warder Library
Photo by Virginia E. McCormick

was dedicated in 1890 it was a major commitment to free public education, and within two years it had an inventory of nearly 15,000 books.[17]

The role of Van Wert merchant and banker J. S. Brumback was similar, on a smaller scale, to Warder's, except that Brumback died while in the process of planning a library building for his community. Both gifts typified the paternalistic style of late-nineteenth-century philanthropists. Brumback's will in 1897 requested that his wife and children fund a library building, and they did so at a cost of $40,000. But his heirs gave a liberal interpretation to this bequest and proposed a county library system to serve the thirty thousand residents of the county, not just the eight thousand in the city of Van Wert. The heirs agreed to provide funds for the building if the county would levy a tax for its maintenance, and the library association, which had been organized in 1893, would contribute their collection of approximately two thousand books. The proposed county library would be governed by a public board representing the county commissioners, the library association, and the Brumback estate. Such a countywide public library system was a new idea that required an enabling act by the Ohio General Assembly in 1898.[18] But it reflected the rising levels of literacy that

BRUMBACK LIBRARY
1901
Richardsonian Romanesque/Gothic Revival
Architect: D. L. Stine
Van Wert (Van Wert Co.)
Photo card from National Register file,
courtesy of Ohio Historic Preservation Office

Cascading entry detail
Photo by Virginia E. McCormick

Reading room accented by a barrel-vaulted
coffered ceiling
Photo from Saida Brumback Antrim and
Ernest Irving, *The County Library*

resulted from free public education and a flourishing American publishing industry fueled by popular writers such as Longfellow, Whittier, Twain,
and Harte.

Brumback Library was also Richardsonian Romanesque in style, designed by D. L. Stine of Toledo, best known as the architect of the Lucas
County courthouse. Executed in Bedford blue sandstone, the massive
arched entry of Brumback Library is flanked by towers—one round and
the other square—with Gothic lancet windows, corbelling, and battlements. The impression of a medieval castle was enhanced by the barrel-
vaulted ceiling of the reading room, supported by classical columns that
formed a side arcade to accommodate the desks from which library staff
served patrons.[19] It is a rare survivor from this period, and it is preserved in
pristine purity.

The building was formally dedicated January 1, 1901, and citizens who
patronized this elegant new library may have been awed by its magnifi-
cence, but Brumback Library lost little time in fulfilling its pledge to taxpayers in the surrounding county. On February 19, a crate of one hundred
books was shipped to the drugstore that had agreed to serve as the Willshire branch library, and within the first year 2,800 books were circulated to

Brumback branch library, Willshire drugstore
Photo from Saida Brumback Antrim and
Ernest Irving, *The County Library*

Brumback branch library patrons, Converse
general store
Photo from Saida Brumback Antrim and
Ernest Irving, *The County Library*

nine branch libraries—usually established in general stores where people traded and stayed to visit when inclement weather discouraged other work. A photograph of the Wetzel general store, acting as a Brumback branch library, suggests that the arrival of a new crate of books from Van Wert was an eagerly awaited occasion that attracted a crowd. A group clustered around the Converse general store, housing another Brumback branch, implies that borrowers included both sexes, all ages, and African Americans as well as Caucasians. Such pictures dramatize the outreach function of Brumback Library and demonstrate a partnership between philanthropy and public funding that would soon become the norm.

The name most closely associated with library construction at the turn of the twentieth century both in Ohio and across the nation is, of course, Andrew Carnegie, the Pittsburgh steel magnate. Only recently have architectural historians such as Abigail A. Van Slyck begun to rescue Carnegie libraries from the research gap that exists between high-style design and vernacular architecture.[20] Although Carnegie's philanthropy began in the 1880s on a small scale in his hometown, in 1899 the East Liverpool and Steubenville Carnegie libraries were the first to be funded in Ohio. The roots of the East Liverpool library date to February 1, 1888, when Will Thompson opened a public reading room stocked with newspapers and periodicals in his music store. Evolving over a decade with support from local businessmen and civic groups, a number of books had been purchased by the spring of 1899 when a local attorney approached Carnegie and received a pledge of $50,000 to construct a library building if the community would provide a suitable lot and at least $3,000 annually for its maintenance and operation.[21] Carnegie had spent part of his boyhood in East Liverpool, and this grant—like the one in Steubenville where he had worked briefly as a telegrapher—reflected his fondness for the years he lived in these communities. The terms of the East Liverpool grant—that Carnegie would provide a building if the community would commit sufficient financial support for its operation—were typical of his philanthropy during the next two decades, when he spent over $41 million building nearly seventeen hundred public libraries across the United States.[22]

East Liverpool Carnegie Library is a handsome building that blends Second-Renaissance and Georgian Revival style. It was designed by Charles Henry Owsley, a British architect who had immigrated to Youngstown in the 1870s.[23] The building's classical portico is crowned by a balustrade and surmounted by a Palladian window decorated with a terra cotta surround

Patrons and crate of books at Brumback
branch library, Wetzel general store
Photo from Saida Brumback Antrim and
Ernest Irving, *The County Library*

and flanked by oculi windows. A trio of round-arched windows on either side is joined by terra cotta pediments richly sculpted in botanical motifs. Corner towers have ogee roofs and flame finials. But the crowning feature is the central octagonal tower with Ionic pilasters, a tile-covered dome, and cupola. This permitted a domed vestibule with a circular balcony leading to reading rooms—a magnificent space with Italian marble wainscoting, solid bronze hardware, and a mosaic-tiled floor reflecting the local ceramic industry. When the building formally opened May 8, 1902, with 2,500 books, thousands of people came out of curiosity but many returned as borrowers. The librarian reported a year later that more books were loaned each month than the total in the library inventory—although this had now increased to nearly six thousand volumes.[24]

There were numerous critics of Carnegie's philanthropy, with influential Columbus minister Rev. Washington Gladden questioning the concept of money from men who exploited their laborers.[25] Carnegie's concept of providing capital funds but requiring communities to commit an amount equaling at least ten percent for operating expenses also had its critics and prevented some towns from acquiring grants. But it did force a continuing commitment and a sense of community ownership.[26] Even though the East Liverpool library had Carnegie Public Library carved on its portico, this was never a requirement from Carnegie, who claimed to prefer the name of the town and the wording Free Public Library.[27] As word of Carnegie's philanthropy became widely known, more cities began seeking funds for libraries, and Ohio became a major beneficiary of his largesse.[28] His generosity ranged from a $6,000 grant to Bristolville in 1911 to $590,000 for fourteen branch libraries in Cleveland.[29]

An interesting example is the Sandusky Carnegie Library, which received a $50,000 grant after a personal contact was made by the president of a group of ladies who had formed a typical local library association. Mrs. J. O. Moss was the wife of a local banker who had business dealings with Carnegie and had earlier provided the Sandusky YMCA a room on the second story of his bank to establish a lending library. Aware of Carnegie's generosity to East Liverpool and Steubenville, Sandusky sought a like amount and engaged Joseph W. Yost—formerly of Columbus but by then associated with Albert D'Oench in New York City—to design their building. This Romanesque Revival structure with some Jacobethan features is crafted of Sandusky blue limestone from the local Wagner quarries.[30]

The symmetrical facade features circular towers on either side of the recessed entry pavilion and steeply pitched gables with tile roofs on either

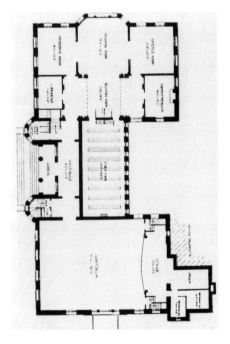

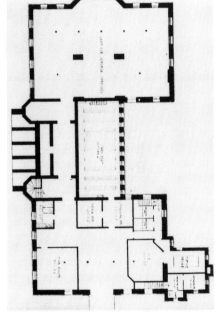

SANDUSKY CARNEGIE LIBRARY

1901

Richardsonian Romanesque

Architects: Albert D'Oench and Joseph W. Yost

Sandusky (Erie Co.)

Photo from *Architectural Review,* 1902

Floor plan shows large community auditorium with stage.

From *Architectural Review,* 1902

Publicizing its summer reading program,
this library is one of the few that serves today
without having undergone major renovation.
Photo by Virginia E. McCormick

side. This design provided on one side a typical large library reading room—with a "cork carpet" to deaden sound—and on the other side a music hall—complete with 338 opera chairs, a stage, Steinway piano, and pipe organ. In addition to reading rooms, the second floor contained a historical society room with exhibit space and a meeting room for the local women's club, with an adjoining kitchen and an art gallery on the walls. Although private donations provided many extras—including exquisite green and amber leaded glass windows on either side of the main entry doors—such elegance and varied use of space was unusual for a Carnegie Library. It was one of only five Richardsonian style buildings among sixty-seven modern libraries that *Architectural Review* featured in 1902—fifty-seven were in the newly popular classical revival form influenced by the Paris École des Beaux-Arts and the Columbian Exhibition.[31] One suspects that Carnegie was not consulted, and he would not have approved of the elaborate plans of the Sandusky library.[32] He was not present for the gala dedication in July 1901, that included the mayor, governor, and President William Oxley Thompson of Ohio State University as the keynote speaker. With or without Carnegie's blessing, Sandusky had created a building whose composite architecture reflected the varied educational uses the community intended,

Classical entry
Photo by Virginia E. McCormick

and it survives as one of the few Carnegie libraries with adequate space to continue serving the library functions of a growing community.

By 1908 James Bertram, Carnegie's private secretary who handled most of the correspondence relating to library grants, began requiring communities to submit their building plans for approval. Although communities were allowed to hire their own architects, Bertram issued guidelines that reflected Carnegie's desire to prevent large entry vestibules that wasted space and elaborate exterior columns and domes.[33] Lima, Ohio, received $34,000 for a library building, but when they submitted a $5,000 request for items to complete it, they were told, "I think it is somewhat impertinent to enter in list of cost of a library the cost of a piano." Rockford, Ohio, received $10,000 but was asked, "With regard to the plans you sent, will you kindly tell me the reason for enclosing the librarian in a small room with walls a foot thick surrounding him?"[34]

There is no record of dispute with the neoclassical library Guy Tilden designed for Canton in 1903–5, but a comparison of the accepted design with the completed building shows the tripartite-arched windows were straightened and the hip roof flattened—perhaps as cost-cutting measures. Tilden was the city's leading architect at the turn of the twentieth century, when industrial growth brought Canton's population from a little over

BUCYRUS PUBLIC LIBRARY
1906
Neoclassical
Architect: Vernon Redding
Bucyrus (Crawford Co.)
Photo by Virginia E. McCormick

Original appearance of the reading room and
circulation desk
Photo card, courtesy of Evelyn V. Gebhardt
and the Bucyrus Public Library

12,000 to nearly 90,000 persons in the short span of thirty years.[35] Tilden already had a local architectural reputation as he had designed a home for Frank Case, the manufacturer of dental reclining chairs who was president of the library board when the contract was awarded. The Canton library design includes a recessed entry supported by fluted columns with Ionic capitals that is crowned by a pediment with the inscription "Open to All."[36]

A similar but more modestly scaled building, completed a year later with a $15,000 Carnegie grant, is Bucyrus Public Library. The Ionic columns of the classical portico and the corner quoins suggest Mansfield architect Vernon Redding was acquainted with Tilden's Canton building. But Redding's placement of the entry on the diagonal to take advantage of a corner lot provides a panoramic facade that makes this moderately sized building impressive.[37] In many respects it is an architectural gem, equaling or surpassing the library building Redding created about the same time at more than twice the cost for his hometown.[38] Although the Bucyrus reading room presented the intimacy of clustered tables and chairs that were far less intimidating than the grand Richardsonian reading rooms a few years earlier, the deeply coffered ceiling and a golden oak fireplace offered readers a pleasant atmosphere that more accurately reflected Carnegie's desires.

The first countywide library in Ohio to receive Carnegie's support was Paulding County Carnegie Library, with a $40,000 grant in 1912 and the building completed in 1914—more than a decade after Van Wert pioneered the concept of a countywide system. The successful outreach of Brumback Library in the adjacent county to the south was critical in convincing Carnegie to fund a countywide system for a community as small as Paulding.[39] It is a spartan neoclassical building with the efficient use of space Carnegie and Bertram desired. The buff brick structure is accented by prominent stringcourses of Indiana Bedford limestone, which is also used in the dentil-trimmed cornice and the entry arch with its keystone flanked by cartouches. Columbus architects Oscar D. Howard and Roy J. Merriam reflect a beaux-arts influence to their classicism.[40] Inside, a central lobby provides access to three reading rooms, and carved oak fireplaces feature a scholar's lamp and laurel wreath motif.

Historians have concluded that Carnegie's generosity contributed more to the public library movement nationwide than either government support or demand from the general public.[41] A 1902 report on library design in *Architectural Review* found that Carnegie-financed libraries were more likely to include children's rooms, lecture halls, and free access to books.[42] His grants influenced the way that librarians, architects, and the public

PAULDING COUNTY CARNEGIE LIBRARY
1912–14
Neoclassical
Architects: Howard and Merriam
Paulding (Paulding Co.)
Historic photo, courtesy of Paulding County
Carnegie Library

Neoclassical entry detail remains unchanged.
Photo by Virginia E. McCormick

viewed libraries. Beaux-arts neoclassicism continued to be popular, not only with architects who had studied abroad but with citizens who believed it best represented the public character and purpose of library buildings. It is important to remember that although seventy-seven Ohio communities received Carnegie library grants by 1923, eighty Ohio communities with populations of a thousand or more had established public libraries without the aid of Carnegie funds.[43] Carnegie was a catalyst, but the movement for public libraries was widespread and construction was slowed only by the economic constraints of World War I and the Great Depression.

Cleveland benefitted enormously from Carnegie's generosity—eventually receiving $590,000 for fourteen branch libraries throughout the city.[44] Of particular interest is Carnegie West Branch Library, a neoclassical building with a unique twist designed by Edward L. Tilton, the New York architect who had become well known a decade earlier for his design for the immigration building at Ellis Island.[45] The bold contrast of limestone and red brick in Carnegie West is similar to the immigration building— a fact that the many Hungarian immigrants in the surrounding neighborhood would have noticed.[46] The triangular site at the intersection of three streets encouraged a triangular plan that Tilton emphasized with horizontal lines of limestone quoins and bands on the classical pillars. The imposing entry supported by pairs of fluted columns puts a creative stamp on classical styling by combining Ionic capitals with the spiral effect of these horizontal bands. Inside, classicism continues with a portion of the frieze from the Parthenon outlining the lobby and Corinthian columns supporting the skylight ceiling of the main reading room. The building's $83,000 cost and 28,000 feet of space were higher and more luxurious that the individual main library buildings in county seat towns throughout the state. But the imposing entry was not accessible to the physically disabled, and reading rooms with massive tables used the interior space inefficiently. A major remodeling in 1979 created a busy children's area with story pit directly accessible from the lobby and formed an area for Spanish resource materials to serve the large Puerto Rican population in the neighborhood— demonstrating the ability to preserve classical aesthetics while modernizing conveniences.[47] It is a sensitive example of librarians and architects collaborating to preserve elegance and charm of the old with the comfort and efficiency of new technology.

But community leaders in Cleveland had grandiose plans that far exceeded Carnegie's generosity. A new central library building was intended to be a key component of the lakeside mall proposed in 1903 by a committee chaired by Daniel Burnham, a leader in the city beautiful movement.[48]

CARNEGIE WEST BRANCH LIBRARY
1910
Neoclassical
Architect: Edward L. Tilton
Cleveland (Cuyahoga Co.)
Photo by Virginia E. McCormick

The unique triangular building established
Library Park in the intersection of three
streets in a Hungarian neighborhood on
Cleveland's west side.
Photo courtesy of Cleveland Public
Library

The bold contrast of red brick with limestone
quoins and banded columns creates a
horizontal effect that resembles Tilton's
immigration building, constructed on Ellis
Island a decade earlier.
Photo by Virginia E. McCormick

In a plan inspired by the Placé de la Concorde in Paris, selected public
buildings—including a federal building, county courthouse, city hall, civic
auditorium, board of education offices, and library—were to be constructed around a park-like mall and unified by the beaux-arts classicism of
their architecture.[49] Delayed by bond issues to raise funds and the labor and
material constraints of World War I, it was 1923 before the cornerstone was
laid for Cleveland Public Library, a library building surpassed in size only
by the Library of Congress and the New York Public Library.

The design was by Frank R. Walker and Harry E. Weeks, MIT-and École
des Beaux-Arts–trained architects who had moved to the city specifically
for the challenge of designing some of the Cleveland Mall buildings.[50] Executed in marble, the six-story library—including a raised basement and
a top floor concealed behind an entablature and balustrade—resembled
the size, shape, and design of the earlier federal building with which it was
paired at the south end of the mall. Massive round-arched windows and

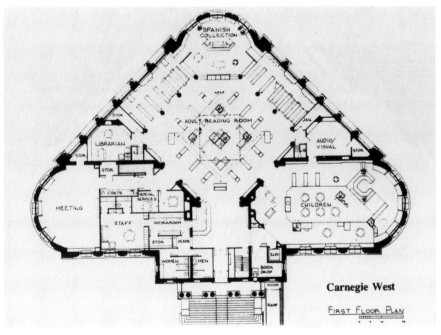

A replica of the Parthenon frieze establishes the classical mode of the interior.
Photo by Virginia E. McCormick

Renovation in 1979 created convenient interior space with the children's reading room accessible directly from the lobby and a designated Spanish resource area for Puerto Rican immigrants in the neighborhood.
Floor plan, courtesy of Cleveland Public Library

entrances on the first floor are surmounted by a fluted colonnade with Corinthian capitals and flanked on either end by pavilions with sculptured cartouches. Classical formality continued inside with a monumental marble staircase to the main reading room with a coffered barrel-vault ceiling. Murals by local artists reflect the city's early public square and the waterfront that made it a commercial power.[51] The building followed the decentralized design Poole advocated in the 1880s. Longtime Cleveland librarian William Brett pioneered the concept of subject matter reading rooms surrounding courtyards for light, with books in adjoining stacks that gave readers easy access—a principle that would become universal for public libraries after World War II.[52]

Cleveland Public Library is a building that offered classical formality with functional practicality for librarians and patrons, but in many ways the city beautiful plan surrounded public buildings with an air of elitism. The library countered this with caravans that delivered books to schools throughout the city—testimony to the institution's outreach mission. But it is impossible to visualize the children seen clustered around a book truck in knickers and on roller skates comfortably visiting the marble halls of the main library.[53] Cleveland was in the forefront of the modern library movement, characterized by public support, open shelves, service to children and schools, and accessibility through branch and traveling libraries.[54]

Like Cleveland, the Public Library of Cincinnati and Hamilton County was reaching out to the rapidly growing suburbs created by electric traction lines that made commuting into the city a realistic option. In the upscale neighborhoods of the western hills, patrons were frustrated by the inadequate space of their branch library, which had operated since 1909 in a room in the local school.[55] In 1930 ground was broken for the Westwood Branch Library, a building designed by Stanley M. Matthews, that won a contest conducted by the local chapter of the American Institute of Architects. It is a modernistic building with clean horizontal lines, not unlike the residences and churches that were then earning fame for Frank Lloyd Wright at Oak Park, Illinois.[56] Its stucco exterior is accented by diamond-shaped brick trim at the entrance, which is reflected in the diamond-shaped lights of the vertical windows above. A hipped roof of glass lights and flat-roofed wings complete the image of strong horizontal lines. The two-story vestibule is bathed with light from above and the warmth of a corner fireplace. To the right is the librarian's discharge desk—with offices and two floors of book stacks in the wing behind it. An adult reading room is directly ahead, and a children's room is to the left. A photograph from the

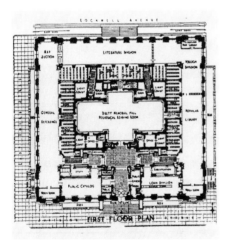

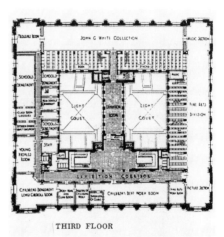

THIRD FLOOR

CLEVELAND PUBLIC LIBRARY
1923–25
Beaux-Arts/Neoclassical
Architects: Walker and Weeks
Cleveland (Cuyahoga Co.)
Photo by Lynn Freska, National Register file,
courtesy of Ohio Historic Preservation Office

First-floor plan shows Brett Memorial Reading
Room and third-floor plan has exhibition
bridge between light courts.
Floor plan from *Library Journal*, 1925

Cleveland library book caravan at Sowinski
School in the 1920s
Photo from C. H. Cramer, *Open Shelves and
Open Minds: A History of the Cleveland Public
Library*, courtesy of Cleveland Public Library

period suggests that neatly dressed young boys with shirts and ties—
although undoubtedly dressed for the photographer—were the type of
children welcome to browse among the precious books here. The community was proud of its building and various organizations contributed to
buy a piano for the meeting room in the basement.[57] During the library's
first year, circulation increased 82 percent—a fact the librarians attributed
both to the new facility and the rising unemployment that countywide
went from less than 6 percent in 1929 to more than 30 percent in 1933.

Like everything else, public library construction halted until the administration of President Franklin D. Roosevelt launched massive public works
programs to combat the Great Depression. Toledo Public Library, begun
in 1938 with assistance from the Public Works Administration (PWA), is
a handsome building designed by the local firm of Alfred A. Hahn and
John J. Hayes. The building is limestone with sculptured aluminum and
glass block windows—the latter a tribute to the national reputation of the
local glass manufacturing industry. It reflects the modernistic design—
what some called the school of American design—related to site, function,

WESTWOOD BRANCH LIBRARY
1930–31
Modernistic
Architect: Stanley M. Matthews
Cincinnati (Hamilton Co.)
Photo courtesy of the Public Library of
Cincinnati and Hamilton County

Entry showing diamond brick detail
Photo by Virginia E. McCormick

Children dressed and posed for a visit to the
new children's reading room
Photo courtesy of the Public Library of
Cincinnati and Hamilton County

and materials, with a simplicity that avoided excessive ornamentation.
Toledo Public Library bears resemblance to outstanding PWA projects such
as the Nevada Supreme Court building in Carson City; the Gallatin County
Courthouse in Bozeman, Montana; the Clay County Courthouse in Liberty,
Missouri; and the Jefferson County office building in Port Arthur, Texas.[58]
With the strong vertical line of its metal windows and the horizontal trim
that wraps all four sides, the exterior exhibits a transition from art deco to
art moderne that is distinguished by sculptural masks and medallions—
such as the log blockhouses reflecting the time when nearby Fort Meigs de-
fended the northwest frontier.[59]

From a visitor's perspective it is glass that makes this building an experience to remember. Originally, a large skylight flooded the central courtyard
with natural light that was enhanced by the translucent quality of the glass
block windows. But the stunning effect is from colored-glass murals—in
the children's department a variety of characters as diverse as Joan of Arc
and Pinocchio come to life. In the central court, murals sixteen to twenty-
six feet in length and six feet in height were crafted by artists and drafts-
men at Libby-Owens Glass; they present mosaics inlaid in slabs of vitro-
lite, an opaque colored glass about three-eighths of an inch thick.[60] They

TOLEDO PUBLIC LIBRARY
1938–40
Art Deco/Art Moderne
Architects: Hahn and Hayes
Toledo (Lucas Co.)
Photo courtesy of the Library Legacy
Foundation of the Toledo–Lucas County
Public Library

Art deco entry detail
Photo by Virginia E. McCormick

Art deco window detail
Photo by Virginia E. McCormick

Fort Meigs sculpture medallion
Photo by Virginia E. McCormick

Libby-Owens glass murals as they originally
appeared in the main lobby
Photo courtesy of the Library Legacy
Foundation of the Toledo–Lucas County
Public Library

FINDLAY–HANCOCK COUNTY
PUBLIC LIBRARY
1991
Modernistic
Architects: Rooney and Clinger
Findlay (Hancock Co.)
Exterior photo, courtesy of the
Findlay–Hancock County Public Library

Architect's rendering, dedication program
1991

reflect industry, commerce, history, literature, religion, arts, music, and philosophy—for this library was organized in the newly popular style of subject-matter departments around the central court.[61] Both beauty and function were important, and Toledo's library was one of the first to have air conditioning for heat and humidity control, an important feature that did not become standard until the mid-1950s.

Modern public libraries play an important role in bridging the diverse information needs of students and businesses searching Internet resources as well as those of children and senior citizens without transportation who rely upon bookmobile visits. Architecturally this is well represented in Findlay–Hancock County Public Library, a 1991 building that was this community's first purpose-built library.[62] The plan by local architects James H. Rooney and Daniel W. Clinger utilizes an urban renewal location near the center of the city, with an underground parking garage that adjoins staff offices and support facilities, including a Friends of the Library gift shop. A flexible design with open boxes and blank walls is flooded with light from the entry atrium, two-story atriums in each corner, and central skylights supplemented by florescent cove lighting. A central circulation desk allows librarians visual supervision of varied spaces, from reference books to periodicals and computer terminals. Defined areas accommodate the children's department, local history resources, and audiovisual materials. In keeping with modern philosophy about the role of libraries in community outreach, a community meeting room can be accessed from the atrium, even on evenings and weekends when the library is closed. A bookmobile garage at the rear of the building offers the convenience of entry from one side and exit from the other. It typifies a trend for local librarians, architects, and community citizens to cooperatively plan modern community libraries—a trend necessary not only to pass a bond issue but to keep abreast of an information age that places one hand on the computer keyboard and the other on the bookmobile steering wheel.

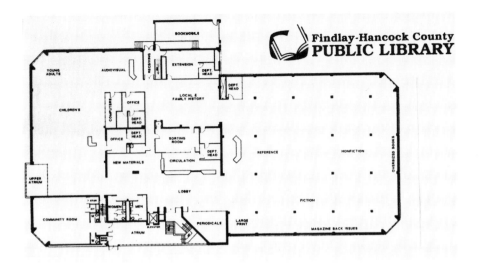

Floor plan reflects modern open-space
concept for flexible use.
Courtesy of the Findlay–Hancock County
Public Library

Bookmobile garage
Photo courtesy of the Findlay–Hancock
County Public Library

Eight | Museums, Opera Houses, &
Conservatories

Although traveling lecturers, actors, and exhibits had long brought culture from a wider world to Ohio towns and cities, before the Civil War few communities began erecting public or private buildings to accommodate such events. One might ask whether opera houses, theaters, and museums were for educational or entertainment purposes—and the answer is clearly that they were for both. Cultural enrichment for adults has always been voluntary and must be sufficiently entertaining to attract patrons. For more than a century the architecture of such buildings has exemplified a community's quest for cultural advancement.

One surviving example of community palaces of culture is Turner's Opera House/Dayton Music Hall/Victory Theatre, a privately financed $225,000 opera house which opened in Dayton in 1866, with dramatist Edwin Forrest portraying the Roman Virginius. Post–Civil War affluence was evident in what the *Dayton Journal* described as an "elegant temple of the Drama and the Muses."[1] This six-story building constructed by John Rouzer in the newly popular Second Empire style was accented by round-arched windows and a mansard roof with dormers. An arched arcade led to the typical retail shopping establishments on the ground floor. The building was destroyed by fire five years later, rebuilt as a four-story structure by an incorporated Music Hall Company, damaged in the 1913 flood, burned again in 1917, and restored to its current elegance in 1981. The contemporary theater is true to the original facade with mansard roof and ground floor retail space delineated by columns, but the charm that won public

TURNER'S OPERA HOUSE / VICTORY THEATRE
1866
Second Empire
Builder: John Rouzer
Dayton (Montgomery Co.)
Lithograph from National Register file,
courtesy of Ohio Historic Preservation Office

Opening bill for Turner's Opera House
January 1, 1866
Advertisement from *Dayton Journal*

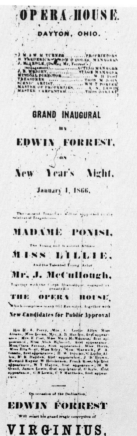

OPERA HOUSE.
DAYTON, OHIO.

GRAND INAUGURAL

EDWIN FORREST,

New Year's Night.

January 1, 1866.

MADAME PONISI,

MISS LILLIE,

Mr. J. McCullough,

THE OPERA HOUSE,

New Candidates for Public Approval

EDWIN FORREST

VIRGINIUS,
THE ROMAN FATHER.

Reconstruction of 1875, after fire destroyed
Turner's Opera House, used as the Music Hall
and Miami Commercial College
Lithograph from 1875 Montgomery
County Atlas

support for its restoration is the auditorium's lavish Victorian interior complete with gilded boxes and sparkling chandeliers.[2]

In Cincinnati—which in the 1870 census ranked as the seventh largest
city in the United States and relished its reputation as the Queen City of the
West—the erection of a music hall in 1877 provided a unique cultural center that managed to integrate the cultural elite with the city's immigrant
German American population and rising industrialization. Designed by
Samuel Hannaford, Cincinnati's most prominent nineteenth-century architect, this Victorian Gothic structure occupied an entire city block, with industrial exposition halls linked to the auditorium on either side. It is a com-
manding facade with Romanesque corbelling and a rose window accenting
the central gable and square towers flanking the entry. Stone stringcourses
unify the design horizontally and one enters the building through segmental arches created by piers.[3]

It was instigated by a gift of two million dollars from Reuben R. Springer,
contingent upon local citizens matching it, and a major purpose of the

Renovated Victory Theatre as it appears today
Photo by Linda Leas, National Register file,
courtesy of Ohio Historic Preservation Office

Renovated interior
Photo by Bill Swartz, National Register file,
courtesy of Ohio Historic Preservation Office

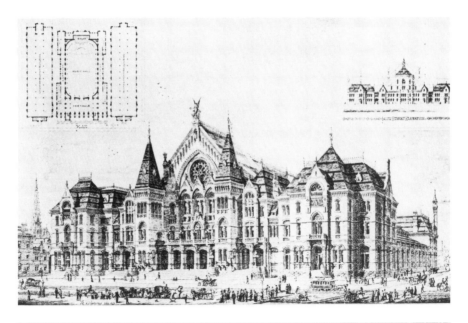

CINCINNATI MUSIC HALL
1877
Victorian Gothic
Architect: Samuel Hannaford
Cincinnati (Hamilton Co.)
Architectural drawing from National Register
file, courtesy of Ohio Historic Preservation
Office

Interior as it appeared late in the
nineteenth century
Lithograph from National Register file,
courtesy of Ohio Historic Preservation
Office

Exterior, including exhibition wings, as it
appears today
Photo by Sandy Underwood, National
Register file, courtesy of Ohio Historic
Preservation Office

Interior as renovated in 1972
Photo from National Register file, courtesy
of Ohio Historic Preservation Office

auditorium was to host Sanegerfests—German American singing festivals for which the city was famous. When Cincinnati Music Hall opened April 8, 1878, it was more like a rehearsal for the six-hundred-member chorus performing the *Messiah,* as the stage was shrouded in scaffolding to complete the organ. Seating in the original music hall was in the dress circle or balcony, and iron columns sixty-four feet high supported a coved ceiling. But the masterpiece was the 6,287 pipe organ—the largest in the United States—installed in a case hand-carved by local women volunteers supervised by master woodcarvers Benn Pitman and the Fry brothers. It was in side rooms surrounding the auditorium that lessons began which led to what became the University of Cincinnati's renowned Conservatory of Music.[4] Although nineteenth-century Cincinnatians acknowledged New York as the country's commercial core and Washington as its political focal point, they claimed status as a major cultural center. With Art Hall and Machinery Hall—90 x 293–foot exhibition spaces on either side of the auditorium—the complex was sufficiently grand to attract the Democratic National Convention in 1880, ironically to nominate a candidate who would be defeated by Ohio congressman James Garfield. Remodeled in 1972 to serve as the home of the symphony orchestra, Cincinnati Music Hall continues to win admiration for its aesthetic environment and acoustical excellence, and its preservation insures Cincinnati its position on the national cultural landscape.

A few miles north, Sorg's Opera House at Middletown provides an interesting contrast in changing architectural fashion. Privately financed by the town's wealthiest entrepreneur, Paul J. Sorg—whose plug tobacco plant employed eighteen hundred people at its peak of production—this Richardsonian Romanesque building was also designed by the Hannaford firm. Its massive limestone facade dominated Main Street, following the popular style of retail stores on the ground floor and a central entry to the opera house on the upper floors. The Palladian style windows of the top floor accented by a polychromatic trim of light beige and dark red limestone remain a significant focal point. On the interior, two oval balconies were supported by columns, and decorations included fresco ceilings and mural walls that the reporter covering the opening September 12, 1891, described as "palatial in its proportions and adornments."[5] Such a facility was essential for attracting high quality theatrical and operatic touring companies and it brought Middletown residents William Shakespeare's plays, grand opera, musical comedy, minstrels, and vaudeville before becoming a movie theater in 1929.[6]

SORG'S OPERA HOUSE
1891
Richardsonian Romanesque
Architects: Samuel Hannaford and Sons
Middletown (Butler Co.)
Photo by Virginia E. McCormick

Company L, First Ohio National Guard
Infantry Regiment posed in front of Sorg's
new opera house before leaving for the
Spanish-American War. Note the entry's
Richardsonian Romanesque details.
Courtesy of Middletown Historical Society

MCCONNELLSVILLE OPERA HOUSE
1890–91
Victorian/Romanesque Revival
Architect: H. C. Lindsay
McConnelsville (Morgan Co.)
Courtesy of Morgan County Historical
Society

By the 1890s, county seat communities throughout Ohio were build-ing opera houses to attract traveling cultural events. In small towns, operas were not the major productions—although an opera singer might per-form a concert of arias or small companies an operetta. Buildings like the McConnelsville Opera House hosted a variety of cultural events and en-tertainers, most notably lecturers and musical performers. It, too, pro-vided retail space on the ground floor on either side of the massive stone arch entry to the auditorium above. The Opera House's Romanesque Re-vival architecture is characterized by the square central tower with a steep pyramidal roof and four dormers with round-arched windows. Although 610 chairs were purchased from the Grand Rapids Chair Company, the pressed brick laid by master mason George Kimmerle of Columbus, and the frescoing done by William Harris of Cambridge, much of the building's construction was performed locally—the stonework, ironwork, plas-tering, and the steel ceiling provided by Morris Hardware. It was a proud

Massive arched entry and arched window
treatments illustrate Richardsonian
Romanesque style.
Photos by Virginia E. McCormick

Renovated interior welcomes Morgan
County residents to a variety of cultural
programs.
Photo by Terry Young, courtesy
of McConnelsville Opera House, Inc.

day when the opera house opened May 28, 1892, with a performance of Gilbert and Sullivan's *Mikado*—the first building in Morgan County to brighten the night with electric lights.[7] It is equally appropriate that its rededication May 30, 1998 featuring a variety of Morgan county youth and adults in musical numbers and recitations would spark an architectural and cultural rebirth for McConnellsville.

Another building from the 1890s traces its origins directly to Chicago's 1893 Columbian Exposition that commemorated the four hundredth anniversary of Christopher Columbus's arrival in the Americas and indirectly to the Crystal Palace built for London's Great Exhibition in 1851. Franklin Park Conservatory, designed by J. M. Freese, derived from the late Victorian interest in establishing botanical gardens for the cultivation and study of plants, but the building itself owes its existence to technological innovations in the use of glass and steel for construction.[8] The Victorian glass botanical style of the Columbus conservatory features a rectangular dome, which at 47 x 130 feet is less than a fifth the size of the huge Horticultural Hall at the Columbian Exposition whose central dome measured an incredible 180 feet in diameter.[9] The building was built on a park site that formerly served as a Franklin County fairgrounds. Columbus officials traveled to Chicago and may have even salvaged some materials for their conservatory, but the mansard style roof with its square glass-domed tower was unique to Columbus. Renovated in 1992 for the five hundredth anniversary celebration of the Spanish explorer's arrival in the Americas, Franklin Park Conservatory continues to serve as a unique botanical education center.

Among public art museums built specifically for the purpose, one of the most architecturally admired is Dayton Art Institute, completed in 1930 with a two-million-dollar gift from Harriet Gardner Carnell. Designed by Buffalo, New York, architect Edward B. Green, this Italian Renaissance Revival building was influenced by the fifteenth-century villa of Cardinal Farnese.[10] Occupying an impressive eight-acre site on a bluff some sixty feet above the Miami River, this octagonal building utilizes the slope and is constructed so both floors can be approached from ground level. Its most spectacular entrance features curving marble staircases embracing a granite fountain while leading to a triple-arched loggia with simulated Renaissance-style frescoes. On the ground floor two cloisters with thirteenth- to sixteenth-century sculptural columns and capitals offer entry to the art school and lecture halls. Galleries on the upper floor are entered through marble doors that are reproductions of those in Florence's Palazzo Vecchio. Both the vaulted ceiling of the loggia and the coffered ceiling of

FRANKLIN PARK CONSERVATORY
1895
Victorian Glass Botanical
Architect: J. M. Freese
Columbus (Franklin Co.)
Photo from National Register file, courtesy
of Ohio Historic Preservation Office

DAYTON ART INSTITUTE
1928–30
Italian Renaissance Revival
Architect: Edward B. Green
Dayton (Montgomery Co.)
Photo by Virginia E. McCormick

the five-hundred-seat auditorium were painted by J. F. Sturdy of Chicago in the style of Raphael, and the lobby echoes the Italian theme with handmade floor tiles.[11] The entire effect is a bold recognition of the status of Italian art on New World culture—as if an appropriate setting would endow this Midwestern city with instant sophistication. But galleries purposely reflected a variety of artistic cultures, with Carnell donating Ming artifacts for a Chinese temple display and her son, a member of the U.S. embassy staff in Constantinople, contributing an exhibit of Persian glass.

It is testimony to one woman's vision. For when Carnell became president of the Dayton Art Museum in 1922, the concept of the ten-year-old organization was enlarged to become the Dayton Art Institute, modeled on Chicago's integrated museum and art school. By the time the Dayton building was occupied, five hundred students—both youth and adult—were enrolled in day and evening classes in design, interior decorating, lettering, sculpture, commercial art, and architecture. A scholarship was given to the most promising student in each elementary, parochial, and high school in Dayton—including three nonwhite students among the fifty-five receiving scholarships the year the building opened. Lorado Taft, a Chicago sculptor whose *Solitude of the Soul* was commissioned for the sculpture court, gave the keynote address at the January 1930 dedication and compared this building and its contents to the Hebrew Ark of the Covenant which carried before the people the ideals of culture and beauty.[12] It was a worthy simile.

Perhaps the most dramatic illustration of the architectural interpretation of a cultural performance space coming full circle is the recent conscientious restoration of the 1896 Southern Theatre in Columbus and the construction of the Aronoff Center for the Arts, in Cincinnati's newest downtown performance square. The remarkable similarity of the concentric acoustical arches of their auditoriums reveals that a century of technological progress reaffirms the quality of the "Gay Nineties" design and craftsmanship.[13]

The "fireproof" Southern Theatre—constructed with brick, iron, tile, steel, and concrete—was a direct response to the danger of gaslights and the loss of five Columbus theaters to fire between 1889 and 1893. Inspired by Louis Sullivan's Chicago Auditorium, the first theater in the country to be lighted entirely by electricity, the Southern became the first in Columbus with electric illumination, generating its own power to provide it. Two hundred and four electric globes were embedded in the gilded arches cascading to the proscenium. Joseph Dauben, a German immigrant who worked in Chicago before moving to Columbus, showed Sullivan's influence in the

SOUTHERN THEATRE
1896
Sullivanesque/Chicago Style
Architects: Joseph Dauben and David Reibel
Columbus (Franklin Co.)
Photo by Virginia E. McCormick

vertical piers of the Southern's exterior and the Romanesque arched entry embellished with gargoyles and cherubs. And designer Menno G. Detweiler, who had previously worked on buildings for the Chicago World's Fair, incorporated the cascading ceiling arches.[14] The gala open-ing season began with a New York revue, continued with Lillian Russell's Opera Company performing *An American Beauty*, and featured Thomas A. Keene in a quartet of Shakespearean plays.[15]

Hosting touring productions as well as local performance groups, the Southern Theatre is once again defining a role in nurturing local talent by providing compatible space for chamber music, light opera, jazz, and dance ensembles. It is further evidence that the close of the twentieth century is creating facilities for extended learning, with adults feeling free to access electronic resources in the public school environment of a "community education village" and school groups actively engaging in learning about a symphony orchestra in a concert hall setting or studying impressionist painters in a museum gallery. Both historic and modernistic structures are achieving flexibility that stretches the boundaries of our definition of educational architecture to buildings for lifelong learning.

Elaborately carved entry arch
Photo by Virginia E. McCormick

Original interior shows proscenium with
cascading arches of electric lights.
Courtesy of the Columbus Association for
the Performing Arts

Appendix A | Timeline of Selected Educational Highlights in Ohio

1772   Moravian missionaries open a school at Gnadenhuten, which is later abandoned to hostile Indians.

1787   The Northwest Ordinance sets aside section sixteen, ¹⁄₃₆th of each township, for the support of schools, establishing the principle of a relationship between property and public schools, but providing insufficient funds for free public schools.

1789   The first school within the boundaries of Ohio is taught at Belpre by Bathsheba Rouse from New Bedford, Massachusetts.

1793   The first newspaper in the Northwest Territory, *The Centinel of the Northwest Territory,* begins publication in Cincinnati.

1796   The Putnam Family Library, forerunner of the Belpre Farmers' Library, is organized in Washington County.

1802   The Ohio Constitution states that "means of education should be encouraged by legislative enactments." Groups of persons wishing to establish schools and academies are required to be incorporated by the legislature.

        The citizens of Amesville in Athens County establish a system of purchasing books for a lending library that will become famous as the "Coonskin Library."

This listing makes no pretense of being all inclusive but focuses on actions and events that provide context regarding ownership, construction, and operation of educational facilities.

1803	The Erie Literary Society at Burton is the first of many such societies to be incorporated in the state.
1804	Ohio University is chartered at Athens as the first institution of higher education in the state.
1805	The Dayton Library Society is the first library incorporated by the Ohio legislature.
1808	The Dayton Academy, the Worthington Academy, and the Chillicothe Academy are the first of many private schools to be chartered in Ohio to offer advanced as well as primary education.
1809	Miami University is incorporated at Oxford.
1815	The Lancaster Seminary is chartered in Cincinnati, the first in the state to utilize the Lancasterian philosophy of master teachers assisted by student monitors.
1818	The General Assembly establishes a state library and the office of a state librarian.
	The Dominican Fathers establish Saint Joseph's Convent near Somerset, the first Catholic educational institution in the state.
1819	The Medical College of Ohio at Cincinnati becomes the first medical school in the state.
	Anyone wishing to practice as an attorney is required by state law to study law for two years before obtaining a license.
1821	The first public school act passed by the Ohio legislature provides the option for local residents to establish local school districts, but no funding is specified.
	Legislation divides the state into five medical districts, each with three examiners who are required to license anyone who wishes to practice "Physic and Surgery."
1824	A theological seminary founded by Episcopal bishop Philander Chase at Worthington moves three years later to become Kenyon College at Gambier.
	The Ohio legislature appropriates funds to support the state library.
1825	The first property tax for the support of public schools requires townships to establish school districts with directors elected by local voters.
	John Harris begins teaching dental students as part of the practice he operates in his home at Bainbridge.

The Court of Common Pleas is authorized to appoint three examiners in each county to certify the qualifications of teachers, and no teacher without a certificate may be paid from tax funds.

1826   Western Reserve University evolved from the Hudson Academy founded by Congregationalists. It later moved to Cleveland and merged with Case Institute to become Case Western Reserve University. The Hudson buildings remain as Western Reserve Academy.

1827   The Ohio Asylum for Educating the Deaf and Dumb is incorporated at Columbus through the efforts of Presbyterian minister James Hoge.

1828   The Cincinnati Academy of Fine Arts is the first arts society to be chartered in the state.

1829   The Ohio Mechanics Institute at Cincinnati becomes the first to advance the interests of "Mechanics, Manufacturers and Artisans."

The Ohio legislature requires a minimum school year of three months for any public school receiving tax money.

Cincinnati establishes a school charter that sets an urban example of free, tax-supported common schools.

The first association of teachers is organized at Cincinnati as The Western College of Teachers, and it publishes *The Academic Pioneer,* the first educational journal in Ohio.

1830   Elyria High School—although it requires tuition—becomes the first chartered school in Ohio to use the word high school in its name.

The Lancaster Harmonic Society is the first of several musical societies chartered in the state.

1831   The Columbus Female Academy becomes the first incorporated institution strictly for the education of females.

The Historical and Philosophical Society of Ohio is organized at Columbus but moves to Cincinnati in 1848.

The Erodelphian Society at Miami University and the Philomathean Society at Kenyon College become the first college literary societies in the state.

1832   The Granville Literary and Theological Institution, forerunner of Denison University, is founded at Granville by the Ohio Baptist Education Society.

Marietta College is founded as the Marietta Collegiate Institute and Western Teachers' Seminary, primarily to prepare teachers for common schools.

1833   Oberlin College is founded at Oberlin by Congregationalists to educate Christian missionaries, and it becomes the first institution of higher education in Ohio to enroll women and African American students.

1834   Reading, writing, arithmetic, and "other necessary branches" are required in the first state law concerning subjects to be taught in public schools.

Stephen Strong's Manual Labor Seminary in Meigs County is the first chartered to teach vocational skills.

1836   Each school district is required to make an annual report to the county auditor regarding the number of students taught, length of the school term, and sources of funding.

William Holmes McGuffey, a professor at Miami University, publishes the first in a series of readers that will dominate education for the remainder of the century.

The American Lyceum of Education in Cincinnati is chartered to establish a model school for experiments in teacher education.

The first statewide convention of teachers calls for improved common schools, establishment of school libraries, and a state superintendent.

1837   The office of superintendent of common schools is created by the Ohio legislature and Samuel Lewis is appointed the first superintendent, but this office is abolished in 1840.

Muskingum College is founded at New Concord under the auspices of the Associate-Reformed Presbyterian Church.

The Ohio Institution for the Instruction of the Blind opens at the Columbus Presbyterian Church with one teacher and five pupils.

The state superintendent reports that Ohio has 7,748 school districts, of which 3,370 do not have a schoolhouse.

1842   Ohio Wesleyan University is founded at Delaware by the Methodist Church.

Saint Xavier College evolves from the Atheneum, the parish school of the first Catholic church in Cincinnati.

1844   The Cincinnati Astronomical Society is the first of its type to be chartered in Ohio.

Cincinnati first introduces vocal music into the school curriculum.

1845   Baldwin Institute is founded by the Methodist Church and joins with the German-founded Wallace College in 1858 to become Baldwin-Wallace College.

Wittenberg College is founded at Springfield by the Evangelical Lutheran Church.

The Ohio College of Dental Surgery is established at Cincinnati.

The first teacher institute is held in Sandusky County.

1846   The Farmers' College incorporated in Hamilton County is the first to offer scientific studies adapted to agricultural pursuits.

The law department of Cincinnati College becomes the first to have its certificate accepted for a license to practice law in the state.

Legislation is passed authorizing school districts to levy a tax not to exceed $30 for the support of a school library.

1847   The Ohio State Teachers' Association, forerunner of the Ohio Education Association, is founded at Akron to promote improved standards for the teaching profession.

The Akron Act establishes the principle of free graded primary and grammar schools by allowing this city to form a single school district. This model leads to an 1849 law extending the graded concept statewide.

Legislation is passed permitting counties to incorporate teacher institutes supported by public funds.

1848   Legislation provides a state department of common schools for African American and mulatto children, and it permits any town or township with twenty nonwhite children to create its own school district.

1849   Otterbein College is founded at Westerville by the United Brethren Church.

Catholic leaders, led by Bishop Purcell of Cincinnati, protest taxation to support a public school system while covering the costs of sending their own children to parochial schools.

The Farmington Normal School on the Western Reserve becomes the first institution for teacher training chartered in Ohio.

1850   The legislature authorizes a state board of education but fails to implement and fund it.

Ohio reports 11,661 public schools with nearly 500,000 students and 206 academies with about 15,000 students.

Cincinnati, the first school district to provide schooling for immigrant children in their native language, now has three German-English schools with twenty-four teachers and twenty-three hundred students.

Six evening schools with about six hundred students are open five evenings weekly from October to February in Cincinnati, the first school district to offer evening schools for working youth and adults.

Capital University is founded at Columbus, evolving from the German Evangelical Lutheran Seminary.

Heidelberg College is founded at Tiffin by the Evangelical and Reformed Church.

The Western Reserve Eclectic Institute is founded at Hiram by the Disciples of Christ and evolves into Hiram College.

Urbana College is founded by the Swedenborgians.

1851   Dr. Joseph Ray, author of widely used textbooks on mathematics, becomes the first principal of Woodward High School in Cincinnati.

The State Common School Fund is established with revenues from varied sources including peddler's licenses and a tax on auction sales.

1852   Forty-five cities and towns report having graded "union" schools with an enrollment from 92 students at Peru to 15,435 at Cincinnati.

Antioch College is established at Yellow Springs as a liberal nonsectarian Christian college by the Unitarians, with noted educator Horace Mann as its first president.

The Ohio Association for the Promotion of Female Education is organized.

The *Ohio Journal of Education,* later to become the *Ohio Educational Monthly,* begins publication as the official journal of Ohio teachers.

1853   Township school boards, composed of one member from each school subdistrict, replace township trustees in being responsible for local school funds, altering school district boundaries, and holding title to school property.

Legislation provides for the office of state commissioner of common schools elected by the voters of the state.

County boards of school examiners are appointed by the probate judge, and examinations for certification are formalized in each county.

Legislation requires a common education to be free to all youth, abolishing the "rate bills" which previously required students in many districts to pay to supplement the public funds.

The General Assembly requires township boards of education to provide a minimum of six months of schooling each year.

Mt. Union College is chartered at Alliance as a "patriotic and Christian" but nonsectarian institution, later affiliated with the Methodist Church.

School districts are required to levy a 1/10th mill tax for the support of a school library, and every family in the district is entitled to use one volume at a time from the school library.

Legislation for the first time permits tax funds to be used for support of secondary education.

1854   Seven hundred and seventy new common school buildings are constructed statewide at an average cost of $450 each.

The state superintendent interprets the new school law to require separate schools for nonwhite children when thirty or more are enumerated in the school district. When there are too few for a separate school, the tax funds raised on their behalf may be used for private instruction, employment of the regular teacher for evening or vacation sessions, or the children may be admitted to the common school "if no objections are raised."

1855   National Normal School is founded at Lebanon and quickly becomes the largest institution in the state for teacher training.

The number of common schools per county ranges from 26 in Fulton County to 359 in Licking County.

Thirty-one counties report a total of eighty-eight schools for nonwhite students.

1856   Superintendents of city and village school districts organize the Ohio Superintendents Association.

Wilberforce University is established in Greene County by the Methodist Episcopal Church to provide higher education for African American students. In 1863 control is assumed by the African Methodist Episcopal Church.

The Ohio Reform Farm School is established near Lancaster to furnish a half day of labor and a half day of schooling to provide inmates a skill upon release. In 1885 it becomes the Boys Industrial School.

William Rainey Harper, innovative educator and founding president of the University of Chicago, is born at New Concord.

Lake Erie College at Painesville, modeled on Mt. Holyoke, evolves from the Female Seminary at Willoughby.

1857   The number of common schools grows from 4,446 in 1837 to 12,339 this year, and the number of students enrolled rises from 146,440 to 603,347, but the average attendance is about 60 percent of those enrolled.

Eleven Ohio colleges report 1,095 full-time students enrolled and 1,899 degrees conferred to date. Ohio Wesleyan University has the largest current enrollment and Miami University the largest number of graduates.

During the past twenty years 9,718 schoolhouses were reportedly built at a total cost of $2,385,706, or a little less than $250 each.

1858   Caroline Luise Frankenberg, who had formerly taught under Friedrich Froebel, the German innovator in early childhood education, opens the state's first kindergarten at Columbus.

1861   Schools receiving public funds are required to offer a minimum of thirty weeks and a maximum of forty-four weeks of instruction.

1862   President Abraham Lincoln signs the Morrill Act that the U.S. Congress passed to provide land grants for each state to establish colleges offering instruction in agriculture and the mechanical arts.

1864   A state board of school examiners is established with authority to issue state certificates that supersede county certificates.

1866   The College of Wooster is founded by the Presbyterian Church.

1867   Legislation is passed to allow cities and villages to levy a $\frac{1}{10}$th mill tax to support public libraries and for local boards of education to appoint a board of library managers.

The Association of Ohio Colleges is organized to coordinate efforts of both public and private institutions.

1869   The Ohio Girls Industrial School is established near Delaware for "helpless, evil-disposed and vicious girls" committed by county probate courts.

1870   The University of Cincinnati becomes the first in the state to receive municipal tax assistance and develop working relationships with local businesses to prepare graduates for jobs in industry.

The Ohio Agricultural and Mechanical College is chartered at Columbus as the state's land-grant university and evolves into The Ohio State University.

Buchtel College is founded at Akron by the Ohio Universalist Convention.

1871   Anna Ogden opens the first training program in the state for kindergarten teachers as part of the Ohio Central Normal School at Worthington.

1872   An eighteen-room school costing $75,700 for 927 white students and an eight-room school costing $20,298 for nonwhite students are built in the Walnut Hills area of Cincinnati.

1873   Legislation is passed to define methods of conducting and financing teacher institutes.

School districts statewide are required to present bilingual instruction in German and English when seventy-five residents representing at least forty students request it.

The legislature establishes a procedure for advertising and bidding projects for new construction or repairs costing at least $500 in township districts and $1,500 in city districts.

1875   Wilmington College is chartered by the Quakers, although the school began operating four years earlier

The average monthly salary statewide for male teachers is $47 for common schools and $72 for high schools and $31 and $57 for female teachers. The average school term is twenty-eight weeks per year.

1876   Rio Grande College is chartered by the Free Will Baptist Church.

1877   The first state law regarding school attendance makes it compulsory for children eight to fourteen years of age to attend school at least twelve weeks annually, but there are numerous exceptions for those mentally deficient, needed for labor, or living more than two miles from a school.

A county tax is authorized to support industrial education for inmates of children's homes and orphanages.

1878   Ashland College is founded by the German Baptists, commonly referred to as the Dunkard Church.

1880   The Case School of Applied Science, now part of Case Western Reserve University, becomes the first institution in Ohio devoted to higher technical education.

1882   The Ohio Teachers Reading Circle is organized at the instigation of Mrs. D. L. Williams to provide a course of self-improvement for young teachers.

Findlay College is founded by the Church of God.

1885   The Ohio Archaeological and Historical Society is founded at Columbus.

1887   The Ohio legislature repeals all "black laws," including those establishing separate schools for nonwhite students.

1888   The State Board of School Examiners is given power to grant lifetime teaching certificates.

State legislation requires all common schools to teach the effects of alcoholic drinks and narcotics on the human body.

1889   The state specifies a universal curriculum for elementary schools that includes spelling, reading, writing, English grammar, geography, and arithmetic.

Legislation provides truant officers to enforce school attendance and requires all children eight to fourteen to attend at least sixteen weeks of school (twenty weeks in city districts), and students fourteen to sixteen who cannot read and write are required to attend half-day or evening classes.

Legislation includes schoolhouses among public buildings that must have fire safety precautions, including accessible exits.

1890   The legislature creates the Ohio School-Book Board to negotiate with publishers and furnish local boards of education with lists of approved books and contract prices.

1892   Domestic Science is introduced at Woodward High School and Hughes High School in Cincinnati.

The Workman Law abolishes subdistrict school directors and authorizes the township board of education to hire teachers.

The Boxwell examination standardizes the qualifications needed to graduate from district schools and permits students in districts with no high school to enter a nearby high school.

All city schools offering an intermediate or secondary curriculum are required to teach physical culture, including calisthenics.

The state allows local boards of education to open or rent schoolhouses for literary entertainments, school exhibitions, singing schools, or religious exercises.

1894   Cedarville College is founded by the Reformed Presbyterian Church.

Kingsville in Ashtabula County is the first township district authorized to eliminate subdistricts and transport all children to a central township school.

Legislation allows districts to provide free schoolbooks to students and Toledo and Tiffin become the first schools in the state to do so.

Legislation provides for the election of township school boards by popular vote, and for the first time in Ohio the law allows women to vote or be candidates for school board elections.

1895   The Ohio Library Association is established to promote library legislation and cooperative relationships among libraries.

| 1896 | Legislation allows the Cincinnati and Toledo school districts to establish teacher pension funds by deducting 1 percent of their salary. Teachers may retire with a disability and twenty years of service, otherwise thirty years if they are female and thirty-five years if they are male. |

1896   Legislation allows the Cincinnati and Toledo school districts to establish teacher pension funds by deducting 1 percent of their salary. Teachers may retire with a disability and twenty years of service, otherwise thirty years if they are female and thirty-five years if they are male.

Fire safety regulations for public buildings are strengthened with requirements regarding exits and the availability of water for fire fighting.

The state library establishes traveling libraries in cooperation with the Ohio Federation of Women's Clubs and soon begins working with granges in rural areas.

1898   A system of graded schools becomes compulsory for each township, with the option of a centralized school and public transportation of students.

Ohio Northern University is chartered by the Methodists from the Northwestern Ohio Normal School under the leadership of H. S. Lehr.

1899   Steubenville, Sandusky, and East Liverpool become the first communities to receive contributions from Andrew Carnegie for what will eventually become more than one hundred library buildings statewide.

1900   Male teachers in Ohio are paid $34 monthly and female teachers $31 monthly for a school year averaging thirty-one weeks.

1901   The Ohio Congress of Parents and Teachers organizes at Columbus, the fifth state in the nation to do so.

The Brumback Library at Van Wert becomes the first public countywide library.

1902   The Brumbaugh Law defines secondary education, and it classifies three levels of high schools and the minimum standards for each.

The Patterson Law makes it compulsory for school districts having no high school to pay tuition to another district for students qualifying to attend high school.

The first state-assisted normal schools for teacher training are established at Miami University and Ohio University.

1904   A school of library science to train professional librarians is established at Western Reserve University with a $100,000 endowment from Andrew Carnegie.

1905   Cincinnati opens the first public kindergarten in the state.

The Ohio State University establishes an agricultural extension division, with A. B. Graham as superintendent, to improve education in rural schools.

1906 One hundred thousand copies of *Agricultural Extension Bulletin* #5, "Centralized Schools in Ohio," mobilize a statewide movement toward rural school consolidation.

1907 The Ohio State University creates a College of Education committed to preparing professional teachers for high schools and normal schools, as well as instructing educational supervisors and administrators.

1908 The most tragic school fire in U.S. history occurs at Lakeview School at Collinwood in Cuyahoga County, killing 172 students and 2 teachers and putting pressure on the legislature and local school boards to improve fire safety standards.

   The Educational Equalization Fund makes its first appropriations totaling nearly $10,000 to compensate local communities' abilities to finance schools.

1909 Indianola Junior High School at Columbus opens as the first in the state to offer this new transitional concept between elementary and secondary education.

   District boards of education are authorized to offer manual training, domestic science, as well as commercial, agricultural, and vocational courses if they choose to do so.

1910 Bowling Green University is founded as Bowling Green State Normal College, and Kent State University is established as Kent State Normal College.

1914 The county replaces the township as the unit of government responsible for school curriculum and funding, with a county superintendent and county school board responsible for all schools except exempted towns and villages with populations over three thousand persons.

   The elected state commissioner of common schools is replaced by a state superintendent of public instruction appointed by the governor.

   The Bureau of Educational Research is established at The Ohio State University.

   The Columbus Catholic Diocese reports operating sixty parish schools with 12,515 students.

1917 Responding to a national need for skilled workers, the U.S. Congress passes the Smith-Hughes Act to provide funds for training in agriculture, domestic science, industrial arts, and commercial studies.

1918 Anti-German sentiment from the war results in the dismissal of most German teachers, and the following year the state forbids instruction in the German language below the eighth grade.

1919   A statewide retirement system is inaugurated to provide financial security for teachers in schools supported entirely or in part by public funds.

A state-supported institution is established to offer agricultural and mechanical training for the "mentally deficient."

1921   The Bing Act makes school attendance compulsory for youth from six to eighteen years of age or those released to work at age sixteen if they have completed the seventh grade. Rural districts are forced to open a high school or pay tuition and transportation to high school in an adjacent district.

The code for high schools first defines standards for junior high schools and establishes certification for junior high school teachers.

WOSU radio begins providing educational programming to the public.

1922   The Ohio School for the Blind is granted a high school charter.

1923   Legislation requires students to have one hundred minutes of physical education weekly and for each student to have an examination from a school physician or board of health with parents to be notified of any "defects" needing correction.

1925   Dr. Sidney L. Pressley, a psychology professor at The Ohio State University, introduces a "teaching machine" that rewards children with candy for correct responses.

1927   The Ohio School for the Deaf is brought under the supervision of the State Department of Education.

1928   The number of high schools in Ohio reaches its peak at 1,397.

1929   The Ohio School of the Air is established by the State Department of Education.

1930   Statewide, 500 parochial school buildings with 4,000 teachers and 175,000 students reveal a dramatic increase from the 355 teachers and nearly 15,000 students reported in 1900.

1932   Forty-eight school districts report having kindergarten classes, with a combined enrollment of 33,749 students.

1935   The Ohio legislature establishes the School Foundation program to guarantee a basic level of funding per student from state revenues.

State teacher certification requirements are revised to provide a one-year temporary certificate, a four-year provisional certificate, an eight-year professional certificate, and a life certificate in nine categories from kindergarten teaching to county supervision.

| 1936 | The U.S. Congress passes the George-Dean Vocational Act to provide funding for distributive education. |

The school construction program of the Public Works Administration contributes to 259 buildings and 1,203 classrooms in Ohio this year.

Evening classes in "Americanization" enroll 5,673 adults statewide.

| 1937 | Seventy-eight institutions of higher education report an undergraduate enrollment of 58,522 students and award 10,396 degrees. |

| 1940 | The number of one-room schools in the state has decreased to less than nine hundred, down from nearly ten thousand in 1914. |

| 1941 | State law establishes a tenure system to protect certified and experienced teachers from dismissal without cause, but it retains a limited contract for new teachers. |

| 1953 | In an effort to remove politics from the State Department of Education, Ohio voters approve a constitutional amendment for an elected state board of education that has authority to appoint the state superintendent. |

| 1955 | The Manahan Study surveys Ohio schools and makes 106 recommendations for improvements in education. |

Twenty-three members are elected to the first Ohio Board of Education, one representing each congressional district.

| 1956 | wosu-tv begins providing educational television for the public. |

Clemons v. *the Hillsboro Board of Education* results in a court order that all children must be assigned to schools without discrimination by race.

| 1959 | Legislation allows the formation of joint vocational school districts across school district and/or county lines. |

| 1961 | The Ohio Educational Television Network is organized to provide programming directly to school classrooms. |

| 1963 | The Ohio Board of Regents is created to coordinate programs and funding for higher education throughout the state. |

| 1965 | Penta County Joint Vocational School District, combining seventeen districts near Toledo, and the Lake County Joint Vocational School District, serving the entire county, create the first joint vocational schools in Ohio. |

The legislature requires school districts to have construction drawings, specifications, and cost estimates approved by their local board and the superintendent and to have them filed with the state board of education before being advertised for bids.

Community college districts are defined as any county or group of counties with seventy-five thousand or more persons wishing to create a public institution of higher education.

1967   The OCLC, Ohio College Library Center, is incorporated to establish and operate a computerized library center for academic libraries statewide. It later evolves into the much broader On-line Computer Library Center responsible for WORLDCAT, the international on-line library catalog.

Supervision of technical education is transferred from the Ohio Department of Education to the Ohio Board of Regents.

1968   The Ohio Council on Higher Continuing Education is founded, and in 1983 evolves into the Ohio Continuing Higher Education Association to coordinate adult education programs in Ohio colleges and universities.

1969   The Association of Independent Colleges and Universities is organized to coordinate the efforts of private institutions to influence legislation related to higher education.

1970   The shooting of four Kent State University students by Ohio National Guard troops becomes a national symbol of student protests against U.S. participation in the Vietnam War.

There are 252 tax-supported libraries in Ohio.

1972   The Dayton school district is ordered by the federal district court to end de facto segregation, and the following year there are similar decisions in Columbus and Cleveland that result in busing students to achieve racial balance.

Legislation requires all school districts to submit a plan for the identification, placement, staffing, and provision of services to disabled children.

1975   State law requires all public school districts to provide a kindergarten program.

1976   The legislature requires school districts to provide breakfast and lunch programs in accordance with the Child Nutrition Act of 1966.

1978   The federal district court rules against the Ohio High School Athletic Association and requires that girls be given the opportunity to compete in interscholastic sports.

1980   School consolidation has decreased the number of Ohio school districts by more than 75 percent, from 2,643 in 1910 to 615 in 1980.

1981	There are 3,169 elementary schools, 281 junior high schools, 742 high schools, 32 vocational schools, and 780 private schools reported in Ohio.
1983	The legislature requires educators to develop a competency-based program for teaching and evaluating student achievement in basic curriculum areas such as mathematics, language arts, and social sciences.
1985	The Ohio Higher Education Facility Commission is created to enhance the efficiency and economy of planning and financing college and university buildings.
1990	Two hundred and fifty public libraries statewide report holdings nearing thirty-six million volumes.
1991	The *DeRolph* case in the Perry County Common Pleas Court challenges inequity of state funding for education.
1992	Ohio Link, an on-line computer catalog of materials held by academic libraries throughout the state, is created by the Ohio Board of Regents.
	Ohio has forty-nine joint vocational school districts.
	Ohio reports 855 private and parochial schools.
1994	The legislature extends its requirement for competency-based education to arts education, including the visual arts, music, dance, and theater.
	SchoolNet Plus is established by the state to link all Ohio schools through a computer-learning network and eventually provide a computer workstation for every five children in kindergarten through fourth grade.
1995	Expenditures per pupil statewide average $5,379.
	The average teacher in the state has 14.9 years of experience and receives a salary of $36,922.
	Ohio has seventy-one four-year and fifty-three two-year campuses of higher education.
	State funding is provided for the Ohio Public Library Information Network (OPLIN), linking Ohio's two hundred and fifty public libraries, the first comprehensive electronic information network for public libraries in the country.
1996	The Ohio Department of Education is directed in the legislature's capital appropriation to develop a standardized design for school buildings in connection with a state-funded building assistance program.

1997   The Ohio Supreme Court upholds the Perry County decision, declares Ohio's method of funding public schools unconstitutional and gives the Ohio legislature one year to devise a remedy.

1998   Ohio voters defeat a legislative proposal to provide an income tax to support public schools.

1999   The Ohio Board of Regents creates the Ohio Learning Network, an on-line catalog that serves as a clearinghouse of courses and degrees that can be taken via the Internet from colleges and universities throughout Ohio.

Appendix B | Architects/Builders of Featured Buildings

Ater and Kern
    Scioto Township District #2 School, Orient
Baker, Lowell W. (Wilberforce)
    Galloway Hall, Wilberforce University, Wilberforce
Bancroft, Gerard (Granville)
    Granville Academy, Granville
Barnum, Frank S. (Cleveland)
    Watterson School, Cleveland
Baxter, Hodell, Donnelly and Preston (Cincinnati)
    Mariemont High School, Mariemont
Bentz, Carl E. (Columbus)
    Jerome Library, Bowling Green State University, Bowling Green
Bissell, Samuel (Twinsburg)
    Twinsburg Institute, Twinsburg
Blackburn, Joseph M. (Cleveland)
    Ohio School for the Deaf, Columbus
Blythe, Walter (Cleveland)
    Oberlin School, Oberlin
    Sterling, Rockwell, Orchard, and Saint Clair Schools, Cleveland
Brookes, Robert T. (Cleveland and Columbus)
    Towers Hall, Otterbein College, Westerville
Brown, Hiram (Xenia and Yellow Springs)
    "Little Antioch" School, Yellow Springs

Includes early-nineteenth-century builders who worked from plan books but does not include contractors on architect-designed projects.

Brown, Thomas, and Thomas Morrison
  Stoddard Hall, Miami University, Oxford
Burgess and Niple, Ltd. (Columbus)
  Perry Community Education Village, Perry
  Solon Dual School, Solon
Cadwallader, Morris
  Sturges Hall, Ohio Wesleyan University, Delaware
Chambers and Smith (Columbus)
  Union School, Worthington
Collingwood, William, and Ransom Collingwood (Florence)
  Florence Corners School, Florence
Corp, Benjamin (Marietta)
  Cutler Hall, Ohio University, Athens
Dauben, Joseph (Columbus)
  Southern Theatre, Columbus
DeCurtins, Frederick (Celina)
  Immaculate Conception High School, Celina
Earnshaw, John B. (Cincinnati)
  Hughes High School, Cincinnati
Eisenman, Peter (New York)
  Aronoff Center for Design and Art, University of Cincinnati, Cincinnati
  Wexner Center for the Visual Arts, The Ohio State University, Columbus
Fleischman, Richard (Cleveland)
  Ohio Aerospace Institute, Brook Park
Freeman, Geoffrey (Boston)
  Olin Library, Kenyon College, Gambier
Freese, J. M. (Columbus)
  Franklin Park Conservatory, Columbus
Garber, Frederick W. (Cincinnati)
  Withrow High School, Cincinnati
Gee, Edwin M. (Toledo)
  Lincoln Elementary School, Toledo
Gehry, Frank O., and Associates (Santa Monica, California)
  Center for the Visual Arts, University of Toledo, Toledo
Gilbert, Cass (New York)
  Allen Memorial Art Museum, Oberlin College, Oberlin
Good, Jeremiah H. (Tiffin)
  Founders Hall, Heidelberg College, Tiffin
Green, Edward B. (Buffalo, New York)
  Dayton Art Institute, Dayton
Hahn, Alfred A. (Toledo)
  Toledo Public Library, Toledo

Marsh Foundation School, Van Wert

Lesko Associates, Architects, and Planners (Cleveland)
    Butternut Elementary School, North Olmsted
    Massillon Washington High School, Massillon
    Wapakoneta High School, Wapakoneta

Lindsay, H. C. (Zanesville)
    McConnelsville Opera House, McConnelsville

Ludwig, F. A. and Co. (Saint Louis)
    Pontifical College Josephinum, Columbus

Manahan, George (Norwalk)
    Norwalk Female Seminary, Norwalk

Matthews, Stanley M. (Cincinnati)
    Westwood Branch Library, Cincinnati

McLaughlin, James W. (Cincinnati)
    Cincinnati Public Library, Cincinnati

Merriam, Roy J. (Columbus)
    Paulding County Carnegie Library, Paulding
    Piqua High School, Piqua

Merrifield, A. M. (Massachusetts)
    Antioch Hall, Antioch College, Yellow Springs

Milner, A. N. (Coshocton)
    Sycamore Street Union School, Coshocton

Morris, Charles E. (Columbus)
    Madison Township School, Grove City

Mueller, Frederick G. (Hamilton)
    Hamilton Catholic High School, Hamilton

Myer, H. E. (Sandusky)
    Sycamore School, Sandusky

Nash, Rev. Norman (Philadelphia)
    Kenyon Hall, Kenyon College, Gambier

Owsley, Charles Henry (Youngstown)
    Carnegie Public Library, East Liverpool

Packard, Frank L. (Columbus)
    Emerson School, Westerville
    Orton Hall, The Ohio State University, Columbus
    University Hall, Ohio Wesleyan University, Delaware

Parker, Harold (Sandusky)
    McCormick School, Huron

Perkins and Will (Chicago)
    Butternut Elementary School, North Olmsted
    New Albany Learning Community, New Albany
    Perry Community Education Village, Perry

Porter, Simeon (Hudson and Cleveland)
  Chapel, Western Reserve College/Academy, Hudson
  Chapman Hall, Mount Union College, Alliance
  Mayflower, Eagle, and Kentucky Street Schools, Cleveland
  North College Hall, Western Reserve College/Academy, Hudson
  Rayen School, Youngstown
Pretzinger, Albert (Dayton)
  Springfield South High School, Springfield
Redding, Vernon (Mansfield)
  Bucyrus Public Library, Bucyrus
Richards, Bauer and Moorhead (Toledo)
  Penta County Joint Vocational School, Rossford
Richards, McCarty and Bulford (Columbus)
  Ohio School for the Deaf, Columbus
Riebel, David (Columbus)
  Indianola Junior High School, Columbus
  Southern Theatre, Columbus
Ritchey, David, William P. Vanhook, and James T. Slack (Oxford)
  Elliott and Stoddard Halls, Miami University, Oxford
Roberts, Henry (London, England)
  Bexley Hall, Kenyon College, Gambier
Rooney and Clinger (Findlay)
  Findlay–Hancock County Public Library, Findlay
Rouzer, John (Dayton)
  Turner's Opera House, Dayton
Sanborn, Steketee, Otis and Evans (Toledo)
  Saddlemire Student Services Building, Bowling Green State University, Bowl-
    ing Green
SEM Partners (Columbus)
  Worthington Park and Granby Elementary Schools, Worthington
Shepley, Rutan and Coolidge (Boston)
  Warder Public Library, Springfield
Smith, Howard Dwight (Columbus)
  Indianola Junior High School, Columbus
Stine, D. L. (Toledo)
  Brumback Library, Van Wert
Stone, Edward Durell (New York)
  Sinclair Community College, Dayton
Sullivan, Leclider and Jay (Dayton)
  Sinclair Community College, Dayton
Sun, Paul Peng-Chen (Boston)
  Olin Library, Kenyon College, Gambier

Swagler, Michael (Ragersville)
   Ragersville School, Ragersville
Terrell, Elah (Columbus)
   Groveport School, Groveport
   Johnstown School, Johnstown
   Madison Township School, Grove City
Tilden, Guy (Canton)
   Canton Public Library, Canton
Tilton, Edward L. (New York)
   Carnegie West Branch Library, Cleveland
Tinsley, William (Cincinnati and Indianapolis)
   Ascension Hall, Kenyon College, Gambier
   Ohio School for the Blind, Columbus
Wagner and Hickox (Cleveland)
   Prospect and Rockwell Schools, Cleveland
Walker, Frank R. (Cleveland)
   Cleveland Public Library, Cleveland
Weary and Kramer (Akron)
   Akron High School, Akron
Webster, J. R. (Wooster)
   Walnut Street School, Wooster
Weeks, Harry E. (Cleveland)
   Cleveland Public Library, Cleveland
Welch, Frederick C. (Delaware)
   Elliott Hall, Ohio Wesleyan University, Delaware
Wipfer, S. J. (Cleveland)
   Saint Ignatius High School, Cleveland
Wolfe, C. Edward (Sandusky)
   McCormick School, Huron
Yamasaki, Minoru (Detroit)
   Bibbons Conservatory of Music, Oberlin College, Oberlin
   King Memorial Hall, Oberlin College, Oberlin
Yost, Joseph W. (Columbus and New York)
   Emerson School, Westerville
   Newark High School, Newark
   Orton Hall, Ohio State University, Columbus
   Sandusky Carnegie Library, Sandusky
   University Hall, Ohio Wesleyan University, Delaware

Appendix C | Ohio Educational Sites on National Register of Historic Places

This list includes individual nominations and contributing buildings within defined historic districts. Asterisks denote properties featured in this volume.

BROWN COUNTY
Georgetown Public School,
Georgetown
BUTLER COUNTY
Augspurger Schoolhouse,
Woodsdale
*Hamilton Catholic High School,
Hamilton
Hughes School, Hamilton
Independent District #1 School,
Fairfield
*Lane Public Library, Hamilton
Miami University, Oxford
*Elliott Hall
William H. McGuffey Home
*Stoddard Hall
Western Female Seminary
*Sorg's Opera House, Middletown
*Reverend Thomas's Select School,
Shandon
CHAMPAIGN COUNTY
Urbana College, Urbana
Bailey Hall
Barclay Hall
Oak Hall
CLARK COUNTY
*Warder Public Library, Springfield
Wittenberg University, Springfield
Myers Hall
CLINTON COUNTY
Pansy School, Clarksville
College Hall, Wilmington College,
Wilmington
COLUMBIANA COUNTY
*Carnegie Public Library, East
Liverpool
CUYAHOGA COUNTY
Allen Memorial Library, Cleveland
Baldwin-Wallace College, Berea
Dietsch Hall
Kohler Hall
Lindsay-Crossman Chapel
Marting Hall
Merner-Pfeiffer Hall

Beehive School, Cleveland
Berea District School, Berea
Cleveland Mall, Cleveland
*Cleveland Public Library
Cleveland State University, Cleveland
University Hall
Cooper School of Art, Cleveland
Doan School, Cleveland
East Cleveland District #9 School,
Cleveland Heights
Flora Stone Mather College,
Cleveland
Clark Hall
Guilford Hall
Harkness Memorial Chapel
Hayden Hall
Mather Memorial Hall
Hruby Conservatory of Music,
Cleveland
Miles Park Library, Cleveland
Murray Hill School, Cleveland
Notre Dame Academy, Cleveland
Notre Dame College, Cleveland
Ohio City Historic District, Cleveland
*Carnegie West Library
Old Center School, Mayfield
Old District #10 Schoolhouse,
Cleveland
Old Euclid District #4 School,
Lyndhurst
*Saint Ignatius High School,
Cleveland
William E. Telling Residence/
Library, South Euclid
*Watterson School, Cleveland
Western Reserve University,
Cleveland
Adelbert Hall
Zion Lutheran School, Cleveland
DARKE COUNTY
Beehive School, Greenville
Carnegie Library, Greenville
DEFIANCE COUNTY
Defiance Public Library, Defiance

DELAWARE COUNTY
Delaware Public Library, Delaware
Ohio Wesleyan University, Delaware
Austin Hall
Edwards Gymnasium/Pheiffer
Natatorium
*Elliott Hall
Merrick Hall
Perkins Observatory
Sanborn Hall
Selby Field
Slocum Library
*Sturges Hall
Stuyvesant Hall
*University Hall/Gray Chapel
ERIE COUNTY
Barker School, Sandusky
*Campbell Street School, Sandusky
*Florence Corners School, Florence
Jackson Junior High School,
Sandusky
Monroe School, Sandusky
Osborne School, Sandusky
Saint Mary's Girls' Grade School,
Sandusky
Saint Mary's High School, Sandusky
*Sandusky Carnegie Library, Sandusky
*Sycamore School, Sandusky
West Market Street School, Sandusky
FAIRFIELD COUNTY
Crawfis Institute, Sugar Grove
South School, Lancaster
Stanbery Junior High School,
Lancaster
FRANKLIN COUNTY
Capital University, Bexley
Lehman Hall
Leonard Hall
Loy Gymnasium
Mees Music Hall
Rudolph Hall
Central College, Westerville
*Central High School, Columbus
*Emerson School, Westerville

Fairchild Building/Central College
Academy, Westerville
Felton School, Columbus
*Franklin Park Conservatory,
Columbus
J. L. Hamilton Residence/One-Room
District School, Washington
Township
Holy Cross Church School, Columbus
*Indianola Junior High School,
Columbus
Jefferson Avenue Learning
Community, Columbus
North High School, Columbus
*Ohio School for the Blind, Columbus
*Ohio School for the Deaf, Columbus
The Ohio State University, Columbus
Hayes Hall
Ohio Stadium
Old Ohio Union
*Orton Hall
Otterbein College, Westerville
*Towers Hall
Principal's Cottage, Ohio Central
Normal School, Worthington
*Sharon Township Hall/Union
School, Worthington
Shepard Street School, Columbus
*Southern Theatre, Columbus
Washington Township School, Dublin
GALLIA COUNTY
Ewington Academy
GEAUGA COUNTY
Old Burton High School, Burton
Second Burton High School, Burton
GREENE COUNTY
Antioch College, Yellow Springs
*Antioch Hall
Art Complex
Birch Hall
Power Plant
Science Building
Bath Township Consolidated School,
Fairborn

Cedarville Opera House, Cedarville
*Yellow Springs High School/South
    "Colored" School, Yellow Springs
GUERNSEY COUNTY
Claysville School, Claysville
HAMILTON COUNTY
Abbe Meteorological Observatory,
    Cincinnati
*Cincinnati Music Hall, Cincinnati
Cincinnati Observatory, Cincinnati
Clifton School, Cincinnati
*Cummins School, Cincinnati
Eastern Avenue Carnegie Library,
    Cincinnati
Edgecliff College, Cincinnati
    Carriage House
    Emory Hall
    Greenhouses
    Maxwelton House
    Theatre/Ferris House
Elliott House Outdoor Education
    Center, Cincinnati
Immaculate Conception School,
    Cincinnati
Jefferson School, Indian Hill
Jehu John House/Subscription
    School, Harrison
Lady of Mercy High School,
    Cincinnati
Lincoln School, Cincinnati
Madame Fredin's Eden Park School,
    Cincinnati
McCormick Hall, Anderson
    Township
McKinley School, Cincinnati
Mount Adams School, Cincinnati
Professor O. M. Mitchell
    Observatory, Cincinnati
Roudebush Farm Schoolhouse,
    Harrison
Sacred Heart Academy, Cincinnati
Saint Francis De Sales School,
    Cincinnati

Saint Paul's Church School, Cincinnati
*Washington Heights School, Indian
    Hills
Westwood Elementary School,
    Cincinnati
*Westwood Branch Library, Cincinnati
*Withrow High School, Cincinnati
HANCOCK COUNTY
Marion Township District #3 School,
    Findlay
HARDIN COUNTY
Kenton Public Library, Kenton
HARRISON COUNTY
Franklin College Building, New
    Athens
*Ourant's School, Cadiz
HOCKING COUNTY
Logan City Hall/Library, Logan
HOLMES COUNTY
Boyd School, Berlin
Millersburg School, Millersburg
HURON COUNTY
*Norwalk Female Seminary, Norwalk
JEFFERSON COUNTY
Bantam Ridge School, Wintersville
Carnegie Library, Steubenville
Central High School, Mingo
    Junction
Central Public School, Mingo
    Junction
Pleasant Hill School, Steubenville
KNOX COUNTY
Kenyon College, Gambier
    *Ascension Hall
    *Bexley Hall
    Church of the Holy Spirit
    *Kenyon Hall
    Rosse Hall
Knox County Infirmary/Mount
    Vernon Bible College, Mount
    Vernon
Woodward Opera House, Mount
    Vernon

Saint Anthony Catholic School, Saint
Anthony
Saint Bernhard's Catholic School,
Burkettsville
Saint Charles Seminary, Carthagena
Saint Henry Junior High School,
Saint Henry
Saint Rose Catholic School, Saint
Rose
Saint Wendelin School, Wendelin

MIAMI COUNTY

Elizabeth Township Centralized
School, Elizabeth Township
Elizabeth Township One-Room
Schools, Elizabeth Township
Mary Jane Hayner Library, Troy
Piqua High School, Piqua

MONTGOMERY COUNTY

*Dayton Art Institute, Dayton
Huffman Avenue School,
Dayton
Longfellow School, Dayton
Turner's Opera House/Victory
Theatre, Dayton
University of Dayton, Dayton
Saint Mary's Hall

MORGAN COUNTY

*McConnellsville Opera House,
McConnelsville

MORROW COUNTY

Old Union School, Chesterville

MUSKINGUM COUNTY

William Rainey Harper House, New
Concord
Muskingum College, New Concord
Brown Chapel
Cambridge Hall
College Drive United Presbyterian
Church
Gymnasium/Theatre
Johnson Hall
Manse/President's House
Montgomery Hall

Patton Hall
Paul Hall
Roseville High School, Roseville
Stone Academy, Zanesville
West Union School, Norwich

PAULDING COUNTY

*Paulding County Carnegie Library,
Paulding

PERRY COUNTY

West School, Crooksville

PICKAWAY COUNTY

Memorial Hall/Library,
Circleville
*Scioto Township District #2 School,
Orient

PIKE COUNTY

Vanmeter Stone Residence/School,
Piketon

PORTAGE COUNTY

Kent State University, Kent
*Administration Building
*Kent Hall
*Lowry Hall
*Merrill Hall
*Moulton Hall

PREBLE COUNTY

Camden School, Camden

PUTNAM COUNTY

Leipsic City Hall/Opera House/
Library, Leipsic

RICHLAND COUNTY

Lexington School, Lexington
Marvin Memorial Library, Shelby
Soldiers and Sailors Memorial,
Mansfield

ROSS COUNTY

Dr. John Harris Dental School,
Bainbridge
South Salem Academy, South
Salem

SCIOTO COUNTY

*Portsmouth Young Ladies
Seminary, Portsmouth

SENECA COUNTY
  Heidelberg College, Tiffin
    Aigler Alumni Building
    College Hall
    *Founders Hall
    France Hall
    Gerhart-Rust Residence
    Great Hall
    Laird Hall
    Octagon
    Pfleiderer Center
    President's House
    Willard Hall
  *Miami Street School, Tiffin
SHELBY COUNTY
  Botkins Elementary School,
    Botkins
  Fort Loramie School, Fort Loramie
STARK COUNTY
  *Canton Public Library, Canton
  Early-Hartzell House, Alliance
  Lake Township School, Uniontown
  *McKinley High School, Canton
  Mount Union College, Alliance
    *Chapman Hall
    Miller Hall
  *Science Hill School, Alliance
SUMMIT COUNTY
  Akron Jewish Center, Akron
  Akron Public Library, Akron
  Bath Township School, Bath
    Township
  Saint Paul's Sunday School, Akron
  Tallmadge Academy/High
    School/Town Hall, Tallmadge
  *Twinsburg Institute, Twinsburg
  Western Reserve College /Academy,
    Hudson
    Athenaeum
    Cartwright House
    *Chapel
    Crisp Boarding House
    Cutler House

    Ellsworth Hall
    Gymnasium
    Reverend Hosford House
    Morley Cottage
    *North College Hall
    Observatory
    President's House
    President Pierce's House
    Professor Nutting's House
    Professor Seymour's House
    Seymour Hall
TRUMBULL COUNTY
  Carnegie-Sutliff Library, Warren
  Green Township Center School,
    North Bloomfield
  Gustavus Center School, Kinsman
TUSCARAWAS COUNTY
  *Ragersville School, Ragersville
VAN WERT COUNTY
  *Brumback Library, Van Wert
  *Marsh Foundation School,
    Van Wert
    Administration Building
    Business Office/Clinic
    Clymer Hall
    Marsh Hall
    Senior Hall
    Vance Hall
  *Willshire School, Willshire
WARREN COUNTY
  Carnegie Library, Lebanon
  *Harvey's Free Negro School,
    Harveysburg
  *Lebanon Academy, Lebanon
WASHINGTON COUNTY
  Marietta College, Marietta
    *Erwin Hall
    Willcox-Mills House
  Old Saint Mary's School, Marietta
WAYNE COUNTY
  College of Wooster, Wooster
    Douglas Hall
    Frick Library

Galpin Memorial Hall

Hygela Hall

Holden Hall

*Kauke Hall

Kenarden Lodge

President's House

*Scovel Hall

Severance Gymnasium

*Severance Hall

Taylor Hall

*Walnut Street School/Art Center,
Wooster

West End School, Carey

Notes

INTRODUCTION

1. Wayne E. Fuller, *The Old Country School* (Chicago: University of Chicago Press, 1982), 59–78.

2. Helen Hooven Santmyer, *Ohio Town* (1962; rpt. New York: Harper and Row, 1984), 187.

3. George S. Bobinski, *Carnegie Libraries: Their History and Impact on American Public Library Development* (Chicago: American Library Association, 1969), 16–20.

4. Sara Snyder Crumpacker, "Using Cultural Information to Create Schools that Work," *Designing Places for Learning,* ed. Anne Meek (Alexandria, Va.: Association for Supervision and Curriculum Development, 1995), 31–42.

5. This is a quotation from Article 3 of the Northwest Ordinance of 1787. See W. A. Taylor, *Ohio Statesman and Hundred Year Book, 1788–1892* (Columbus: Westbote, 1892), 10.

6. T. C. Holy and W. E. Arnold, *Standards for the Evaluation of School Buildings* (Columbus: Ohio State University Bureau of Educational Research, 1936).

7. John Ruskin, *The Seven Lamps of Architecture* (1849; rpt. New York: Farrar, Straus, and Giroux, 1979).

8. For discussion of this concept see David Watkin, *A History of Western Architecture,* 2d ed. (London: Laurence King, 1996), 458.

9. John Dewey, *The School and Society* (Chicago: University of Chicago Press, 1913), and *Democracy and Education* (New York: Macmillan, 1916), 102–8, 388–95.

10. Anne Taylor, "How Schools Are Redesigning Their Space," in Meek, ed., *Designing Places for Learning,* 67–76.

11. Speech by Governor Gaston Capeton of West Virginia to the 1991 National Convention on Educational Facilities in Washington, D.C. (Published as the preface to Meek's *Designing Places for Learning*).

12. Jerry M. Lowe, "Historical Perspectives," *Guide for Planning Educational Facilities* (Columbus: Council of Educational Facility Planners, 1991), A1–9.

1. Taylor, *Ohio Hundred Year Book,* 10.

2. For an elaboration on inadequate financing for public schools on the Ohio frontier see William McAlpine, "Origin of Public Education in Ohio," *Ohio Archaeological and Historical Society Quarterly* 38 (1929): 409–47; *A History of Education in the State of Ohio* (Columbus: Columbus Gazette, 1876), 80–86; Francis P. Weisenburger, *The Passing of the Frontier, 1825–1850* (Columbus: Ohio Historical Society, 1941), 164–66; E. H. Roseboom and F. P. Weisenburger, *A History of the State of Ohio* (Columbus: Ohio Historical Society, 1986), 141–42.

3. George W. Knight, "History of Educational Progress in Ohio," in Henry Howe, *Historical Collections of Ohio* (Cincinnati: C. J. Krehbiel, 1902), cites records of the Ohio Company (1:137–49). Moravian missionaries had opened a school among the Native American population before the Revolutionary War but this was abandoned during hostilities.

4. Ohio Historic Inventory, BUT-1-10, and National Register nomination; William Stephan Riggs, *The Saga of Paddy's Run* (Oxford, Ohio: n.p., 1945), 21, 124–25, 146–47; *Hamilton Journal-News,* Sept. 16, 1950.

5. Ohio Centennial Educational Committee, "Brief History of Twinsburgh Insti-tute," *Historical Sketches of the Higher Educational Institutions, and also of Benevolent and Reformatory Institutions of the State of Ohio* (Columbus: State Centennial Educational Committee, 1876); George B. Hettinger, "Samuel Bissell: Humanitarian and Educator, 1797–1895" (D.Ed. diss., University of Akron, 1981); Luman Lane, *A History of Twinsburgh from 1820* (Akron: Beebe and Elkins, Printers, 1861), 60–62. The 1860 U.S. Population Census, Summit County, Ohio, Twinsburg, 267, includes in the Bissell household eleven males and five females from fifteen to twenty-two years of age, four of them Indians and several of the males apparently working on the farm in addition to their studies. The 1861 catalog for the Twinsburgh Institute lists tuition for "the ordinary branches" at three dollars per twelve-week term, with an additional dollar for Latin, Greek, and higher mathematics, as well as a supplementary three dollars for German and French.

6. Edward A. Miller, "History of the Educational Legislation in Ohio from 1803 to 1850," 27 *Ohio Archaeological and Historical Publications* (1919): 154. The terms "academy," "seminary," "institute," and "high school" were used interchangeably during this period and do not reliably define the sex of the students or the level of education offered.

7. Worthington Academy subscription list, May 17, 1805, Griswold Papers, 1802–1809, Worthington Historical Society. Robert W. Steele, president of the Dayton Board of Education, described the Dayton Academy built in 1808 as a "highly creditable building," in a letter to Anson Smyth, State Commissioner of Education, Dec. 1, 1858, in *Fifth Annual Report of the State Commissioner of Common Schools* (Columbus: Richard Nevins, 1859), 120. It would appear that these three academies had similar brick buildings.

8. Contract between the trustees of the Worthington Academy and Daniel Bishop, Sept. 29, 1808, Griswold Papers, 1802–1809, Worthington Historical Society.

9. Although no photograph of the Worthington Academy survives, an 1820 Masonic Lodge of almost identical size and style now stands in Worthington as the Ohio Masonic Museum.

10. This same John Kilbourn later moved to Columbus and published the earliest series of gazetteers for the state of Ohio.

11. *(Worthington) Western Intelligencer,* July 17, 1811.

12. This method was associated with the English educator Joseph Lancaster, and the first U.S. school to copy this model opened in New York City in 1806. Dell Upton, "Lancasterian Schools, Republican Citizenship, and the Spatial Imagination in Early-Nineteenth-Century America," *Journal of the Society of Architectural Historians* 55 (Sept. 1996): 238–53.

13. Charles Frederic Goss, *Cincinnati: The Queen City* (Cincinnati: S. J. Clarke Publishing, 1912), 379–80. It was not uncommon for Lancasterian schools to have several hundred scholars at long rows of benches in a single room with the master's desk on a raised platform at one end and lining either side space for students to stand in semicircles for recitation with a monitor.

14. Ohio Historic Inventory, LIC-18–15, and National Register nomination; William T. Utter, *Granville: The Story of an Ohio Village* (Granville: Granville Historical Society, 1956), 154–56. Although no contract has been found, Horace King, *Granville, Massachusetts to Ohio* (Granville: Sentinel Publishing, 1989), is persuasive that this is the work of master builder Gerard Bancroft, whose two brothers were trustees when the academy was built (192–94).

15. Acts of the Thirty-Third General Assembly, Dec. 17, 1834.

16. Ohio Historic Inventory, MEG-367–9, and National Register nomination; Edgar Ervin, *Pioneer History of Meigs County, Ohio, to 1949: Including Masonic History of the Same Period* (Pomeroy, Ohio: Meigs County Pioneer Society, 1949), 110, 284; Taylor, *Ohio Hundred Year Book,* 321.

17. Paul Venable Turner, *Campus: An American Planning Tradition* (Cambridge, Mass.: MIT Press, 1990), 90–100.

18. Hudson Academy evolved into Western Reserve College, but when the institution moved to Cleveland in 1882, the buildings at Hudson remained as Western Reserve Academy. National Register nomination; Frederick C. Waite, *Western Reserve University: The Hudson Era* (Cleveland: Western Reserve University Press, 1943), 184–201; Richard Campen, *Architecture of the Western Reserve, 1800–1900* (Cleveland: Press of Case Western Reserve University, 1971); Eric Johannesen, *Ohio College Architecture before 1870* (Columbus: Ohio Historical Society, 1969), 20–23; William Henry Perrin, *History of Summit County, Ohio* (Chicago: Baskin and Battey, 1881), 446–66; (Hudson) *Ohio Observer,* Aug. 24, 1836.

19. Turner, *Campus,* 305.

20. Asher Benjamin, *The Practical House Carpenter* (1830; rpt. New York: Dover Publications, 1988); Eric Johannesen, "Simeon Porter: Ohio Architect," *Ohio History* 74 (Summer 65): 169–90.

21. (Hudson) *Ohio Observer,* Aug. 26, 1835.

22. For elaboration regarding the Yale Row see Turner, *Campus,* 45.

23. Ohio Historic Inventory, WAR-744–6, and National Register nomination; Hazel Spencer Phillips, *Traditional Architecture—Warren County* (Lebanon: Warren County Historical Society, 1969).

24. Karl J. Kay, *History of National Normal University* (Wilmington, Ohio: Wilmington College, 1929).

25. National Register nomination; *History of Warren County, Ohio* (Chicago: W. H. Beers, 1881), 652–60; "First Free Black School in Ohio," Harveysburg Community Historical Society. This was one of the earliest and longest operating schools for African American youth, but it was not the first in Ohio. Several earlier schools were recorded in Cincinnati. The first to accept black students was the Lancaster Seminary in 1815, and in 1826 the first black school was taught by a black teacher named Schooley. See Walter McKinley Nicholes, "The Educational Development of Blacks in Cincinnati from 1800 to the Present" (D.Ed. diss.,

University of Cincinnati, 1977), 21–27; L. D. Easton, "The Colored Schools of Cincinnati," in *History of the Schools of Cincinnati and Other Institutions, Public and Private*, ed. Isaac M. Martin (Cincinnati: Cincinnati Public Schools, 1900); and Frederick A. McGinnis, *The Education of Negroes in Ohio* (Wilberforce: Wilberforce Press, 1941), 39.

26. The 1880 U.S. Population Census, Warren County, Ohio, Massie Township, Harveysburg, 348–54. From 1849 to 1887 Ohio law maintained separate school systems for white and nonwhite youth. See Nicholes, "Educational Development of Blacks," 63–64.

27. S. S. Scranton, *History of Mercer County, Ohio* (Chicago: Biographical Publishing, 1902), 65–68; Howe, *Historical Collections of Ohio*, 2:241; *First Report of the Trustees of the Emlen Institute* (Philadelphia: Culbertson and Bache, 1875).

28. J. F. Everhart, *History of Muskingum County, Ohio, 1794–1882* (Columbus: J. F. Everhart, 1882), 148–53; Howe, *Historical Collections of Ohio*, 2:335.

29. Howe, *Historical Collections of Ohio*, 1:964, 1:970.

30. Ohio Historic Inventory, HUR-69–3, and National Register nomination; Talbot Hamlin, *Greek Revival Architecture in America* (1944; rpt. New York: Dover Publications, 1964), 282.

31. An advertisement in the *Huron Reflector*, Sept. 3, 1850, shows the school's intent to offer both primary- and secondary-level courses. The 1850 U.S. Population Census, Huron County, Ohio, Norwalk, shows the Hayes household included a half a dozen boarding students, but most were undoubtedly day scholars in a building of this size (4).

32. Ohio Historic Inventory, SCI-50–13, and National Register nomination; folder of historic materials at Stepping Stone House, which today serves as a woman's shelter.

33. Robert L. Straker, *Horace Mann and Others* (Yellow Springs: Antioch Press, 1963).

34. David A. Simmons, "Little Antioch," *Timeline* 13 (Sept.–Oct. 1996): 52–53; Cosmelia Hirst, "Little Antioch School," *Yellow Springs News*, Oct. 15, 1926, 8; Arthur R. Kilner, *History of One- and Two-Room Schoolhouses in Greene County, Ohio* (Xenia, Ohio: privately printed, 1983), 51.

35. Henry Barnard, *School Architecture, Or, Contributions to the Improvement of Schoolhouses in the United States*, 6th ed. (Cincinnati: H. W. Derby, 1854), 234–35, 260–63.

36. His son Guy Tilden became one of northeastern Ohio's best-known architects. Joseph G. Butler, *History of Youngstown and the Mahoning Valley, Ohio* (New York: American Historical Society, 1921), 1:291–93; Mahoning Valley Historical Society, will is quoted in MSS 1863, National Register nomination.

37. Dewey, *School and Society*, in an April 1899 lecture (31–32). John Dewey's philosophy that occupation maintains a balance between the intellectual and practical phases of experience led directly to the movement for federal and state funding to support vocational education which culminated in Congressional passage of the Smith-Hughes Act in 1917.

38. "First Year Book," Marsh Foundation School, 1927; *Van Wert Times*, Aug. 16, 1920; W. A. Wegandt, "Van Wert Citizens Vie with Each Other in Public Philanthropies," *Cleveland Plain Dealer Magazine*, Jan. 20, 1935, 4.

Two | ONE-ROOM SCHOOLS

1. The Venice school is described in the *History and Biographical Cyclopedia of Butler County, Ohio* (Cincinnati: Western Biographical Publishing, 1882), 453. The Washington

County school is described in Donald A. Hutslar, *The Architecture of Migration: Log Construction in the Ohio Country, 1750–1850* (Athens: Ohio University Press, 1986), app. F, 506–9.

2. Miller, "History of Educational Legislation in Ohio," 17–18.

3. Andrew Guillford, *America's Country Schools* (Washington, D.C.: Preservation Press, 1984), 35; Wayne E. Fuller, "Everybody's Business: The Midwestern One-Room School," *Timeline* 10 (Sept.–Oct. 1993): 32–47.

4. Fuller, *Old Country School,* 2, quoting Adell Krebs, "Saga of a Country School," manuscript, Wisconsin State Historical Society.

5. Hamlin Garland, *A Son of the Middle Border* (Lincoln: Bison Press, 1979), 95.

6. Tuscarawas County Deed Record 6:113.

7. National Register nomination; *History of Early Tuscarawas County Schools* (Dover: Tuscarawas County Retired Teachers' Association, 1978), 6–7; Clayton Renner, *Ragersville Centennial History* (Ragersville, Ohio: n.p., 1930), 12–18; Ed DeGraw, "Ragersville: 150 Exciting Yesterdays," *Dover Times Reporter,* July 30, 1980, D29.

8. Guillford, *America's Country Schools,* 167.

9. National Register nomination; Ohio Historic Inventory HAS-302–10.

10. Guillford, *America's Country Schools,* 172.

11. Ohio Historic Inventory, HAM-18–57, and National Register nomination; Eleanor Gholson Taft, *Hither and Yon on Indian Hill* (Cincinnati: Indian Hill Garden Club, 1962), 77–80; Geoffrey J. Giglierano and Deborah A. Overmyer, *The Bicentennial Guide to Greater Cincinnati: A Portrait of Two Hundred Years* (Cincinnati: Cincinnati Historical Society, 1988), 555.

12. Wayne E. Fuller, *One-Room Schools of the Middle West* (Lawrence: University Press of Kansas, 1994), contends that most of these large bells were rarely rung and that teachers continued to use handbells to call children to class (21–26).

13. Nelson L. Bossing, "History of Educational Legislation in Ohio, 1851–1925," *Ohio Archaeological and Historical Society Publications* 39 (1930): 78–399.

14. Hiram H. Barney, *First Annual Report of the State Commissioner of Common Schools* (Columbus: Statesman Steam Press, 1855), 45–46.

15. Smyth, *Fifth Annual Report of the State Commissioner of Common Schools*, 38.

16. National Register nomination; Robert L. Zorn, "Poland's Little Red Schoolhouse," typescript, rededication program, Sept. 20, 1987, Poland Township Historical Society.

17. National Register nomination.

18. Ohio Historic Inventory, MER-219–14, and National Register nomination.

19. James Johonnot, *Schoolhouses: Architectural Designs by S.E. Hewes* (New York: J. W. Schermerhorn, 1872), 85–97. Double-seat student desks came into use in mid-century to replace the benches common in early one-room schools. Cleveland first used them in 1845 according to Andrew Freese, *Early History of the Cleveland Public Schools* (Cleveland: Robison, Savage and Co, 1876), 29.

20. Orson S. Fowler, *The Octagon House, A Home for All* (1853; rpt. New York: Dover Publications, 1973); Leland M. Roth, *A Concise History of American Architecture* (New York: Harper and Row, 1980), 122.

21. Carl F. Schmidt, *The Octagon Fad* (Scottsville, NY: privately printed, 1958).

22. Barnard, *School Architecture,* 73–75. This design featured a central skylight that was apparently not incorporated at Florence Corners, although the louvered cupola would have made window lights possible.

23. Schmidt, *Octagon Fad,* does not cite a source for his statement that this school was built by "Rant" Collingwood, but he personally measured this building and talked to local residents (102–3). The assertion is supported by the fact that William Collingwood and his sixteen-year-old son, William H., are listed as stonemasons in the 1850 U.S. Population Census, Erie County, Ohio, Florence Township, 421. The household included the elder William's thirteen-year old Joseph and eleven-year-old Ransom. More than a decade later Ransom Collingwood enlisted in Company B of the 3d Ohio Volunteer Infantry.

24. Anna Franklin, *Sandusky Register,* May 5, 1958, 12.

25. *History of Lorain County, Ohio* (Philadelphia: Williams Brothers, 1879), 336–38; G. Frederick Wright, *A Standard History of Lorain County* (Chicago: Lewis Publishing, 1916), 3–8, 533–36. The distinctive color of this sandstone was more blue-gray than beige-brown.

26. National Register nomination. Today this building is well maintained as a private residence, but the cupola has been removed.

27. LeRoy Brown, *Thirtieth Annual Report of the State Commissioner of Common Schools* (Columbus: Myers Bros., 1884), 23.

28. Oak Grove School Contract, Hoopple Ridge, Oct. 15, 1885, vertical file manuscript (VFM), Ohio Historical Society.

29. National Register nomination.

30. Anson Smyth, *Seventh Annual Report of the State Commissioner of Common Schools* (Columbus: Richard Nevins, 1861), 141.

31. Virginia E. McCormick and Robert W. McCormick, *A. B. Graham: Country Schoolmaster and Extension Pioneer* (Worthington, Ohio: Cottonwood Publications, 1984), 54–56.

32. Fletcher B. Dressler, *Rural Schoolhouses and Grounds* (Washington, D.C.: United States Bureau of Education, 1914), Bulletin No. 12.

33. Frank W. Miller, *Sixty-First Annual Report of the Superintendent of Public Instruction* (Springfield, Ohio: The Springfield Publishing, 1915), 9.

Three | FROM GRADED "UNION SCHOOLS" TO "OPEN-SPACE" ELEMENTARY BUILDINGS

1. Miller, "History of Educational Legislation in Ohio," 64–68. From 1840 to 1850 Akron's population increased 96 percent, Secretary of State, *Census of Ohio by Counties and Minor Civil Divisions, 1900* (Columbus: Fred J. Heer, State Printer, 1901), 11.

2. Freese, *Cleveland Public Schools,* 19–21, 83–87. William J. Akers, *Cleveland Schools in the Nineteenth Century* (Cleveland: W. M. Gayne Printing House, 1901), utilizes school managers minutes (15–18); William Ganson Rose, *Cleveland: The Making of a City* (Cleveland: The World Publishing, 1950), uses newspaper descriptions (176). Salary disparities between male and female teachers were standard at the time.

3. Johannesen, "Simeon Porter," *Ohio History;* Freese, *Cleveland Public Schools,* 88–101.

4. Akers, *Cleveland Schools in the Nineteenth Century,* 71–72.

5. Ibid., 131, 136. Urban districts sometimes offered as many as five primary grades and three intermediate or grammar levels. *A History of Education in the State of Ohio* (Columbus: Columbus Gazette, 1876), 117.

6. *Thirty-Fourth Annual Report of the Board of Education* (Cleveland: Fairbanks, Benedict, 1871), 29, 80–84. The *Cleveland Plain Dealer,* Sept. 5, 1868, describes the dedication of the "Hudson Street School," designed by Charles W. Heard and Walter Blythe—then partners—and gives the floor plan and room dimensions pictured for Rockwell (3).

7. *Fortieth Annual Report of the Board of Education* (Cleveland: Robison, Savage, 1877), 48–53; Akers, *Cleveland Schools in the Nineteenth Century,* 163; Leonard P. Ayres and May Ayres, *School Buildings and Equipment* (Cleveland: Survey Committee of Cleveland Foundation, 1916), 11–36. By 1873 Charles W. Heard was largely retired, although he was listed in city directories in partnership with his sons L. Allen Heard and C. Wallace Heard. It is not known whether the firm was still in contract with the Board of Education and responsible for this design.

8. *Annual Report of the Secretary of State on the Condition of Common Schools* (Columbus: Osgood and Blake, 1853). In 1854 Barnard's *School Architecture* was made available to every school district for $1.25 a copy, half of its retail price.

9. Barney, *First Annual Report of the State Commissioner of Common Schools,* 58.

10. Report of the New Philadelphia school district to the secretary of state, contained in the 1853 annual report. A daily average of eighty pupils per teacher suggests this district might have been utilizing some form of the Lancasterian method with older students perhaps hearing recitations of younger scholars in the separate recitation rooms.

11. Ohio Historic Inventory, COS-22–15, and National Register nomination; William E. Hunt, *Historical Collections of Coshocton County, Ohio* (Cincinnati: Robert Clarke, 1876), 132–33; N. N. Hill, *History of Coshocton County, Ohio* (Newark, Ohio: A. A. Graham, 1881), 440; H. Money, "Coshocton City Schools, 1807–1937," typescript, Coshocton Public Library; *Coshocton Tribune,* May 3, 1931; *Coshocton Times Reporter,* Apr. 26, 1971.

12. Ohio Historic Inventory, FRA-22–3, and National Register nomination; receipts relating to the Worthington District School from Mar. 26, 1855 to Aug. 30, 1858, MSS 193, box 6, folder 7, Griswold Papers, Ohio Historical Society.

13. *Columbus Gazette*, Feb. 1, 1861. This two-story, 16½ x 33–foot building was in the block between Third and Fourth Streets, between Long and Spring.

14. Barney, *First Annual Report of the Commissioner of Common Schools*, 34–35.

15. Smyth, *Fifth Report of the State Commissioner of Common Schools*, 73.

16. Barney, *First Annual Report of the Commissioner of Common Schools*, 58–63.

17. The 1870 U.S. Population Census, Crawford County, Ohio, Bucyrus.

18. Ursula Mills, "History of the Union School Building," *Bucyrian,* 1908, the first yearbook published by the senior class of the Bucyrus High School; 1911 photograph, Bucyrus High School, Bucyrus Historical Society, *Scroggs House News* 3 (Fall 1998): 3. This building was more than twenty feet longer than Antioch Hall, but it did not compare with Joseph M. Blackburn's 270–foot Ohio School for the Deaf

19. "Specifications of the Union School Building of Bucyrus, Crawford County, Ohio" prepared by Blackburn and Koehler, Architects, 1868, Ohio Historical Society.

20. General and Local Laws and Joint Resolutions Passed by the General Assembly, Ohio Historical Society, microfilm 249, 66:92–93.

21. *History of Crawford County* (Chicago: Baskin and Battey, 1881), 412–13. By 1880 the school had an enrollment of 949 students—with 85 in the high school department, 142 in the grammar department, 183 in the intermediate department, 427 in the primary department, and 112 in the German-English school. From 1870 to 1873, as an "experiment," the board employed Miss Marcella Swingley as "lady superintendent"—a progressive idea that was apparently not universally accepted by local citizens and lasted only three years.

22. Ohio Historic Inventory, HAM-903–31, and National Register nomination; *Forty-Third Annual Report of the Common Schools of Cincinnati* (Cincinnati: W. A. Stach, Baldwin, 1873).

23. Samuel Hannaford, "School Architecture," in Martin, ed., *History of the Schools of Cincinnati,* 188–92, and in John B. Shotwell, *A History of the Schools of Cincinnati* (Cincinnati:

The School Life Company, 1902), 317–29; "Samuel Hannaford," in Henry F. Withey and Elsie R. Withey, *Biographical Dictionary of American Architects (Deceased)* (Los Angeles: Hennessey and Ingalls, 1970), 261–62; John Clubbe, *Cincinnati Observed: Architecture and History* (Columbus: The Ohio State University Press, 1992), 55.

24. Ohio Historic Inventory, ERI-124–3, and National Register nomination; Report of Ulysses T. Curran, Superintendent, Sandusky, Ohio Public Schools, in *Historical Sketches of Public Schools in Cities, Villages, and Townships of the State of Ohio* (Columbus: State Centennial Educational Committee, 1876).

25. *Local History of the Public School System of the City of Sandusky from 1838 to 1894* (Sandusky: J. F. Mack and Bro., Printers, 1894), 136; Report of Tenth Ward School, 1893–1894; Lewis C. Aldrich, *History of Erie County, Ohio* (1889, rpt.; Evansville Ind.: Unigraphic, 1978), 336–42; *Portraits from the Past* (Sandusky: Sandusky Area Sesquicentennial Committee, 1968), 30–33; Ellie Damm, *Treasures by the Bay: The Historic Architecture of Sandusky, Ohio* (Cranbury, N.J.: Associated University Presses, 1989), 100.

26. National Register nomination; Martha Leonard, *Westervelt Hall: Its First Century* (pamphlet printed by the Times Press, Dec. 12, 1982); Anthony J. Mealy, *Oberlin News Tribune*, Bicentennial Edition, 1983; Geoffrey Blodgett, *Oberlin Architecture, College and Town: A Guide to Its Social History.* (Oberlin: Oberlin College and Kent State University Press, 1985), 108–9.

27. LeRoy Brown, *Thirty-Second Annual Report of the State Commissioner of Common Schools* (Columbus: Myers Bros., 1886), 428–30.

28. Conceived by Lewis Miller, cofounder of the Lake Chautauqua Institute, and first built by Jacob Snyder in 1868 for the First Methodist Church of Akron, the auditorium sanctuary/classroom style quickly became popular with Protestant congregations that emphasized Sunday schools. A. Robert Jaeger, "The Auditorium and Akron Plans—Reflections of a Half Century of American Protestantism," (master's thesis, Cornell University, 1984).

29. Ohio Historic Inventory, SEN-440, and National Register nomination.

30. Rick Cochran, *The Story of Tiffin University* (Tiffin, Ohio: Tiffin University, 1976).

31. Ohio Historic Inventory, ERI-174–3, and National Register nomination; Brown, *Thirty-Second Annual Report of the State Commissioner of Common Schools*, 410–12, 418–22; *Portraits from the* Past; Damm, *Treasures by the Bay*, 102. *History of Sandusky Schools* showed that the Eighth Ward School (Campbell Street School) had 551 pupils in eleven primary and grammar classrooms during 1893–94 (136).

32. Mariana Griswold Van Rensselaer, *Henry Hobson Richardson and His Works* (1888; rpt. New York: Dover Publications, 1969), discusses Richardson's enormous influence on public buildings such as schools and libraries. Paul Clifford Larson, ed., *The Spirit of H.H. Richardson on the Midland Prairies* (Ames: Iowa State University Press, 1988), examines the characteristics of Richardson's work assimilated by Midwestern architects (15–16, 37).

33. "Frank L. Packard," "Joseph W. Yost," in Withey and Withey, *Biographical Dictionary,* 451–52, 676; Charles B. Galbreath, "Frank L. Packard," *Ohio Archaeological and Historical Society Publications* 33 (1924): 106–8.

34. Ohio Historic Inventory, FRA-654–4, and National Register nomination; *Westerville Public Opinion,* Mar. 19, 1896, 1; Julia Morris, "Emerson School: Building Tour," typescript, bicentennial project, 1976; Betty Daft, "Final Bells Toll for 1896 School," *Columbus Dispatch*, June 4, 1976, B-4; Mike Harden, "Emerson School: Memories to Fill a Whole Century," *Columbus Dispatch,* May 19, 1996, I-1; Harold Hancock, *History of Westerville* (Westerville, Ohio: n.p., 1973), 103–6.

35. National Register nomination.

36. National Register nomination; *Wooster Daily Record,* June 28, 1983, Feb. 2, 1984, Apr. 25, 1985; restoration photographs and records at Wayne Center for the Arts in cooperation with the Rubbermaid Corporation.

37. Peter W. Williams, *Houses of God: Region, Religion, and Architecture in the United States* (Urbana: University of Illinois Press, 1997), 17; Louis A. Hoying et al., *Pilgrims All: A History of Saint Augustine Parish, Minster, Ohio* (Minster: Saint Augustine Press, 1982).

38. Ohio Historic Inventory, AUG-13–14, and National Register nomination; *Sidney Daily News,* Bicentennial Edition, July 1, 1976, 86; C. W. Williamson, *History of Western Ohio and Auglaize County* (Columbus: W. M. Linn and Sons, 1905), 831–33; William J. McMurray, *History of Auglaize County, Ohio* (Indianapolis: Historical Publishing, 1923), 1:293–94.

39. The Chickasaw building later became a VFW hall and is pictured in "Yesterday's Dreams—Today's Realities: Chickasaw, Ohio, 1838–1988," edited by Marie McClurg for the community's sesquicentennial celebration.

40. *Laws of Ohio,* microfilm 249, 91:632–33. This legislation was crafted to apply only to this township, but the precedent was established that transportation to school could be provided with public funds.

41. A. B. Graham, *Centralized Schools in Ohio* (Columbus: Ohio State University Extension Bulletin, 1906).

42. National Register nomination.

43. G. Frederick Wright, *A Standard History of Lorain County, Ohio* (Chicago: Lewis Publishing, 1916), 162; *Wellington Enterprise,* Aug. 18, 1915, 3, 8.

44. "Frank S. Barnum," in Withey and Withey, *Biographical Dictionary,* 39.

45. National Register nomination; Eric Johannesen, *Cleveland Architecture, 1876–1976* (Cleveland: Western Reserve Historical Society, 1979), 47; *Ohio Architect and Builder,* 1911.

46. *Cleveland Plain Dealer,* Mar. 5, 1908. This was front-page news in Cleveland for several days to come.

47. Johannesen, *Cleveland Architecture,* 96.

48. John J. Donovan, *School Architecture: Principles and Practices* (New York: Macmillan, 1921), 590–93; William C. Bruce, *Grade School Buildings* (Milwaukee: Bruce Publishing, 1925); John M. Killits, *Toledo and Lucas County, Ohio* (Chicago: S. J. Clarke Publishing, 1923), 1:363–84.

49. Donovan, *School Architecture,* 289–90.

50. McCormick School is discussed as an example of art moderne style in Stephen C. Gordon, *How to Complete the Ohio Historic Inventory* (Columbus: Ohio Historic Preservation Office, Ohio Historical Society, 1992), 114.

51. Ohio Historic Inventory, ERI-1–4; Audrey Mackiewicz, Huron Historical Society, "McCormick School, Ohio St., Huron, Ohio" to author, July 5, 1998. The Huron Historical Society has compiled a video from a home movie made during the construction of this unique building and it is available at Huron Library.

52. The 1,965 school projects funded by the Public Works Administration from 1933 to 1939 allowed the government to wield significant influence on school building design. C. W. Short and R. Stanley Brown, *Public Buildings: A Survey of Architecture, 1933–1939* (Washington, D.C.: Public Works Administration, 1939), xx–xxi.

53. *Open-Space Schools* (Washington, D.C.: American Association of School Administrators, 1971), 14, 41, 108–9.

54. Ibid., 56–57.

55. *American School and University* 62 (Nov. 1989): 54–55. The "Architectural Portfolio" recognition program sponsored annually since 1984 features outstanding elementary, middle, secondary, and higher education buildings constructed during the year, as judged by creative use of interior and exterior space, appropriateness to the region and the site, accessibility to the community, flexibility, and ability to expand.

56. This is the concept recommended by Gary T. Moore and Jeffery A. Lackney, *Educational Facilities for the Twenty-First Century* (Milwaukee: Center for Architecture and Urban Planning Research, 1994).

57. Sutter Park Elementary School (1986) and Bluffsview Elementary School (1990) employed essentially the same design; McCord Middle School (1986) used a variation.

58. This plan was cited for recognition in *American School and University* 66 (Nov. 1993): 38; "Solon Dual School," *Burgess and Niple Facets* (Winter 1991), (Spring 1993): 1–2.

Four | SECONDARY SCHOOLS

1. Thomas Hughes will, Dec. 4, 1824, Hamilton Co. Will Record 1:465, quoted in *The Hughes Alumnal* (Cincinnati: Robert Clarke, 1870), 9–12.

2. Turner, *Campus,* discusses the concept of noble edifices conveying instant credibility and prestige (117). Kenyon Hall, although large enough to qualify, did not exhibit the architectural purity of "venerable" Gothic style. However, Antioch Hall, completed about the same time as Hughes High School and Woodward High School, certainly did.

3. Barnard, *School Architecture,* 260–63; John P. Foote, *The Schools of Cincinnati and Its Vicinity* (Cincinnati: C. F. Bradley and Company's Power Press, 1855), 11–19; Shotwell, *History of the Schools of Cincinnati,* 122–35; Martin, ed., *History of the Schools of Cincinnati,* 42–43; Goss, *Queen City,* 399–404; Giglierano and Overmyer, *Bicentennial Guide to Greater Cincinnati,* 237.

4. *Twenty-Seventh Annual Report of the Common Schools of Cincinnati* (Cincinnati: Gazette Printing, 1856), 79–87; Shotwell, *History of the Schools of Cincinnati,* 135–52; Martin, ed., *History of the Schools of Cincinnati,* 37–41; Goss, *Queen City,* 406–12; Giglierano and Overmyer, *Bicentennial Guide to Greater Cincinnati,* 564.

5. *Twenty-Fifth Annual Report of the Common Schools of Cincinnati* (Cincinnati: Gazette Printing, 1854), 43–45; *Twenty-Sixth Annual Report of the Common Schools of Cincinnati* (Cincinnati: Gazette Printing, 1855), 88–90.

6. Johannesen, "Simeon Porter," *Ohio History;* Akers, *Cleveland Schools in the Nineteenth Century,* 181.

7. Kilner, *History of One- and Two-Room Schoolhouses,* 52–53; Cosmelia Hirst, "Yellow Springs When Young," *Yellow Springs News,* Oct. 15, 1926, 9–11; National Register nomination.

8. Bossing, "History of Educational Legislation in Ohio," 78–219, 223–399.

9. *Pioneer and General History of Geauga County* (Chardin: Geauga County Historical Society, 1953), 231–33; Acts of the Ohio General Assembly, Mar. 26, 1884.

10. LeRoy Brown, *Thirty-First Annual Report of the State Commissioner of Common Schools* (Columbus: Myers Bros., 1885), 432.

11. LeRoy Brown, *Thirty-Second Annual Report of the State Commissioner of Common Schools* (Columbus: Myers Bros., 1886), 406.

12. Ibid., 323, 386–91, 399–40.

13. National Register nomination.

14. Bossing, "History of Educational Legislation in Ohio," 132–33.

15. National Register nomination.

16. John Fleischman, "Raiders of the Lost Art," *Historic Preservation* 49 (May–June 1997): 86.

17. Secretary of State, *Census of Ohio by Counties and Minor Civil Divisions, 1900,* 11.

18. William H. Pierson, Jr., *American Buildings and Their Architects* (Garden City, N.Y.: Doubleday, 1970), 248–55.

19. Carey Boggess, "The New High School," *Springfield High School Herald* 7 (June 1911): 8; "Springfield South High School Rededication Program," Oct. 19, 1980; "Albert Pretzinger," *Memoirs of the Miami Valley,* ed. John C. Hover et al. (Chicago: Robert O. Law, 1919), 3:509–10; *Art Work of Springfield, Ohio* (Chicago: Gravure Illustrations, 1927); Benjamin F. Prince, *A Standard History of Springfield and Clark County, Ohio* (Chicago: American Historical Society, 1922), 177–80.

20. Elsie Ayres Johnson, *Highland Pioneer Sketches and Family Genealogies* (Springfield, Ohio: H. K. Skinner and Son, 1971), 67–69.

21. "William B. Ittner," in Withey and Withey, *Biographical Dictionary*, 316–17.

22. F. R. Harris and William B. Ittner, *The Complete School at Greenfield, Ohio* (Saint Louis: William B. Ittner, 1928), 5; Grace Atkinson Blake, *Art Catalog, Edward Lee McClain High School, Greenfield, Ohio* (1918; rev., Greenfield: Greenfield Printing and Publishing, 1980); *Greenfield Republican*, May 21, 1914, laying cornerstone, Sept. 2, 1915, high school dedication, Nov. 8, 1923, vocational and elementary schools; *McClain High School Dragon,* souvenir issue Dec. 1915.

23. *High School Buildings and Grounds* (Washington, D.C.: United States Bureau of Education, 1922), Bulletin 23; William C. Bruce, *High School Buildings* (Milwaukee: American School Board Journal, 1919), 2:119–22; Donovan, *School Architecture,* 230, 317, 649–52.

24. Harris and Ittner, *Complete School at Greenfield,* 33.

25. *Laws of Ohio,* microfilm 249, 95:71–73.

26. Frederick W. Garber began his career as a draftsman in a Cincinnati ironworks. But after studying at MIT, Garber established a partnership with his brother-in-law Clifford B. Woodward that became recognized for its outstanding schools, churches, offices, and hospitals. *AIA Journal* 16 (1951): 17–18.

27. "East High School, Cincinnati, Ohio," *The American Architect–The Architectural Review* (Apr. 26, 1922): 340–45.

28. National Register nomination; Giglierano and Overmyer, *Bicentennial Guide to Greater Cincinnati*, 359.

29. National Register nomination; Edward T. Heald, *The Stark County Story* (Canton: Stark County Historical Society, 1952).

30. Austin W. Lord and Albert Kelsey, "The Plan of the City of Columbus," typescript, February 1908.

31. National Register nomination; Jeffrey T. Darbee and Nancy A. Recchie, "Education Is the Safeguard of Liberty: A Historical Analysis of Central High School, Columbus, Ohio" (Columbus: Benjamin D. Rickey, 1995), 18.

32. Darbee and Recchie, "Education Is the Safeguard of Liberty," 12–23; William B. Ittner, "The New Washington Gladden High School of Columbus, Ohio," *The American Architect–The Architectural Review*" (Oct. 25, 1922): 348–52. For whatever reason, the initial plan to name this school for Congregational minister and social activist Rev. Washington Gladden was never realized.

33. Emerson Burkhart interview, *Columbus Citizen,* Aug. 16, 1943. The principal had the mural whitewashed four years after its completion, but as part of Central High School's conversion to the Center of Science and Industry it has been removed and restored.

34. Ohio Historic Inventory, BUT-762–9, and National Register nomination; Ralph H. Hetterich, "Hamilton Catholic Hi Is a Beautiful Structure," *Hamilton Journal-News,* Nov. 10, 1923. Hetterich was a member of the first graduating class of this high school, which had been functioning for fifteen years when this building was erected. He served as a member of the design team and wrote this description for the dedication.

35. "Report of the Committee on an Equal Division of the Twelve Years in the Public Schools between the District and High Schools," *National Education Association Proceedings,* July 8–12, 1907, Los Angeles, National Education Association, 705–10.

36. Ohio Historic Inventory, FRA-1292–13.

37. This was Howard Dwight Smith's last commission as architect for the Columbus schools. He joined the faculty of The Ohio State University, where he was already recognized for his design of Ohio Stadium, and became the university's architect until his retirement. A biographical folder of his work is available in The Ohio State University Archives.

38. National Register nomination.

39. Ohio Historic Inventory, MER-36–8, and National Register nomination.

40. A sketch of the DeCurtins family appears in *Mercer County, Ohio History* (Dallas: Taylor Publishing, 1978), although no descendants by that surname have lived in the county for some time (786). There is no doubt that Anton and his sons built churches, carved and painted interior furnishings, and built organs and pews, but there is no evidence that Anton should be referred to as an architect. Fred was raised by a maternal uncle after he was orphaned at the age of ten, appearing in the 1900 U.S. Population Census, Mercer County, Ohio, Marion Township (vol. 107, ED [Enumeration District] 86, p. 9).

41. *Milestones: A History of the State Board of Education in Ohio* (Columbus: Ohio Board of Education, 1989) contains a review of educational legislation from 1956 to 1989; *Toledo Blade,* Mar. 27, May 12, Sept. 3, 1964, Mar. 12, 1965, Apr. 27, 1967, June 2, 1976, June 23, 1978.

42. "Learning in an Open Environment," descriptive brochure produced by the architectural firm of Baxter, Hodell, Donnelly, and Preston about the design of Mariemont High School; *Open-Space Schools* (Washington, D.C.: American Association of School Administrators, 1971). The design was given an award in 1971 by the Ohio Society of the American Institute of Architects.

43. Kurt Iversen, "An Open High School Plan," *Cincinnati Enquirer,* Dec. 6, 1970, F-1; Mary McCarthy, "Open Policy School," *Cincinnati Post and Times-Star,* Oct. 6, 1970, 8.

44. C. E. Sherman, *Original Ohio Land Subdivisions* (1925; rpt. Columbus: Ohio Topographic Survey Report, 1976), 171–73.

45. "Remembering Our Heritage . . . Reaching for the Future," Wapakoneta High School dedication program, Oct. 29, 1989; *American School and University* 63 (Nov. 1990): 153.

46. *American School and University* 65 (Nov. 1992): 132.

47. "Laurence Bradford Perkins," in *Contemporary Architects,* ed. Muriel Emmanuel (New York: Saint James Press, 1993), 746–47; Ralph Johnson, *of Perkins and Will: Buildings and Projects* (New York: Rizzoli International Publications, 1995), 52–67.

48. The concept was praised in "Community Education Village for Perry Local Schools," *American School and University* 62 (Nov. 1989); as educators cited the high school as "an extraordinary project" when it opened in 1993, *American School and University* 67 (Nov.

1994): 54–55; and architects commended it in Nicolai Ouroussoff, "All in One," *Architectural Record* 183 (July 1995).

49. *Columbus Dispatch,* May 19, 1996. This community authority financed streets and fire facilities for the new subdivisions.

50. See Pierson, *American Buildings,* and Turner, *Campus,* for elaboration on the Jeffersonian rectangle as the predominant early-twentieth-century form of the beaux-arts campus plan (317–34; 191).

51. Dedication materials, New Albany Learning Community, Sept. 6, 1996; Lisa K. Zellner, "Education with a Vision toward the Future," *Suburban News,* Aug. 28, 1996; Gary T. Moore and Jeffery A. Lackney, "Design Patterns for American Schools: Responding to the Reform Movement," in Meek, ed., *Designing Places for Learning,* 11–22.

Five | COLLEGES AND UNIVERSITIES

1. Ohio Historic Inventory, ATH-6–7, ATH-7–7, ATH-8–7, and National Register nomination; William E. Peters, *Legal History of Ohio University, Athens, Ohio* (Cincinnati: Western Methodist Book Concern, 1910), 87, 99–106.

2. Johannesen, *Ohio College Architecture,* 7. The Ellias Hasket Derby mansion in Salem, Massachusetts, designed by Samuel McIntire and Charles Bulfinch is featured in Fiske Kimball, *Domestic Architecture of the American Colonies and of the Early Republic* (New York: Dover Publications, 1966), 201.

3. This is based on research of Frank J. Roos, assistant professor of fine arts, "Cutler Hall and the Early History of Ohio University," typescript, Sept. 1971, Ohio University Archives.

4. Roos, "Cutler Hall"; and Thomas N. Hoover, *The History of Ohio University* (Athens: Ohio University Press, 1954), 32–33.

5. Turner, *Campus,* 37.

6. Ohio Historic Inventory, BUT-159–1, BUT-162–1, and National Register nomination; Johannesen, *Ohio College Architecture,* 9–10; *Historical and Biographical Cyclopedia of Butler County, Ohio* (Cincinnati: Western Biographical Publishing, 1882), 58–77.

7. Walter Havinghurst, *The Miami Years, 1809–1959* (New York: G. P. Putnam's Sons, 1958), 37.

8. "Minutes of the Board of Trustees," Miami University, Sept. 25–26, 1827. National Register File, Elliott and Stoddard.

9. George F. Smythe, *Kenyon College: Its First Century* (New Haven: Yale University Press, 1924), 21–30; Turner, *Campus,* 110.

10. Philander Chase, *Bishop Chase's Reminiscences: An Autobiography* (Boston: James B. Dow, 1848). For elaboration of this concept, see Turner, *Campus,* 4.

11. Williams, *Houses of God,* 14.

12. Richard G. Salomon, "Philander Chase, Norman Nash, and Charles Bulfinch: A Study in the Origins of Old Kenyon," MSS 14, box 544, Ohio Historical Society, PA; Johannesen, *Ohio College Architecture,* 10–14; Roth, *Concise History of American Architecture,* 110.

13. Kenyon College issue, *American Antiques Journal* 1, no. 9 (Sept. 1946) 8; Johannesen, *Ohio College Architecture,* 13–14. Despite the elegance of this building, Henry Roberts was known in England for his pioneering efforts for working-class housing in London.

14. John Douglas Forbes, *Victorian Architect: The Life and Work of William Tinsley.* (Bloomington: Indiana University Press, 1953), 3–8, 90; "William Tinsley," in Withey and Withey, *Biographical Dictionary,* 602.

15. Professor Earl Warner, Ohio Wesleyan class of 1926, "Elliott Hall—Ohio Wesleyan University," typescript, 1984, Ohio Wesleyan University Archives; E. T. Nelson, *Fifty Years of History of the Ohio Wesleyan University* (Cleveland: Cleveland Printing and Publishing, 1895), 20–21; Henry C. Hubbart, *Ohio Wesleyan's First Hundred Years* (Delaware: Ohio Wesleyan University, 1943), 7. Records in the university archives indicate that Welch was assisted in the construction by David Floyd and Benjamin and Evan Morgan. For a brief view of Methodist origins in the United States see Russell E. Richey, *Early American Methodism* (Bloomington: Indiana University Press, 1991).

16. Sturges Hall, Ohio Wesleyan University Archives; Johannessen, *Ohio College Architecture,* 18–20.

17. Turner, *Campus,* 38–46; Hamlin, *Greek Revival Architecture,* 173.

18. Johannesen, "Simeon Porter: Ohio Architect," *Ohio History.*

19. "A Walking Guide to Western Reserve Academy," Hudson, Ohio, National Register File. Williams, *Houses of God,* notes the Episcopal Church emphasis on Gothic churches and Congregational preference for Greek Revival.

20. Arthur G. Beach, *A Pioneer College: The Story of Marietta* (Chicago: John F. Cuneo, 1935), 70; *History of Washington County* (Cleveland: H. Z. Williams and Bros., 1881), 401. Johannesen, *Ohio College Architecture,* 24–25, questions a recent paper on Erwin Hall by George Blazer naming William Curtis as the architect but citing no source. Rufus E. Harte indisputably supervised construction.

21. Johannesen, *Ohio College Architecture,* 27–28; National Register nomination; E. I. F. Williams, *Heidelberg: Democratic Christian College, 1850–1950* (Menasha, Wis.: George Banta Publishing Company, 1952), 39–42; Heidelberg College catalog, 1852, 25; *The Heidelberg Bulletin* 14 (Aug. 1929): 4–7.

22. Robert L. Straker, *Horace Mann and Others* (Yellow Springs, Ohio: Antioch Press, 1963), 18–21.

23. Carroll L. V. Meeks, "Romanesque Before Richardson in the United States," *Art Bulletin* 35 (1953), 17–33; Robert Dale Owen, *Hints on Public Architecture* (1849; rpt. New York: DaCapo Press, 1978).

24. W. Boyd Alexander, "The Architectural Ancestry of Antioch Hall," *Antioch Alumni Bulletin,* Feb. 1938; Johannesen, *Ohio College Architecture,* 31–34; Turner, *Campus, 133;* National Register nomination.

25. National Register nomination; Mrs. Peter S. Hitchcock, "Lake Erie Female Seminary from the Beginning," *The Historical Society Quarterly of Lake County* 5 (Feb. 1963); Margaret Manor Butler, *A Pictorial History of the Western Reserve, 1796–1860* (Cleveland: Early Settlers Association of the Western Reserve, 1963), 76, 397.

26. Johannesen, *Ohio College Architecture,* 34–35.

27. Newell Y. Osborne, *A Select School* (Alliance, Ohio: Mount Union College, 1967), 80–85.

28. Johannesen, "Simeon Porter," *Ohio History.*

29. National Register nomination; Johannesen, *Ohio College Architecture,* 37–39; Homer J. Clark et al., *A Condensed History of Mount Union College* (Alliance, Ohio: Mount Union College, 1866), 20.

30. Elias F. Drake, a Xenia attorney, purchased the three parcels comprising this property in 1850 and in December 1851 conveyed the property including Towana House and improvements such as stables, thirty-three lots for cottages, engine and boiler, piano, kitchen and dining room furniture, and carpets and chamber furniture to the Xenia Springs Company, whose articles of association are appended to the deed record. Greene County Deed Records, 26:642–44, 27:594–96.

31. B. W. Arnett and S. T. Mitchell, *The Wilberforce Alumnal: A Comprehensive Review of the Origin, Development and Present Status of Wilberforce University* (Xenia, Ohio: Xenia Gazette, 1885); photograph 4141, sc 1489, Ohio Historical Society.

32. Ibid.; George W. Knight, *The History of Higher Education in Ohio* (Washington, D.C.: Government Printing Office, 1891), 214–25; Joshua H. Jones, "Wilberforce University," *Greene County, 1803–1908* (Xenia, Ohio: Aldine Publishing House, 1906), 179–86; M. A. Broadstone, ed., *History of Greene County, Ohio* (Indianapolis: B. F. Bowen, 1918), 475–83; R. S. Dills, *History of Greene County* (Dayton: Odell and Mayers, 1881), 455–60.

33. *Wilberforce University Bulletin,* 1900–1901, 80; "Minutes, Trustees of the Combined Normal and Industrial Department of Wilberforce University," Aug. 17, Nov. 3, 1904; Frederick A. McGinnis, *A History and an Interpretation of Wilberforce University* (Blanchester, Ohio: Brown Publishing, 1941), 72–73. Professor Lowell W. Baker resigned from Wilberforce in the fall of 1904 to become a "government supervising architect" for the rapidly growing city of Youngstown, Ohio, and was paid $550 by the trustees for the "plans, specifications and detailed drawings," although the work was completed by his successors.

34. Franklin M. Reck, *The 4-H Story: A History of 4-H Club Work* (Ames: Iowa State University Press, 1951), 3–47.

35. *Wilberforce University Bulletin,* 1917–1918, 23, and 1930–1931, 21.

36. Ohio Historic Inventory, fra-646-4, and National Register nomination; Harold Hancock, "Towers from Ashes: The Story of the Building of Towers Hall," *Otterbein Miscellany* (May 1967); sesquicentennial history, Daniel Hurley, *Otterbein College: Affirming Our Past/Sharing Our Future* (Westerville, Ohio: Otterbein College, 1996), 28–30; Johannesen, *Ohio College Architecture,* 42–44.

37. The best analysis of Tinsley's influence on design is Forbes, *Victorian Architect.*

38. The restoration of these literary society rooms is described in *Otterbein Towers* 55 (Summer 1982): 4–5; Hurley, *Otterbein College,* 54.

39. *Westerville Public Opinion,* Sept. 3, 1891.

40. Galbreath, "Frank L. Packard," *Ohio Archaeological and Historical Society Publications;* Joseph W. Yost and Frank L. Packard, *Portfolio of Architectural Realities* (Columbus: Yost and Packard, c. 1900), includes both Orton Hall and University Hall in this photographic portfolio of work completed during their partnership.

41. Turner, *Campus,* 142–50.

42. "The Geological History of Ohio Lies in the Stones of Orton Hall," The Ohio State University Geology Department, n.d., The Ohio State University Archives; Robert E. Samuelson et al., *Architecture Columbus* (Columbus: American Institute of Architects, 1976), 108; James F. Henry, "The Gargoyles of Orton Hall," *Columbus Dispatch Magazine,* Jan. 18, 1948.

43. Thomas C. Mendenhall, ed., *History of The Ohio State University* (Columbus: Ohio State University Press, 1920), vol. 1, 1870–1910; William A. Kinnison, *Building Sullivant's Pyramid: An Administrative History of The Ohio State University, 1870–1907* (Columbus: Ohio State University Press, 1970).

44. This relates to the biblical reference in 1 Kings 7:21.

45. *Ohio Wesleyan Transcript*, 27, June 20, 1893, 1–2; Mary J. Kookootsedes, "A History of Gray Chapel," typescript, 1958, and Heidi Johns, "University Hall, Past and Present," typescript, 1991, both in Ohio Wesleyan University Archives.

46. Lansing C. Holden, a practicing architect in New York City, was the brother of the college president. About the same time George C. Nimmons, a Wooster native then working as an architect in Chicago, designed Taylor Hall and the library building in similar Gothic style. "Lancing C. Holden," "George C. Nimmons," in Withey and Withey, *Biographical Dictionary*, 295, 442.

47. Ralph Adams Cram, "The Work of Messrs. Cope and Stewardson," *Architectural Record* 12 (Nov. 1904): 407–38. Walter Cope and the brothers Emlyn L. and John Stewardson earned recognition for collegiate buildings at Bryn Mawr and Haverford College as well as Princeton. "Walter Cope," "Emyln L. Stewardson," "John Stewardson," in Withey and Withey, *Biographical Dictionary;* 39–40, 573, 574.

48. National Register nomination; Waldo H. Dunn, "The Builder of Wooster," *Wooster Alumni Bulletin* 1 (Jan. 1924): 15–17; Lucy L. Notestein, *Wooster of the Midwest* (1937; rpt. Kent, Ohio: Kent State University Press, 1971); University of Wooster, Catalog, 1902–3, 23–28.

49. Phillip R. Shriver, "From Normal School to University," in *A Book of Memories: The Kent State University, 1910–1992,* ed. William H. Hildebrand, Dean H. Keller, and Anita D. Herington (Kent, Ohio: Kent State University Press, 1993), 15–50.

50. "George F. Hammond," in Withey and Withey, *Biographical Dictionary,* 261–62.

51. Turner, *Campus,* 167 discusses the concept of the university as the city beautiful and relates it to campuses such as Duke University and Stanford University. George Francis Hammond was undoubtedly influenced by the concurrently evolving plans for the Cleveland Mall.

52. Phillip R. Shriver, *The Years of Youth: The Kent State University, 1910–1960* (Kent: The Kent State University Press, 1960), 31–32, 36–39, 43, 48–49, 53, 57–58; *Portage Heritage* (Ravenna, Ohio: Portage County Historical Society, 1957).

53. Turner, *Campus,* 204–9.

54. Geoffrey Blodgett, "Oberlin College Architecture: A Short History," (Oberlin, Ohio: Oberlin College, 1979).

55. "Cass Gilbert," in Withey and Withey, *Biographical Dictionary,* 233–35.

56. Roland M. Baumann, "Guide to the Architectural Records in the Oberlin College Archives," Oberlin College, 1996. Architectural plans for this building are in the "Papers of Cass Gilbert," Record Group 6, number 55, and the "Art Building Construction Papers" are in Record Group 9, number 26, Oberlin College Archives, Oberlin College. Blodgett, *Oberlin Architecture,* 26–27; Campen, *Architecture of the Western Reserve,* 238; Roth, *Concise History of American Architecture,* 348.

57. Geoffrey Blodgett, "Cass Gilbert, Architect: Conservative at Bay," *Journal of American History* 72 (Dec. 1985): 615–36, and "President King and Cass Gilbert: The Grand Collaboration," *Oberlin Alumni Magazine* 79 (Winter 1983): 15–19. It is ironic that the majority of Gilbert's work was in the neoclassical mode, yet he is perhaps best remembered for the steel-frame, terra cotta–clad Woolworth Building in New York City.

58. Ohio Historic Inventory, FRA-2167–3; John P. Kleinz, "The Pontifical College Josephinum," *The Priest* (1956): 568–72; *Barquilla del Santa Maria,* Diocese of Columbus, Apr. 1985, 25–40; "The Jessing Legacy," Pontifical College Josephinum, 1988; *Worthington News,* Apr. 17, Aug. 21, 1930, June 2, Nov. 26, Dec. 3, 1931.

59. Jerome Library file, Bowling Green State University Archives.

60. Student Services Building file, Bowling Green State University Archives.

61. Turner, *Campus*, 251, 264–67.

62. "Colleges for the Community," *Architectural Forum* 111 (Nov. 1959): 132–33.

63. "Campus City, Chicago," *Architectural Forum* 123 (Sept. 1965): 23–44.

64. C. Chester Bussey, *Origin and Development of Sinclair Community College, Dayton, Ohio, 1887–1970* (Dayton: Montgomery County Community College District, 1970); Sinclair Community College website, June 15, 1998; "Edward Durell Stone," in Emmanuel, ed., *Contemporary Architects,* 927–28.

65. Baumann, "Guide to the Architectural Records," Record Group 10, number 28, Conservatory of Music, Oberlin College Archives, contains an extensive photo collection; Campen, *Architecture of the Western Reserve,* 239; Norman Lloyd, "Report from the Conservatory," *Oberlin Alumni Magazine* 60 (May 1964): 4–9; Blodgett, *Oberlin Architecture,* 46–49; "Minoru Yamasaki," in Emmanuel, ed., *Contemporary Architects,* 1069–71.

66. Paul Peng-Chen Sun and Geoffrey Freeman represent the well-known architectural firm of Shepley, Bulfinch, Richardson, and Abbott, whose principals are deceased.

67. Barbara Zollinger Turner, "Two Ambitious New Post-Modern Projects," *Columbus Monthly* 12 (Nov. 1986): 143.

68. Allen Freeman, "Stylistic Shotgun Wedding on a Midwestern Campus," *Architecture* 77 (Feb. 1988): 78–81; "Kenyon College Library," *American School and University* 60 (Nov. 1987): 158; Dedication program, 18 Oct. 1986, Olin and Chalmers Library, Kenyon College Archives. The Gordon Keith Chalmers bequest for the 1962 library building and the Olin Foundation contribution of $5.5 million for the new library dictated that these buildings maintain separate identities.

69. Citation winner, *American Schools and Universities* 66 (Nov. 1993): 50; Website, Ohio Aerospace Institute; Description, Richard Fleischman, Architects.

70. Andreas C. Papadakis, ed., *Wexner Center for the Visual Arts* (New York: St. Martin's Press Academy Editions, 1989). All these essays are helpful but in particular see Charles Jencks, "Eisenman's White Holes," 22–39, and Kurt W. Foster, "A Framework for the Future," 73–79. See also "Eisenman Builds," *Progressive Architecture* 70 (Oct. 1989): 68–89; "Peter Eisenman," in Emmanuel, ed., *Contemporary Architects,* 275–78; and "Wexner Center for the Visual Arts," in Peter Eisenman, *Eisenman Architects: Selected and Current Works* (Mulgrave, Victoria, Australia: The Master Architect Series, The Images Publishing Group, 1995), 112–19.

71. Jack L. Nasar, *Design by Competition: Making Design Competition Work* (Cambridge, Mass.: Cambridge University Press, 1999).

72. Visitor's guide, The University of Toledo Center for the Visual Arts at the Toledo Museum of Art; Michael Webb, "A Man Who Made Architecture an Art of the Unexpected," *Smithsonian* 17 (Apr. 1987): 48–58; "Frank O. Gehry," in Emmanuel, ed., *Contemporary Architects,* 341–44.

73. Thomas Fisher, "Art as Architecture," *Progressive Architecture* 76 (May 1995): 72–77; "Center for the Visual Arts, University of Toledo, Ohio," *Architectural Record* 181 (July 1993): 78–85; Annette LeCuyer, "Frank Gehry Art School for Toledo University [*sic*], Ohio," *The Architectural Review* 193 (Aug. 1993): 28–31; *Toledo Blade,* Apr. 21, 1991, Feb. 3, 1993.

74. David Gosling, "Eisenman Architects: Aronoff Center for Design and Art, University of Cincinnati, 4," *Architectural Design* 67 (Sept.–Oct. 1997): iii–xi.

75. Joseph Giovannini, "Campus Complexity," *Architecture* 85 (Aug. 1996): 116

76. Kurt W. Forster, "Rising from the Land, Sinking into the Ground," in *Eleven Authors in Search of a Building: A Building by Eisenman Architects,* ed. Cynthia C. Davidson (New York: Monacelli Press, 1996), 114–33; Silvia Kolbowski "Fringe Benefits," in *Eleven Authors in Search of a Building,* 136–43.

77. Jeffrey Kipnis, "P-TR's Progress," in Davidson, ed., *Eleven Authors in Search of a Building,* 170.

78. *New York Times,* Oct. 14, 1996, B-1, B-5; "University of Cincinnati Master Plan," University of Cincinnati Website.

79. Gosling, "Eisenman Architects," *Architectural Design.* Unlike distant critics, as the Ohio Eminent Scholar in Urban Design at the University of Cincinnati, Professor Gosling is intimately acquainted with the building.

Six | SPECIAL EDUCATIONAL INSTITUTIONS

1. *History of the Ohio Institution for the Education of the Deaf and Dumb.* There is not an author or publisher, but this book was apparently written by Superintendent G. L. Smead in 1876. See also *Historical and Biographical Souvenir of the Ohio School for the Deaf* (Columbus: C. C. Johnson, Printers, 1898); *Manual and History of the State School for the Deaf* (Columbus: School Printing Department, 1911).

2. *Thirty-Eighth Annual Report of the Ohio Institution for the Education of the Deaf and Dumb* (Columbus: Columbus Printing, 1864), 28–35; *Thirty-Ninth Annual Report of the Ohio Institution for the Education of the Deaf and Dumb,* 26–31; *Laying of the Cornerstone of the Ohio Institution for the Education of the Deaf and Dumb* (Columbus: Richard Nevins, 1864).

3. *Forty-First Annual Report of the Ohio Institution for the Education of the Deaf and Dumb,* 9–10; *Forty-Second Annual Report of the Ohio Institution for the Education of the Deaf and Dumb,* 5–6. Several sources have erroneously credited George Bellows, Sr., as the architect of this building, apparently from a verbal comment to a reporter after the building had burned and his son had become a well-known artist. The 1864 annual report of the deaf school trustees and superintendent describes Blackburn's hiring and his design for the building. A handwritten ledger at the Ohio Historical Society stamped "J. M. Blackburn, Architect and Superintendent" contains construction expenditures. The only entry for George Bellows, Sr., is a payment on February 24, 1868, of $7.80 for "sundry charges"—an insignificant amount in comparison with the hundreds and thousands being paid to various suppliers and construction workers (51). Further, Bellows cannot be credited with completing the job when Blackburn was dismissed since the 1869 report credits Trustee H. F. Booth with managing the project's completion.

4. The forty-fourth trustees report (1870) was the first to contain a lithograph by John Barrick (a deaf-mute former student), a floor plan, and a complete description of the building, but these were repeated in subsequent reports for several years.

5. The new building opened May 21, 1874. *History of the Ohio Institution for the Education of the Blind.* There is not an author or publisher, but this was apparently an 1876 report by Superintendent G. L. Smead. Samuelson et. al., *Architecture Columbus,* 165.

6. *Thirty-Sixth Annual Report of the Ohio Institution for the Education of the Blind* (Columbus: Nevins and Myers, 1873), 9; *Thirty-Eighth Annual Report of the Ohio Institution for the Education of the Blind,* 8–11.

7. "George H. Bulford," "Clarence E. Richards," in Withey and Withey, *Biographical Dictionary,* 92, 506.

8. *Columbus Dispatch,* Oct. 18, 1899, 8; Samuelson et al., *Architecture Columbus,* 172–73.

9. *Historical and Biographical Souvenir;* James J. Burns, *Educational History of Ohio* (Columbus: Historical Publishing, 1905), 269–72.

Seven | LIBRARIES

1. Mike Lafferty, "Belpre Library Is a Pioneer 200 Years Old," *Columbus Dispatch,* Apr. 8, 1995.

2. George W. Knepper, *Ohio and Its People* (Kent, Ohio: Kent State University Press, 1989), 197; William T. Utter, *A History of the State of Ohio: The Frontier State, 1803–1825* (Columbus: Ohio State Archaeological and Historical Society, 1942), 413–14; Sarah J. Cutler, "The Coonskin Library," *Ohio State Archaeological and Historical Quarterly* 26 (1917): 58–77.

3. Virginia E. McCormick and Robert W. McCormick, *New Englanders on the Ohio Frontier: Migration and Settlement of Worthington, Ohio* (Kent, Ohio: Kent State University Press, 1998), 53, citing Scioto Company Minutes for Dec. 23, 1803.

4. Kenneth A. Breisch, *Henry Hobson Richardson and the Small Public Library in America* (Cambridge: MIT Press, 1997), 7–8.

5. Fowler, *Octagon House;* Barnard, *School Architecture,* 73–75.

6. James E. Schwartz, "Lane Public Library: Commemorating the Years, 1866–1997," Lane Public Library, Hamilton, Ohio; "Greater Hamilton Edition," *Hamilton Republican-News,* Feb. 3, 1947, 100; *Hamilton Telegraph,* Nov. 15, 1866; *Centennial History of Butler County, Ohio* (N.p.: B. F. Bowen, 1905), 243–44.

7. W. H. Venable, "Public Libraries of Cincinnati," in *Public Libraries in the United States of America: Their History, Condition, and Management* (Washington, D.C.: United States Bureau of Education, 1876), 898–917; "James W. McLaughlin," in Withey and Withey, *Biographical Dictionary,* 413. McLaughlin was one of the Queen City's most esteemed architects, that same year winning commissions for the art museum at Eden Park and the city opera house.

8. Ohio cities with public libraries in 1876 were Akron, Chillicothe, Cincinnati, Circleville, Cleveland, Columbus, Fremont, Hamilton, Medina, Springfield, and Toledo. Bureau of Education Report, "General Statistics of all Public Libraries in the United States," in *Public Libraries in the United States,* 1105–13. Ohio had an additional thirty-eight subscription libraries and 173 academic libraries.

9. Abigail A. Van Slyck, "'The Utmost Amount of Effectiv [*sic*] Accommodation': Andrew Carnegie and the Reform of the American Library," *Journal of the Society of Architectural Historians* 50 (Dec. 1991): 359–83.

10. Justin Windsor, "Library Buildings," in *Public Libraries in the United States of America,* 466, 472.

11. Librarians of this period, such as Justin Windsor and William Frederick Poole, did not allow public access to the shelves of books that patrons could borrow but required retrieval by pages. Scholars, however, could work at tables in reading alcoves among the books they were using. There is irony in the reversal for modern libraries that allow public access to books available for loan but closed stacks in reference libraries and rare book rooms designed for scholarly research.

12. William Frederick Poole, "Small Library Buildings," *Library Journal* 10 (1885): 250; Kenneth A. Breisch, "William Frederick Poole and Modern Library Architecture," in *Modern Architecture in America: Visions and Revisions,* ed. R. G. Wilson and S. G. Robinson (Ames: Iowa State University Press, 1991), 52–72.

13. Breisch, *Richardson and the Small Public Library in America,* 13–14.

14. John P. Gibboney and John L. Eberts, "The Influence of H. H. Richardson on the Architecture of Springfield, Ohio," typescript, National Register nomination. Richardson designed a residence for the Warder family in Washington, D.C., and the Springfield, Ohio, residence of Governor Asa Bushnell. Although Richardson died four years before this library was built, his son-in-law's firm, Shepley, Rutan, and Coolidge perpetuated his style. "George F. Shepley," in Withey and Withey, *Biographical Dictionary,* 550–51. See Larson, ed., *Spirit of H. H. Richardson,* regarding Richardson's influence on Midwestern architecture in the decade following his death (19).

15. John Ruskin, *The Stones of Venice* (New York: Dutton, 1907).

16. Breisch, *Richardson and the Small Public Library in America,* 194–201.

17. When the library was recently replaced by a larger modern facility, this building became the home of a countywide literacy training program.

18. Ohio General Assembly, Apr. 26, 1898.

19. Saida Brumback Antrim and Ernest Irving Antrim, *The County Library: The Pioneer County Library and the County Library Movement in the United States* (Van Wert: Pioneer Press, 1914); Mary B. Maturi and Richard J. Maturi, *Cultural Gems: An Eclectic Look at Unique United States Libraries* (Cheyenne, Wyo.: Twenty-First-Century Publications, 1996). The Brumback Library is the subject of the first and the inspiration for the second reference mentioned here, the latter of which features the library on the cover.

20. Abigail A. Van Slyck, *Free to All: Carnegie Libraries & American Culture, 1890–1920* (Chicago: University of Chicago Press, 1995).

21. Chleo Deshler Goodman, "History of Carnegie Public Library of East Liverpool," typescript, May 1962, National Register nomination.

22. Bobinski, *Carnegie Libraries,* 78; David A. Simmons, "Carnegie Libraries in Ohio," *Ohio Historical Society Echoes* (Apr. 1981): 5–6. Mary Ellen Armentrout, an Otterbein College librarian who is currently researching Carnegie libraries in Ohio, places this figure at $56 million and 1,679 libraries in the United States, *The Chronicle of Higher Education,* Aug. 8, 1997, B2.

23. "Charles H. Owsley," in Withey and Withey, *Biographical Dictionary,* 451.

24. Goodman, "History of Carnegie Public Library of East Liverpool."

25. Reverend Gladden's article "Tainted Money" was published in *Outlook* in 1895, and the questions he raised about the ethics of accepting such philanthropy are discussed by Van Slyck, *Free to All,* 19.

26. Ralph Munn, "Hindsight on the Gifts of Carnegie," *Library Journal* 76 (Dec. 1, 1951): 1966–70. Van Slyck, *Free to All,* discusses the conflicts this policy raised with women's groups that had been the primary force in operating voluntary library associations prior to this time (77).

27. Bobinski, *Carnegie Libraries,* indicates that only 27 percent of the libraries funded by Carnegie used his name on their building (105).

28. Simmons places the number of Carnegie libraries in Ohio at 109 in 81 communities, Armstrong at 115. Bobinski, *Carnegie Libraries,* says Ohio ranked third among all states in the total funds received and fifth in the number of libraries, with 105 buildings in 77 communities (16–20). The discrepancy probably lies in the distinction between community and

college libraries—both funded by Carnegie in Ohio—and between single buildings and communities that had several branches funded by Carnegie.

29. Bobinski, *Carnegie Libraries,* app.; Robert M. Lester, *Carnegie Grants for Library Buildings* (New York: Carnegie Corporation, 1943).

30. Ohio Historic Inventory, ERI-19–3, and National Register nomination; Hewson Lindsay Peeke, *Centennial History of Erie County* (Cleveland: Firelands Historical Society, 1925), 286–87; Damm, *Treasures by the Bay,* 107.

31. *Sandusky Register,* July 10, 1901, 7. A picture and floor plans of this library appear in Charles C. Soule, "Modern Library Buildings," *Architectural Review* 9 (Jan. 1902): 1–60.

32. East Liverpool had requested and been denied an art school to support their ceramic industry as part of their Carnegie library grant.

33. In 1915 the Carnegie Foundation issued six possible designs for small community libraries with a basement and single story. James Bertram, "Notes on the Erection of Library Buildings," in Van Slyck, *Free to All,* 38–39. New York architect Edward L. Tilton became friends with Bertram and obtained numerous commissions for Carnegie library buildings, including Carnegie West Branch Library in Cleveland and the one at Warren, Ohio.

34. Bobinski, *Carnegie Libraries,* 67, 64.

35. Eric Johannesen, "The Architectural Legacy of Guy Tilden of Canton," *Ohio History* 82 (Summer–Fall 1973): 124–41.

36. National Register nomination; Heald, *The Stark County Story,* 519–20.

37. *Bucyrus Journal,* May 13, 1904; *Bucyrus Telegraph-Forum,* sesquicentennial issue, June 21, 1971; "Bucyrus Public Library," special newspaper supplement for grand opening of library addition, Oct. 15, 1989; John E. Hopley, *History of Crawford County, Ohio, and Representative Citizens* (Chicago: Richmond-Arnold Publishing, 1912); Maturi and Maturi, *Cultural Gems.*

38. The Mansfield library was completed in 1908 with a $37,000 Carnegie grant. It is pictured in Simmons, "Carnegie Libraries in Ohio," 6; "Vernon Redding," in Withey and Withey, *Biographical Dictionary,* 498.

39. "Paulding County Carnegie Library History," prepared by Director Susan Hill for the eighty-fifth anniversary celebration; National Register nomination. There are numerous historic ties between the Van Wert and Paulding communities, with George Marsh, father of George H. Marsh who established Van Wert's charitable foundation, being one of the pioneers who platted Paulding in 1850.

40. The Columbus architectural firm of Howard and Merriam is perhaps best known for designing the Rutherford B. Hayes Memorial Library in Fremont, the first presidential library in the country. Hank Harvey, "The Libraries That Carnegie Built," *Toledo Blade Magazine,* Jan. 12–18, 1986, 7–14.

41. Samuel E. Morrison, Henry S. Commager, and William E. Leuchtenburg, *The Growth of the American Republic* (New York: Oxford University Press, 1969; 6th ed.), 312–13.

42. Van Slyck, *Free to All,* 28–34.

43. Bobinski, *Carnegie Libraries,* 195.

44. Ibid., app.

45. "Edward L. Tilton," in Withey and Withey, *Biographical Dictionary,* 601. Tilton trained with the famed New York firm of McKim, Mead, and White, studied at the Paris École des Beaux-Arts, and worked in partnership with William A. Boring on the Ellis Island building. Late in his career he specialized in the design of library buildings.

46. Wilton S. Tifft, *Ellis Island* (Chicago: Contemporary Books, 1990), 48–53; *Cleveland Plain Dealer,* May 5, 23, 25, 1910. The National Register nomination for the Ohio City

Historic District in Cleveland contains historical material on this community west of the river that was incorporated in 1836, had an industrial boom both before and after the Civil War, and has been home to successive waves of immigrants from Irish to Hungarian to Puerto Rican. See Steve Ferguson, "Secret on Cleveland's West Side," reprinted by the Ohio City Redevelopment Association from *Western Reserve Magazine.*

47. Historical folder, Carnegie West Branch Library; 1910 Annual Report, Cleveland Public Library, 61–65. The renovation is described in *New Public Library Buildings,* vol. 2 (New York: Library Journal Special Report, 1980).

48. As early as 1895 the Cleveland Architectural Club held a competition to design a plan to group public buildings in a manner similar to the neoclassical buildings in the Court of Honor at the Columbian Exposition. William H. Wilson, *The City Beautiful Movement* (Baltimore: Johns Hopkins University Press, 1989), 61–62; Roth, *Concise History of American Architecture,* 215–20.

49. Daniel Burnham, John Carrere, and Arnold Brunner, *Report on the Group Plan of Public Buildings of the City of Cleveland, Ohio* (Cleveland, 1903); Arnold Brunner, "Cleveland's Group Plan," *Proceedings of the Eighth National Conference on City Planning, Cleveland, June 5–7, 1916* (New York: Douglas C. McMurtrie, 1916), 14–24.

50. Frank R. Walker and Harry E. Weeks were both natives of Pittsfield, Massachusetts, but they spent their architectural careers in Cleveland. "Frank R. Walker," "Harry E. Weeks," in Withey and Withey, *Biographical Dictionary,* 624–25, 640. The definitive portrayal of their work is Eric Johannesen, *A Cleveland Legacy: The Architecture of Walker and Weeks* (Kent, Ohio: Kent State University Press, 1999), 5–12.

51. National Register nomination, Cleveland Mall; *Guide to Cleveland and Cuyahoga County* ([Cleveland]: Federal Writer's Project, 1936), pt 1, 190–200, pt. 2, 226–29.

52. See Johannesen, *Cleveland Legacy,* 68–71. William Brett was killed in a traffic accident before the library was completed, but the concept of subject matter divisions thrived under his successor, Linda Eastman. Floor plans are included in Linda A. Eastman, "Cleveland's New Public Library," *Library Journal* 50 (June 1, 1925): 491–92, and "Some Features of the New Cleveland Library," *Library Journal* 50 (Nov. 15, 1925): 943–48. See also C. H. Cramer, *Open Shelves and Open Minds: A History of the Cleveland Public Library* (Cleveland: Case Western Reserve University, 1972), 138–45; Donald Oehlerts, *Books and Blueprints: Building America's Public Libraries* (New York: Greenwood Press, 1991), 86–87.

53. Cramer, *Open Shelves,* 119. Van Slyck, *Free to All,* emphasizes the role of branch libraries and bookmobiles in responding to social reformers of the Progressive Era (101).

54. A. E. Bostwick, *The American Public Library* (New York: D. Appleton, 1910), 8–9.

55. Lyle Koehler, *A History of Westwood in Ohio* (Cincinnati: Westwood Civic Association, 1981), 59–78; *A Decade of Service, 1930–1940* (Cincinnati: Public Library of Cincinnati and Hamilton County, 1941), 36; *Achievement in Western Hills* (Cincinnati: Ohio Book, 1932), 100.

56. The National Register nomination for the Westwood Historic District compares this library to Frank Lloyd Wright's Unitarian church at Oak Park, but it is a comparison of overall impression rather than architectural details.

57. *Cincinnati Enquirer,* May 26, 1931, 7.

58. Short and Brown, *Public Buildings,* 26, 52, 54, 66.

59. *Toledo Blade,* Dec. 14, 1938, May 10, 1940, Sept. 5, 1940; Russell J. Schunk, "The Toledo Public Library," *Library Journal* 66 (Feb. 15, 1941): 155–58.

60. J. D. Hinr, "Glass Murals of the Toledo Public Library," typescript, 1948, Toledo Public Library; "Varied Applications of Glass Mark Toledo Library Building," *Ohio Architect*

1 (Sept. 1940), 12; J. R. Hildebrand, "Glass Goes to Town," *National Geographic* 83 (Jan. 1943): 1–48.

61. Oehlerts, *Books and Blueprints,* 95.

62. Historical background in the dedication program, Findlay–Hancock County Public Library, 1991, indicates Findlay established a public library in 1905 in the basement of the courthouse and later moved it to an old post office building. Carnegie offered the community $35,000 for a library building, but they were unable to provide a site and the 10 percent annually for operating expenses. Since 1968 *Library Journal* has devoted a portion of its December issue to summarizing new and renovated library construction nationally, with statistics regarding costs and space, architects, and pictures of exceptional buildings or features. This library was featured in *Library Journal* 117 (Dec. 1992): 58, 65.

Eight | MUSEUMS, OPERA HOUSES, AND CONSERVATORIES

1. *Dayton Journal,* Jan. 1, 1866.

2. National Register nomination; Charlotte R. Conover, *Dayton, Ohio: An Intimate History* (New York: Lewis Historical Publishing, 1932); "John Rouzer," *The History of Montgomery County, Ohio* (Chicago: W. H. Beers, 1882), 606; "Victory Theatre Becomes a Winner," *Commercial Remodeling* (Dec. 1981).

3. National Register nomination; Joseph S. Stern, Jr., "The Queen of the Queen City: Music Hall," *Cincinnati Historical Society Bulletin* 31 (Spring 1973): 7–27; Judith Spraul, "Cultural Boosterism: The Construction of Music Hall," *Cincinnati Historical Society Bulletin* 34 (Feb. 1976): 189–203; Robert Thomas Gifford, "The Cincinnati Music Hall and Exhibition Buildings" (master's thesis, Cornell University, 1973); "Springer Music Hall and Exposition Buildings," *American Architect and Building News*, Apr. 27, 1878; *Cincinnati Commercial,* May 14, 1878.

4. *Cincinnati Daily Enquirer,* Apr. 9, 1878, 8; Goss, *Queen City,* 466–70; Giglierano and Overmyer, *Bicentennial Guide to Greater Cincinnati,* 100–101; Shotwell, *History of the Schools of Cincinnati,* 468.

5. *Middletown Daily Signal,* Sept. 14, 1891.

6. Ohio Historic Inventory, BUT-125–8, and National Register nomination; Sam Ashworth, *A History of Sorg's Opera House, Middletown, Ohio* (Middletown: Fool's Press, 1991), 5–6, 23–24, 31–34, 44, 53, 58–59; George Crout, *Historic South Main Street* (Middletown, Ohio: City of Middletown, 1977).

7. National Register nomination; *McConnelsville Democrat,* July 18, 1890, June 19, 1891, July 24, 1891, Aug. 14, 1891, Sept. 21, 1891, Nov. 6, 1891, May 28, 1892, and collections of Opera House, from Galen Finley, owner/manager from 1962 to 1992 during its renovation. Note that this building opened with electric lights four years before any Columbus theater was so equipped.

8. National Register nomination; *Columbus Dispatch,* Nov. 26, 1894, 6; Ronald M. Traub, "A Myth Laid to Rest: The Origins of the Franklin Park Conservatory," paper for Architecture 694 seminar, Ohio State University, Autumn 1974. Traub effectively disproves the myth that the Columbian Exposition building was dismantled and moved to Columbus.

9. Huber H. Bancroft, *The Book of the Fair* (Chicago: Bounty Books, 1893). Horticultural Hall was 250 by 1,000 feet.

10. "Edward B. Green," in Withey and Withey, *Biographical Dictionary,* 249.

11. The Sunday *Dayton Journal,* Jan. 5, 1930, devoted an entire section to pictures and articles describing the opening of this building. See also Conover, *Dayton, Ohio,* 211–27; "Dayton Art Institute," *Architectural Forum* 56 (June 1932), 556–58; *Art Digest* 4 (Feb. 1, 1930): 14, 8 (Aug. 1934): 18; *Art News* 28 (Mar. 29, 1930): 28; *Museum News* 7 (Mar. 15, 1930): 2; Campen, *Architecture of the Western Reserve,* 177.

12. *Dayton Journal,* Jan. 8, 1930, 1.

13. Edward Keegan, "Street Performance," *Architecture* 85 (Nov. 1996): 120–27; "Cesar Pelli," in Emmanuel, ed., *Contemporary Architects,* 613–15. Argentinian architect Cesar Pelli utilized the modern technology of perforated aluminum in the proscenium arches of the Aronoff Center, but the design derives from the Chicago Auditorium that also inspired the Southern Theatre.

14. At the time the Southern Hotel and attached Southern Theatre were designed, Joseph Dauben was serving as the building inspector for the city of Columbus and David Riebel was the architect for the Columbus Board of Education. Both were concerned for safety in public buildings. National Register nomination; Roth, *Concise History of American Architecture,* 178–80; Robert Albrecht, "From Dazzling Beautiful to Brink of Extinction . . . and Back," Nancy Gilson, "Cascading Arches Point to Architectural Significance," *Columbus Dispatch,* Sept. 20, 1998, H6–7; Rosa Stolz, "Southern Theatre History," Columbus Association for the Performing Arts, Sept. 1998; Debbie Gebolys, "Grand Dame of Downtown," *Columbus Dispatch,* Nov. 30, 1977, H1; Barbara Zuck, "Southern Theatre: A Rare Find," *Columbus Dispatch,* Apr. 4, 1982; Marcia A. Siena, "The History of the Great Southern Theater, Columbus, Ohio" (master's thesis, Ohio State University, 1957); Phil Sheridan, *Those Wonderful Old Downtown Theaters* (Columbus: privately printed, 1978), 175–86.

15. *Columbus Dispatch,* Sept. 21, 1896, Oct. 1, 1896, Dec. 10–12, 1896.

Selected Bibliography

TYPESCRIPT MANUSCRIPTS AND NEWSPAPER FEATURES

Baumann, Roland M. "Guide to the Architectural Records in the Oberlin College Archives." Oberlin College, 1996.

Bicentennial Edition, *Sidney Daily News,* July 1, 1976.

Boggess, Carey. "The New High School." *Springfield High School Herald,* June 7, 1911.

"Bucyrus Public Library." Special edition, *Bucyrus Telegraph-Forum,* Oct. 15, 1989.

Daft, Betty. "Final Bells Toll for 1896 School." *Columbus Dispatch,* June 4, 1976.

"Dayton Art Institute." Special edition, *Dayton Journal,* Jan. 5, 1930.

DeGraw, Ed. "Ragersville: 150 Exciting Yesterdays," *Dover Times Reporter,* July 30, 1980.

"East High School, Cincinnati, Ohio." *The American Architect–The Architectural Review,* Apr. 26, 1922.

"First Free Black School in Ohio." Harveysburg Community Historical Society.

Gibbony, John P., and John L. Eberts, "The Influence of H. H. Richardson on the Architecture of Springfield, Ohio." Typescript. National Register nomination for Warder Library.

Gilson, Nancy. "Cascading Arches Point to Architectural Significance." *Columbus Dispatch,* Sept. 20, 1998.

Goodman, Chleo Deshler. "History of Carnegie Public Library of East Liverpool." Typescript, May 1962, National Register nomination for East Liverpool Carnegie Library.

Harden, Mike. "Emerson School: Memories to Fill a Whole Century." *Columbus Dispatch,* May 19, 1996.

Hetterich, Ralph H. "Hamilton Catholic Hi Is a Beautiful Structure." *Hamilton Journal News,* Nov. 10, 1923.

Henry, James F. "The Gargoyles of Orton Hall." *Columbus Dispatch Magazine,* Jan. 18, 1948.

Hinr, J. D. "Glass Murals of the Toledo Public Library." Typescript, 1948. Toledo Public Library.

Hirst, Cosmelia. "Little Antioch School." *Yellow Springs News,* Oct. 15, 1926.

———. "Yellow Springs When Young." *Yellow Springs News,* Oct. 15, 1926.

Ittner, William B. "The New Washington Gladden High School at Columbus, Ohio," *The American Architect–The Architectural Review,* Oct. 22, 1922

Iversen, Kurt. "An Open High School Plan." *Cincinnati Enquirer,* Dec. 6, 1970.

Johns, Heidi. "University Hall, Past and Present." Typescript, 1991. Ohio Wesleyan University archives.

Kookootsedes, Mary J. "A History of Gray Chapel." Typescript, 1958. Ohio Wesleyan University archives.

Lafferty, Mike. "Belpre Library Is a Pioneer 200 Years Old." *Columbus Dispatch,* Apr. 8, 1995.

Leonard, Martha. "Westervelt Hall: Its First Century." 1927. Rpt. *Oberlin College Times,* Dec. 12, 1982

Marsh Foundation School Yearbook, Van Wert, 1927.

McCarthy, Mary. "Open Policy School." *Cincinnati Post and Times-Star,* Oct. 6, 1970.

McClurg, Marie, ed. "Yesterday's Dreams—Today's Realities: Chickasaw, Ohio, 1838–1988." Mercer County Historical Society.

Mealy, Anthony J. Bicentennial Edition. *Oberlin News Tribune,* 1983.

Money, H. "Coshocton City Schools. 1807–1893." Typescript. Coshocton Public Library.

Morris, Julia. "Emerson School: Building Tour." Westerville Public Library.

"Remembering Our Heritage . . . Reaching for the Future." Wapakoneta High School dedication program, Oct. 29, 1989.

Roos, Frank J. "Cutler Hall and the Early History of Ohio University." Typescript. Ohio University Archives.

Salomon, Richard G. "Philander Chase, Norman Nash, and Charles Bulfinch: A Study in the Origins of Old Kenyon." Ohio Historical Society, PA box 544.

"The Geological History of Ohio Lies in the Stones of Orton Hall." Geology department. Typescript. Ohio State University archives.

Traub, Ronald M. "A Myth Laid to Rest: The Origins of the Franklin Park Conservatory." Architecture 694 term paper, Autumn 1974, Ohio State University.

Warner, Earl. "Elliott Hall—Ohio Wesleyan University." Ohio Wesleyan University Archives.

Wegandt, W. A. "Van Wert Citizens Vie with Each Other in Public Philanthropies." *Cleveland Plain Dealer Magazine,* Jan. 20, 1935.

Zellner, Lisa K. "Education with a Vision toward the Future." *Suburban News,* Aug. 28, 1996.

Zorn, Robert L. "Poland's Little Red Schoolhouse." Poland Township Historical Society, Rededication Program, 20 Sept. 1987.

Zuck, Barbara. "Southern Theatre a Rare Find." *Columbus Dispatch,* 4 Apr. 1982.

BOOKS, THESES, AND JOURNAL ARTICLES

Achievement in Western Hills. Cincinnati: Ohio Book, 1932.

Akers, William J. *Cleveland Schools in the Nineteenth Century.* Cleveland: W. M. Gayne Printing House, 1901.

Aldrich, Frederic C. *The School Library in Ohio with Special Emphasis on Its Legislative History.* New York: Scarecrow Press, 1959.

Aldrich, Lewis C. *History of Erie County, Ohio.* 1889. Rpt. Evansville, Ind.: Unigraphic, 1978.

Alexander, W. Boyd. "The Architectural Ancestry of Antioch Hall." *Antioch Alumni Bulletin* (Feb. 1938).

Annual Report of the Board of Education. Cleveland: Board of Education, 1871–77.

Annual Report of the Board of Trustees of the Ohio Institution for the Education of the Blind. Columbus: State Printer, 1873–75.

Annual Report of the Board of Trustees of the Ohio Institution for the Education of the Deaf and Dumb. Columbus: State Printer, 1864–70.

Annual Report of the Common Schools of Cincinnati. Cincinnati: Board of Education, 1853–75.

Annual Report of the Secretary of State on the Condition of Common Schools. Columbus: Osgood and Blake, 1853.

Annual Report of the State Commissioner of Common Schools. Columbus: State Department of Education, 1854–1912.

Annual Report of the State Superintendent of Public Instruction. Columbus: State Department of Education, 1912–41.

Antrim, Saida Brumback, and Ernest Irving Antrim. *The County Library: The Pioneer County Library and the County Library Movement in the United States.* Van Wert, Ohio: Pioneer Press, 1914.

"Architectural Portfolio." *American School and University.* 1984–.

Arnett, B. W., and S. T. Mitchell. *The Wilberforce Alumnal: A Comprehensive Review of the Origin, Development, and Present Status of Wilberforce University.* Xenia, Ohio: Xenia Gazette, 1885.

Arp, Julius B. *Rural Education and the Consolidated School.* Yonkers-on-Hudson, N.Y.: World, 1918.

Art Work of Springfield, Ohio. Chicago: Gravure Illustrations, 1927.

Ashworth, Sam. *A History of Sorg's Opera House, Middletown, Ohio.* Middletown: Fool's Press, 1991.

Ayres, Leonard P., and May Ayres. *School Buildings and Equipment.* Cleveland: Survey Committee of Cleveland Foundation, 1916.

Bancroft, Huber H. *The Book of the Fair.* Chicago: Bounty Books, 1893.

Barnard, Henry. *School Architecture, Or, Contributions to the Improvement of School Houses in the United States.* 6th ed. Cincinnati: H. W. Derby, 1854.

Beach, Arthur G. *A Pioneer College: The Story of Marietta.* Chicago: John F. Cuneo, 1935.

Benjamin, Asher. *The Practical House Carpenter.* 1830. Rpt. New York: Dover Publications, 1988.

Blake, Grace Atkinson. *Art Catalog, Edward Lee McClain High School, Greenfield, Ohio.* 1918. Rev. ed. Greenfield: Greenfield Printing and Publishing, 1980.

Blodgett, Geoffrey. "Cass Gilbert, Architect: Conservative at Bay." *Journal of American History* 72 (Dec. 1985).

———. *Oberlin Architecture, College and Town: A Guide to Its Social History.* Oberlin, Ohio: Oberlin College and Kent State University Press, 1985.

———. "Oberlin College Architecture: A Short History." Oberlin: Oberlin College, 1979.

———. "President King and Cass Gilbert: The Grand Collaboration." *Oberlin Alumni Magazine* 79 (Winter 1983).

Bobinski, George S. *Carnegie Libraries: Their History and Impact on American Public Library Development.* Chicago: American Library Association, 1969.

Bossing, Nelson L. "History of Educational Legislation in Ohio, 1851–1925." *Ohio Archaeological and Historical Society Publications* 39 (1930).

Bostwick, A. E. *The American Public Library.* New York: D. Appleton, 1910.

Breisch, Kenneth A. *Henry Hobson Richardson and the Small Public Library in America.* Cambridge, Mass.: MIT Press, 1997.

———. "William Frederick Poole and Modern Library Architecture." *Modern Architecture in America: Visions and Revisions,* edited by R. G. Wilson and S. G. Robinson. Ames: Iowa State University Press, 1991.

"Brief History of Twinsburgh Institute." *Historical Sketches of the Higher Educational Institutions, and also of Benevolent and Reformatory Institutions.* Columbus: State Centennial Educational Committee, 1876.

Briggs, Warren R. *Modern American School Buildings.* New York: J. Wiley and Sons, 1899.

Broadstone, M. A., ed. *History of Greene County, Ohio.* Indianapolis: F. Bowen, 1918.

Bruce, William C. *Grade School Buildings.* Milwaukee: Bruce Publishing, 1925.

———. *High School Buildings.* Milwaukee: American School Board Journal, 1919.

Brunner, Arnold. "Cleveland's Group Plan." *Proceedings of the Eighth National Conference on City Planning.* New York: Douglas C. McMurtrie, 1916.

Burnham, Daniel, John Carrere, and Arnold Brunner. *Report on the Group Plan of Public Buildings of the City of Cleveland, Ohio.* Cleveland: N.p., 1903.

Burns, James J. *Educational History of Ohio.* Columbus: Historical Publishing, 1905.

Bussey, C. Chester. *Origin and Development of Sinclair Community College, Dayton, Ohio, 1887–1970.* Dayton: Montgomery County Community College District, 1970.

Butler, Joseph G. *History of Youngstown and the Mahoning Valley, Ohio.* New York: American Historical Society, 1921.

Butler, Margaret M. *A Pictorial History of the Western Reserve, 1796–1860.* Cleveland: Early Settlers Association of the Western Reserve, 1963.

Calkins, David L. "Black Education and the Nineteenth-Century City: An Institutional Analysis of Cincinnati's Colored Schools, 1850–1887." *Cincinnati Historical Society Bulletin* 33 (1975).

Campen, Richard. *Architecture of the Western Reserve, 1800–1900.* Cleveland: Press of Case Western Reserve University, 1971.

"Campus City, Chicago." *Architectural Forum* 123 (Sept. 1965).

Caudill, William W. *Toward Better School Design.* New York: F. W. Dodge, 1954.

"Center for the Visual Arts, University of Toledo, Ohio." *Architectural Record* 181 (July 1993).

Chase, Philander. *Bishop Chase's Reminiscences: An Autobiography.* Boston: James B. Dow, 1848.

Clark, Homer J., et al. *A Condensed History of Mount Union College.* Alliance: Mount Union College, 1866.

Clark, Theodore M. *Rural School Architecture.* Washington, D.C.: Government Printing Office, 1880.

Clubbe, John. *Cincinnati Observed: Architecture and History.* Columbus: Ohio State University Press, 1992.

Cochran, Rick. *The Story of Tiffin University.* Tiffin: Tiffin University, 1976.

"Colleges for the Community." *Architectural Forum* 111 (Nov. 1959).

Conover, Charlotte R. *Dayton, Ohio: An Intimate History.* New York: Lewis Historical Publishing, 1932.

Cram, Ralph Adams. "The Work of Messrs. Cope and Stewardson." *Architectural Record* 12 (Nov. 1904).

Cramer, C. H. *Open Shelves and Open Minds: A History of the Cleveland Public Library.* Cleveland: Case Western Reserve University, 1972.

Cremin, Lawrence A. *American Education: The National Experience, 1783–1871.* New York: Harper and Row, 1980.

———. *The Metropolitan Experience, 1876–1980.* New York: Harper and Row, 1988.

Crout, George. *Historic South Main Street.* Middletown, Ohio: City of Middletown, 1977.

Crumpacker, Sara Snyder. "Using Cultural Information to Create Schools that Work." *Designing Places for Learning,* edited by Anne Meek. Alexandria, Va.: Association for Supervision and Curriculum Development, 1995.

Cutler, S. J. "The Coonskin Library." *Ohio State Archaeological and Historical Quarterly* 26 (1917).

Cutler, William W. "Cathedral of Culture: The Schoolhouse in American Educational Thought and Practice since 1820." *History of Education Quarterly* 29 (1989).

Damm, Ellie. *Treasures by the Bay: The Historic Architecture of Sandusky, Ohio.* Cranbury, N.J.: Associated University Presses, 1989.

Darbee, Jeffrey T., and Nancy A. Recchie. "Education Is the Safeguard of Liberty: A Historical Analysis of Central High School, Columbus, Ohio." Columbus: Benjamin D. Rickey, 1995.

Davidson, Cynthia C., ed. *Eleven Authors in Search of a Building: A Building by Eisenman Architects.* New York: Monacelli Press, 1996.

"Dayton Art Institute." *Architectural Forum* 56 (June 1932).

A Decade of Service, 1930–1940. Cincinnati: Public Library of Cincinnati and Hamilton County, 1941.

Dewey, John. *Democracy and Education.* New York: Macmillan, 1916.

———. *The School and Society.* Chicago: University of Chicago Press, 1913.

Dills, R. S. *History of Greene County.* Dayton: Odell and Mayers, 1881.

Donovan, John J. *School Architecture: Principles and Practices.* New York: Macmillan, 1921.

Dressler, Fletcher B. *American School Houses.* Washington, D.C.: United States Bureau of Education, 1911.

———. *Rural Schoolhouses and Grounds.* Washington, D.C.: United States Bureau of Education, 1914.

Dunn, Waldo H. "The Builder of Wooster." *Wooster Alumni Bulletin* 1 (Jan. 1924).

Eastman, Linda A. "Cleveland's New Public Library." *Library Journal* 50 (June 1925).

Easton, L. D. "The Colored Schools of Cincinnati." *History of the Schools of Cincinnati and Other Educational Institutions, Public and Private,* edited by Isaac M. Martin. Cincinnati: Cincinnati Public Schools, 1900.

Edwards, Newton. *The School in the American Social Order.* Boston: Houghton Mifflin, 1963.

"Eisenman Builds." *Progressive Architecture* 70 (Oct. 1989).

Eisenman, Peter. *Eisenman Architects: Selected and Current Works.* Mulgrove, Victoria, Australia: The Master Architect Series, Images Publishing Group, 1995.

Emmanuel, Muriel, ed. *Contemporary Architects.* New York: Saint James Press, 1993.

Ervin, Edgar. *Pioneer History of Meigs County, Ohio, to 1949: Including Masonic History of the Same Period.* Pomeroy, Ohio: Meigs County Pioneer Society, 1949.

Eveleth, Samuel F. *School-House Architecture.* New York: The American News, 1870.

Everhart, J. F. *History of Muskingum County, Ohio, 1794–1882.* Columbus: J. F. Everhart, 1882.

First Report of the Trustees of the Emlen Institute. Philadelphia: Culbertson and Bache, 1875.

Fisher, Thomas. "Art as Architecture." *Progressive Architecture* 76 (May 1995).

Fleischman, John. "Raiders of the Lost Art." *Historic Preservation* 49 (May–June 1997).

Foote, John P. *The Schools of Cincinnati and Its Vicinity.* Cincinnati: C. F. Bradley and Company's Power Press, 1855.

Forbes, John Douglas. *Victorian Architect: The Life and Work of William Tinsley.* Bloomington: Indiana University Press, 1953.

Fowler, Orson S. *The Octagon House: A Home for All.* 1853. Rpt. New York: Dover Publications, 1973.

Freeman, Allen. "Stylistic Shotgun Wedding on a Midwestern Campus." *Architecture* 77 (Feb. 1988).

Friedman, Donald. *Historical Building Construction: Design, Materials, and Technology.* New York: W. W. Norton, 1995.

Fuller, Wayne E. "Everybody's Business: The Midwestern One-Room School." *Timeline* 10 (Sept.–Oct. 1993).

———. *The Old Country School.* Chicago: University of Chicago Press, 1982.

———. *One-Room Schools of the Middle West.* Lawrence: University Press of Kansas, 1994.

Gaines, Ervin, Marian Huttner, and Frances Peters. "Library Architecture: The Cleveland Experience." *Wilson Library Bulletin* 56 (Apr. 1982).

Galbreath, Charles B. "Frank L. Packard." *Ohio Archaeological and Historical Society Publications* 33 (1924).

———. *Sketches of Ohio Libraries.* Columbus: Fred J. Heer, State Printer, 1902.

Garland, Hamlin. *A Son of the Middle Border.* Lincoln: Bison Press, 1979.

General and Local Laws and Joint Resolutions Passed by the General Assembly. Columbus: State Printer, 1803– .

Gifford, Robert Thomas. "The Cincinnati Music Hall and Exhibition Buildings." Master's thesis, Cornell University, 1973.

Giglierano, Geoffrey J., and Deborah A. Overmyer. *The Bicentennial Guide to Greater Cincinnati: A Portrait of Two Hundred Years.* Cincinnati: Cincinnati Historical Society, 1988.

Giljahn, Jack W., and Thomas R. Matheny. *A Guide for the Adaptive Use of Surplus Schools.* Columbus: Columbus Landmarks Foundation, 1981.

Giovannini, Joseph. "Campus Complexity." *Architecture* 85 (Aug. 1996).

Goldstone, Harman H. "The Marriage of New Buildings with Old." *Historic Preservation* 23 (Jan. 1971).

Gordon, Stephen C. *How to Complete the Ohio Historic Inventory.* Columbus: Ohio Historic Preservation Office, Ohio Historical Society, 1992.

Goss, Charles Frederic. *Cincinnati: The Queen City.* Cincinnati: S. J. Clarke Publishing, 1912.

Gottfried, Herbert, and Jan Jennings. *American Vernacular Design, 1870–1940.* Ames: Iowa State University Press, 1988.

Graham, A. B. *Centralized Schools in Ohio.* Columbus: Ohio State University Extension Bulletin, 1906.

Grant, H. Roger. *Ohio in Historic Postcards: Self-Portraits of a State.* Kent, Ohio: Kent State University Press, 1997.

Gross, Ronald, and Judith Murphy. *Educational Change and Architectural Consequences: A Report on Facilities for Individualized Instruction.* New York: Educational Facilities Laboratories, 1968.

Guillford, Andrew. *America's Country Schools.* Washington, D.C.: Preservation Press, 1984.

Hamlin, Talbot. *Greek Revival Architecture in America.* 1944. Rpt. New York: Dover Publications, 1964.

Hancock, Harold. *History of Westerville.* Westerville, Ohio: N.p., 1973.

———. "Towers from Ashes: The Story of the Building of Towers Hall." *Otterbein Miscellany* (May 1967).

Hannaford, Samuel. "School Architecture." *History of the Schools of Cincinnati and Other Educational Institutions, Public and Private,* edited by Isaac M. Martin. Cincinnati: Cincinnati Public Schools, 1900.

Harris, F. R., and William B. Ittner. *The Complete School at Greenfield, Ohio.* Saint Louis: William B. Ittner, 1928.

Harrison, Wallace K., and C. E. Dobbin. *School Buildings of Today and Tomorrow.* New York: Architectural Book Publishing, 1931.

Havinghurst, Walter. *The Miami Years, 1809–1959.* New York: G. P. Putnam's Sons, 1958.

Heald, Edward T. *The Stark County Story.* Canton: Stark County Historical Society, 1952.

Hettinger, George B. "Samuel Bissell: Humanitarian and Educator, 1797–1895." Ph.D. diss., University of Akron, 1981.

High School Buildings and Grounds. Washington, D.C.: United States Bureau of Education, 1922.

Hildebrand, J. R. "Glass Goes to Town." *National Geographic* 83 (Jan. 1943).

Hildebrand, William H., Dean H. Keller, and Anita D. Herington, eds. *A Book of Memories: The Kent State University, 1910–1992.* Kent: Kent State University Press, 1993.

Hill, N. N. *History of Coshocton County, Ohio.* Newark, Ohio: A. A. Graham, 1881

Historical and Biographical Cyclopedia of Butler County, Ohio. Cincinnati: Western Biographical Publishing, 1882.

Historical and Biographical Souvenir of the Ohio School for the Deaf. Columbus: C. C. Johnson, Printers, 1898.

Historical Sketches of Public Schools in Cities, Villages, and Townships of the State of Ohio. Columbus: State Centennial Educational Committee, 1876.

History of Crawford County, Ohio. Chicago: Baskin and Battey, 1881.

History of Early Tuscarawas County Schools. Dover: Tuscarawas County Retired Teachers' Association, 1978

A History of Education in the State of Ohio. Columbus: Columbus Gazette, 1876.

History of Lorain County, Ohio. Philadelphia: Williams Brothers, 1879.

History of Montgomery County, Ohio. Chicago, W. H. Beers, 1882.

History of the Ohio Institution for the Education of the Blind. Columbus: N.p., 1876.

History of Warren County, Ohio. Chicago: W. H. Beers, 1881.

History of Washington County, Ohio. Cleveland: H. Z. Williams and Bros., 1881.

Hitchcock, Mrs. Peter S. "Lake Erie Female Seminary from the Beginning." *The Historical Society Quarterly of Lake County* 5 (Feb. 1963).

Holy, T. C., and W. E. Arnold. *Standards for the Evaluation of School Buildings.* Columbus: Ohio State University Bureau of Educational Research, 1936.

Hoover, Thomas N. *The History of Ohio University.* Athens: Ohio University Press, 1954.

Hopley, John E. *History of Crawford County, Ohio, and Representative Citizens.* Chicago: Richmond-Arnold Publishing, 1912.

Hover, John C., et al., eds. *Memoirs of the Miami Valley.* Chicago: Robert O. Law, 1919.

Howe, Henry. *Historical Collections of Ohio.* Cincinnati: C. J. Krehbiel, 1902.

Hubbart, Henry C. *Ohio Wesleyan's First Hundred Years.* Delaware, Ohio: Ohio Wesleyan University, 1943.

The Hughes Alumnal. Cincinnati: Robert Clarke, 1870.

Hunt, William E. *Historical Collections of Coshocton County, Ohio.* Cincinnati: Robert Clarke, 1876.

Hurley, Daniel. *Otterbein College: Affirming Our Past/Sharing Our Future.* Westerville, Ohio: Otterbein College, 1996.

Hutslar, Donald A. *The Architecture of Migration: Log Construction in the Ohio Country, 1750–1850.* Athens: Ohio University Press, 1986.

Jaeger, A. Robert. "The Auditorium and Akron Plans—Reflections of a Half Century of American Protestantism." Master's thesis, Cornell University, 1984.

Jencks, Charles. "Eisenman's White Holes." *Wexner Center for the Visual Arts,* edited by Andreas C. Papadakis. New York: St. Martin's Press Academy Editions, 1989.

Johannesen, Eric. "The Architectural Legacy of Guy Tilden of Canton." *Ohio History* 82 (Summer–Autumn 1973).

———. *Cleveland Architecture, 1876–1976.* Cleveland: Western Reserve Historical Society, 1979.

———. *A Cleveland Legacy: The Architecture of Walker and Weeks.* Kent, Ohio: Kent State University Press, 1999.

———. *Ohio College Architecture before 1870.* Columbus: Ohio Historical Society, 1969.

———. "Simeon Porter: Ohio Architect." *Ohio History* 74 (Summer 1965).

Johnson, Elsie Ayres. *Highland Pioneer Sketches and Family Genealogies.* Springfield, Ohio: H. K. Skinner and Son, 1971.

Johnson, Ralph. *Of Perkins and Will: Buildings and Projects.* New York: Rizzoli International Publications, 1995.

Johonnot, James. *Schoolhouses: Architectural Designs by S. E. Hewes.* New York: J. W. Schermerhorn, 1872.

Jones, Joshua H. *Wilberforce University. Greene County, 1803–1908.* Xenia, Ohio: Aldine Publishing House, 1906.

Kay, Karl J. *History of National Normal University.* Wilmington, Ohio: Wilmington College, 1929.

"Kenyon College." *American Antiques Journal* 1 (Sept. 1946).

"Kenyon College Library." *American School and University* 60 (Nov. 1987).

Killits, John M. *Toledo and Lucas County, Ohio.* Chicago: S. J. Clarke Publishing, 1923.

Kilner, Arthur R. *History of One- and Two-Room Schoolhouses in Greene County, Ohio.* Xenia, Ohio: privately printed, 1983.

Kimball, Fiske. *Domestic Architecture of the American Colonies and of the Early Republic.* New York: Dover Publications, 1966.

King, Horace. *Granville, Massachusetts to Ohio.* Granville: Sentinel Publishing, 1989.

Kinnison, William A. *Building Sullivant's Pyramid: An Administrative History of The Ohio State University, 1870–1907.* Columbus: Ohio State University Press. 1970.

Kleinz, John P. "The Pontifical College Josephinum." *The Priest* (1956).

Knepper, George W. *Ohio and Its People.* Kent: Kent State University Press, 1989.

Knight, George W. "History of Educational Progress in Ohio." *Historical Collections of Ohio,* edited by Henry Howe. Cincinnati: C. J. Krehbiel, 1902.

———. *The History of Higher Education in Ohio.* Washington, D.C.: Government Printing Office, 1891.

Koehler, Lyle. *A History of Westwood in Ohio.* Cincinnati: Westwood Civic Association, 1981.

Lane, Luman. *A History of Twinsburgh from 1820.* Akron: Beebe and Elkins, Printers, 1861.

Larson, Paul Clifford, ed. *The Spirit of H. H. Richardson on the Midland Prairies.* Ames: Iowa State University Press, 1988.

Laying of the Cornerstone of the Ohio Institution for the Education of the Deaf and Dumb. Columbus: Richard Nevins, 1864.

LeCuyer, Annette. "Frank Gehry Art School for Toledo University, [*sic*] Ohio." *The Architectural Review* 193 (Aug. 1993).

Lester, Robert M. *Carnegie Grants for Library Buildings.* New York: Carnegie Corporation, 1943.

Lloyd, Norman. "Report from the Conservatory," *Oberlin Alumni Magazine* 60 (May 1964).

Local History of the Public School System of the City of Sandusky from 1838 to 1894. Sandusky: J. F. Mack and Bro., Printers, 1894.

Lowe, Jerry M. "Historical Perspectives." *Guide for Planning Educational Facilities.* Columbus: Council of Educational Facility Planners, 1991.

Manual and History of the State School for the Deaf. Columbus: School Printing Department, 1911.

Martin, Isaac M., ed. *History of the Schools of Cincinnati and Other Institutions, Public and Private.* Cincinnati: Cincinnati Public Schools, 1900.

Mattingly, Paul H., and Edward W. Stevens. *Schools and the Means of Education Shall Forever Be Encouraged: A History of Education in the Old Northwest.* Athens: Ohio University Press, 1987.

Maturi, Mary B., and Richard J. Maturi. *Cultural Gems: An Eclectic Look at Unique United States Libraries.* Cheyenne, Wyo.: Twenty-First-Century Publications, 1996.

Matzolff, Clement L. *Ohio University, The Historic College of the Old Northwest.* Athens: Ohio University Press, 1910.

McAlpine, William. "Origin of Public Education in Ohio." *Ohio Archaeological and Historical Society Quarterly* 38 (1929).

McCormick, Virginia E., and Robert W. McCormick. *A. B. Graham: Country Schoolmaster and Extension Pioneer.* Worthington, Ohio: Cottonwood Publications, 1984.

———. *New Englanders on the Ohio Frontier: Migration and Settlement of Worthington, Ohio.* Kent, Ohio: Kent State University Press, 1998.

McGinnis, Frederick A. *The Education of Negroes in Ohio*. Wilberforce, Ohio: Wilberforce University Press, 1941.

———. *A History and an Interpretation of Wilberforce University*. Blanchester, Ohio: Brown Publishing, 1941.

McMurray, William J. *History of Auglaize County, Ohio*. Indianapolis: Historical Publishing, 1923.

McQuade, Walter, ed. *Schoolhouse*. New York: Simon & Schuster, 1958.

Meek, Anne, ed. *Designing Places for Learning*. Alexandria, Va.: Association for Supervision and Curriculum Development, 1995.

Meeks, Carroll L. V. "Romanesque before Richardson in the United States." *Art Bulletin* 35 (1953).

Mendenhall, Thomas C., ed. *History of the Ohio State University*. Columbus: Ohio State University Press, 1920.

Mercer County, Ohio History. Dallas: Taylor Publishing, 1978.

Middleton, Robin. *The Beaux-Arts and Nineteenth-Century French Architecture*. Cambridge, Mass.: MIT Press, 1982.

Milestones: A History of the State Board of Education in Ohio. Columbus: Ohio Board of Education, 1989.

Miller, Edward A. "History of the Educational Legislation in Ohio from 1803 to 1850." *Ohio Archaeological and Historical Publications* 27 (1919).

Moore, Gary T., and Jeffery A. Lackney. *Educational Facilities for the Twenty-First Century*. Milwaukee: Center for Architecture and Urban Planning Research, 1994.

Morrison, Samuel E., Henry S. Commager, and William E. Leuchtenburg. *The Growth of the American Republic*. 6th ed. New York: Oxford University Press, 1969.

Munn, Ralph. "Hindsight on the Gifts of Carnegie." *Library Journal* 76 (Dec. 1951).

Nasar, Jack L. *Design by Competition: Making Design Competition Work*. Cambridge, Mass.: Cambridge University Press, 1999.

National Education Association. *High School Buildings and Grounds*. Washington, D.C.: Government Printing Office, 1922.

Neff, S. Ernest, ed., *The Bucyrian*. Bucyrus, Ohio: Bucyrus High School, 1908.

Nelson, E. T. *Fifty Years of History of the Ohio Wesleyan University*. Cleveland: Cleveland Printing and Publishing, 1895.

New Public Library Buildings. Vol. 2. New York: Library Journal Special Report, 1980.

Nicholes, Walter McKinley. "The Educational Development of Blacks in Cincinnati from 1800 to the Present." D.Ed. diss., University of Cincinnati, 1977.

Notestein, Lucy L. *Wooster of the Midwest*. 1937. Rpt., Kent, Ohio: Kent State University Press, 1971.

Oehlerts, Donald. *Books and Blueprints: Building America's Public Libraries*. New York: Greenwood Press, 1991.

Ohio Centennial Educational Committee. *Historical Sketches of the Higher Educational Institutions, and also the Benevolent and Reformatory Institutions of the State of Ohio*. Columbus: State Centennial Educational Committee, 1876.

Open-Space Schools. Washington, D.C.: American Association of School Administrators, 1971.

Osborne, Newell Y. *A Select School.* Alliance, Ohio: Mount Union College, 1967.

Ouroussoff, Nicolai. "All in One." *Architectural Record* 183 (July 1995).

Overman, William D. "Education in Ohio since 1900." *History of the State of Ohio,* edited by Carl Wittke. Columbus: Ohio Archaeological and Historical Society, 1942.

Owen, Robert Dale. *Hints on Public Architecture.* 1849. Rpt. New York: DaCapo Press, 1978.

Papadakis, Andreas C., ed. *Wexner Center for the Visual Arts.* New York: St. Martin's Press Academy Editions, 1989.

Peeke, Hewson Lindsay. *Centennial History of Erie County.* Cleveland: Firelands Historical Society, 1925.

Perkins, Lawrence B., and Walter D. Conkling. *Schools.* New York: Reinhold, 1949.

Perrin, William Henry. *History of Summit County, Ohio.* Chicago: Baskin and Battey, 1881.

Peters, William E. *Legal History of Ohio University, Athens, Ohio.* Cincinnati: Western Methodist Book Concern, 1910.

Phillips, Hazel Spencer. *Traditional Architecture—Warren County.* Lebanon: Warren County Historical Society, 1969.

Pierson, William H., Jr. *American Buildings and Their Architects.* Garden City, N.Y.: Doubleday, Inc., 1970.

Pioneer and General History of Geauga County. Chardin: Geauga County Historical Society, 1953.

Poole, William Frederick. "Small Library Buildings." *Library Journal* 10 (1885).

Portage Heritage. Ravenna, Ohio: Portage County Historical Society, 1957.

Portraits from the Past. Sandusky: Sandusky Area Sesquicentennial Committee, 1968.

Prince, Benjamin F. *A Standard History of Springfield and Clark County, Ohio.* Chicago: American Historical Society, 1922.

Public Libraries in the United States of America: Their History, Condition, and Management. Washington, D.C.: United States Bureau of Education, 1876.

Ramsey, Marjorie E., ed. *Recommended Kindergarten Guidelines.* Columbus: Ohio Department of Education, 1978.

Ranck, Samuel H. "Library Architecture and Building Planning." *Bulletin of the American Library Association* 30 (May 1936).

Reck, Franklin M. *The 4-H Story: A History of 4-H Club Work.* Ames: Iowa State University Press, 1951.

Renner, Clayton. *Ragersville Centennial History.* Ragersville, Ohio: n.p., 1930.

"Report of the Committee on an Equal Division of the Twelve Years in the Public Schools between the District and High Schools." *National Education Association Proceedings.* Los Angeles: National Education Association, 1907.

Richey, Russell E. *Early American Methodism.* Bloomington: Indiana University Press, 1991.

Rose, William Ganson. *Cleveland: The Making of a City.* Cleveland: World Publishing, 1950.

Roseboom, E. H., and F. P. Weisenburger. *A History of the State of Ohio.* Columbus: Ohio Historical Society, 1986.

Rosenberg, Janis. "A Landscape of Enculturation: The Vernacular of Elementary School Buildings and Playgrounds, 1840–1930." Ph.D. diss., University of Pennsylvania, 1984.

Ross, Elizabeth Dale. *The Kindergarten Crusade: The Establishment of Preschool Education in the United States.* Athens: Ohio University Press, 1976.

Roth, Leland M. *A Concise History of American Architecture.* New York: Harper and Row, 1980.

Ruskin, John. *The Seven Lamps of Architecture.* 1849. Rpt. New York: Farrar, Straus, and Giroux, 1979.

Samuelson, Robert E., et al. *Architecture Columbus.* Columbus: American Institute of Architects, 1976.

Santmyer, Helen Hooven. *Ohio Town.* 1962. Rpt., New York: Harper and Row, 1984.

Schmidt, Carl F. *The Octagon Fad.* Scottsville, N.Y.: privately printed, 1958.

Schroeder, Fred E. H. "Educational Legacy: Rural One-Room Schoolhouses," *Historic Preservation* 29 (July–Sept. 1977).

———. "Schoolhouse Reading: What You Can Learn from Your Rural Schools," *History News* 36 (Apr. 1981).

Schunk, Russell J. "The Toledo Public Library." *Library Journal* 66 (Feb. 1941).

Scranton, S. S. *History of Mercer County, Ohio.* Chicago: Biographical Publishing, 1902.

Shaw, Robert J., ed. *Libraries: Building for the Future.* Chicago: American Library Association, 1967.

Sheridan, Phil. *Those Wonderful Old Downtown Theaters.* Columbus: privately printed, 1978.

Sherman, C. E. *Original Ohio Land Subdivisions.* 1925. Rpt. Columbus: Ohio Topographic Survey Report, 1976.

Short, C. W., and R. Stanley Brown. *Public Buildings: A Survey of Architecture, 1933–1939.* Washington, D.C.: Public Works Administration, 1939.

Shotwell, John B. *A History of the Schools of Cincinnati.* Cincinnati: The School Life Company, 1902.

Shriver, Phillip R. "From Normal School to University." *A Book of Memories: The Kent State University, 1910–1992,* edited by William H. Hildebrand, Dean H. Keller, and Anita D. Herington. Kent, Ohio: Kent State University Press, 1993.

———. *The Years of Youth: The Kent State University, 1910–1960.* Kent, Ohio: Kent State University Press, 1960.

Siena, Marcia A. "The History of the Great Southern Theater, Columbus, Ohio." Master's thesis, Ohio State University, 1957.

Simmons, David A. "Carnegie Libraries in Ohio." *Ohio Historical Society Echoes* 7 (Apr. 1981).

———. "Little Antioch." *Timeline* 13 (Sept.–Oct. 1996).

Smythe, George F. *Kenyon College: Its First Century.* New Haven: Yale University Press, 1924.

Soule, Charles C. "Modern Library Buildings." *Architectural Review* 9 (Jan. 1902).

Spraul, Judith. "Cultural Boosterism: The Construction of Music Hall." *Cincinnati Historical Society Bulletin* 34 (Feb. 1976).

Straker, Robert L. *Horace Mann and Others.* Yellow Springs, Ohio: Antioch Press, 1963.

Stern, Josesph S., Jr. "The Queen of the Queen City: Music Hall." *Cincinnati Historical Society Bulletin* 31 (Sept. 1973).

Taft, Eleanor Gholson. *Hither and Yon on Indian Hill.* Cincinnati: Indian Hill Garden Club, 1962.

Taylor, Anne. "How Schools Are Redesigning Their Space." *Designing Places for Learning,* edited by Anne Meek. Alexandria, Va.: Association for Supervision and Curriculum Development, 1995.

Taylor, W. A. *Ohio Statesman and Hundred Year Book, 1788–1892.* Columbus: Westbote, 1892.

Tifft, Wilton S. *Ellis Island.* Chicago: Contemporary Books, 1990.

Tilton, Edward L. "The Architecture of the Small Library." *Public Libraries* 16 (Feb. 1911).

Turner, Barbara Zollinger. "Two Ambitious New Post-Modern Projects." *Columbus Monthly* 12 (Nov. 1986).

Turner, Paul Venable. *Campus: An American Planning Tradition.* Cambridge, Mass.: MIT Press, 1990.

Upham, Alfred H. *Old Miami, the Yale of the Early West.* Hamilton, Ohio: Whitaker-Mohler Printing, 1947.

Upton, Dell. "Lancasterian Schools, Republican Citizenship, and the Spatial Imagination in Early-Nineteenth-Century America." *Journal of the Society of Architectural Historians* 55 (Sept. 1996).

Utter, William T. *Granville: The Story of an Ohio Village.* Granville: Granville Historical Society, 1956.

———. *A History of the State of Ohio: The Frontier State, 1803–1825.* Columbus: Ohio State Archaeological and Historical Society, 1942.

Van Rensselaer, Mariana Griswold. *Henry Hobson Richardson and His Works.* 1888. Rpt. New York: Dover Publications, 1969.

Van Slyck, Abigail A. *Free to All: Carnegie Libraries and American Culture, 1890–1920.* Chicago: University of Chicago Press, 1995.

———. "'The Utmost Amount of Effectiv [*sic*] Accommodation': Andrew Carnegie and the Reform of the American Library." *Journal of the Society of Architectural Historians* 50 (Dec. 1991).

"Varied Applications of Glass Mark Toledo Library Building." *Ohio Architect* 1 (Sept. 1940).

Venable, W. H. "Public Libraries of Cincinnati." *Public Libraries in the United States of America: Their History, Condition, and Management.* Washington, D.C.: United States Bureau of Education, 1876.

Waite, Frederick C. *Western Reserve University: The Hudson Era.* Cleveland: Western Reserve University Press, 1943.

Watkin, David. *A History of Western Architecture.* 2d. ed. London: Laurence King Publishing, 1996.

Webb, Michael. "A Man Who Made Architecture an Art of the Unexpected." *Smithsonian* 18 (Apr. 1987).

Weisenburger, Francis P. *The Passing of the Frontier, 1825–1850.* Columbus: Ohio Historical Society, 1941.

Wheeler, Joseph L., and Alfred M. Githens. *The American Public Library Building.* New York: C. Scribner's Sons, 1941.

Whiffen, Marcus. *American Architecture since 1780: A Guide to the Styles.* Cambridge, Mass.: MIT Press, 1981.

Williams, Edward I. F. *Heidelberg: Democratic Christian College, 1850–1950.* Menasha, Wis.: George Banta Publishing, 1952.

Williams, Peter W. *Houses of God: Region, Religion, and Architecture in the United States.* Urbana: University of Illinois Press, 1997.

Williams, Stephen Riggs. *The Saga of Paddy's Run.* Oxford, Ohio: N.p., 1945.

Williamson, C. W. *History of Western Ohio and Auglaize County.* Columbus: W. M. Linn and Sons, 1905.

Wilson, William H. *The City Beautiful Movement.* Baltimore: Johns Hopkins University Press, 1989.

Windsor, Justin. "Library Buildings." *Public Libraries in the United States of America: Their History, Condition, and Management.* Washington, D.C.: United States Bureau of Education, 1876.

Withey, Henry F., and Elsie R. Withey. *Biographical Dictionary of American Architects (Deceased).* Los Angeles: Hennessey and Ingalls, Inc., 1970.

Wright, G. Frederick. *A Standard History of Lorain County, Ohio.* Chicago: Lewis Publishing, 1916.

Yost, Joseph W., and Frank L. Packard. *Portfolio of Architectural Realities.* Columbus: Yost and Packard, ca. 1900.

Index

Educational Architecture in Ohio
was designed by Will Underwood;
composed in 11/14 Monotype Garamond
using QuarkXPress by The Book Page, Inc.;
printed by sheet-fed offset lithography on 70-
pound Fortune Matte enamel stock, Smyth sewn
and bound over binder's boards in Pearl Linen with
Rainbow endpapers, and wrapped with dustjackets
printed in two colors on 100-pound enamel stock
finished with polypropylene matte film lamination
by Thomson-Shore, Inc.; and published by
The Kent State University Press
KENT, OHIO 44242